A Place for Us

A PLACE FOR US

West Side Story and New York

Julia L. Foulkes

THE UNIVERSITY OF CHICAGO PRESS

CHICAGO AND LONDON

The University of Chicago Press, Chicago 60637
The University of Chicago Press, Ltd., London
© 2016 by Julia L. Foulkes
All rights reserved. Published 2016.
Printed in the United States of America

25 24 23 22 21 20 19 18 17 16   1 2 3 4 5

ISBN-13: 978-0-226-30180-8 (cloth)
ISBN-13: 978-0-226-30194-5 (e-book)
DOI: 10.7208/chicago/9780226301945.001.0001

Library of Congress Cataloging-in-Publication Data

Names: Foulkes, Julia L., author.
Title: A place for us : "West Side story" and New York / Julia L. Foulkes.
Description: Chicago ; London : The University of Chicago Press, 2016 |
Includes bibliographical references and index.
Identifiers: LCCN 2016011299 | ISBN 9780226301808 (cloth : alk. paper) |
ISBN 9780226301945 (e-book)
Subjects: LCSH: Bernstein, Leonard, 1918–1990. West Side story. | New York
(N.Y.)—In motion pictures. | Robbins, Jerome.
Classification: LCC ML410.B566 F68 2016 | DDC 792.6/42—dc23 LC record
available at http://lccn.loc.gov/2016011299

♾ This paper meets the requirements of ANSI/NISO Z39.48-1992
(Permanence of Paper).

To Brisa,
my dancing daughter

CONTENTS

PROLOGUE

"There's a place for us"

The making of *West Side Story*, both the musical and the film, required research. To fit the story of *Romeo and Juliet* to a moment (the 1950s), a social issue (juvenile delinquency), and a place (New York), choreographer and director Jerome Robbins, composer Leonard Bernstein, librettist Arthur Laurents, film director Robert Wise, and screenwriter Ernest Lehman scoured the newspapers for the latest articles on gang battles, listened to the music pouring out of apartment windows, visited dance halls and homes in Spanish Harlem, and clipped pictures that evoked the drama of life in the city, its seesaw between possibility and barrier, hope and despair. Balancing documentation and fiction, sociology and artistry, the real and the unreal, they transformed that research into the story of Tony and Maria, Bernardo and Anita, the Jets and the Sharks.

Since its Broadway debut in 1957, the tragic but vibrant story they created has moved far beyond the place and time it depicts to become a worldwide phenomenon. There have been an estimated forty thousand productions of the musical. It remains on the schedule of a summer stock theater in Long Island and a dinner theater in Chicago; is produced in schools from Anchorage, Alaska, to Tampere, Finland; and in 1997 was the first authorized Broadway musical to appear in China. The 1961 film extended the success of the musical to audiences far beyond the stage, and racked up its own awards. In Tokyo, the movie played continuously for five years in the 1960s. *West Side Story* has become emblematic of the best of musicals, both Broadway and Hollywood. It is a cultural touchstone, often used as a corollary to *Romeo and Juliet*, yet with its own distinct character: Israeli and Palestinian teenagers in the West Bank put on the musical as an act of peace-making; Puerto Rican actors John Leguizamo and Jennifer Lopez reimagine the story as parody or fantasy; and journalists describe political fights in Congress as battles between the Jets and the Sharks.

The success of these productions is certainly due to their artistic mastery and innovation, but not only that. *West Side Story* captured its moment. The research the creators conducted deepened their portrayal of the central issues but, even more, caught the spirit, anxiety, and aspirations that spiraled beyond those issues. As much as the show was about juvenile delinquency or Puerto Rican migration to the US mainland, it was even more about the passion of young love, the wounds of bigotry and betrayal, and the yearning to belong. New York of the 1950s embodied these larger themes. It had attained new prominence on the world stage after World War II as the headquarters of the United Nations; the building of Lincoln Center for the Performing Arts and the Guggenheim Museum helped cement its status as a capital of culture. But belonging in New York, finding a place to be and to thrive, remained elusive for many, particularly the waves of Puerto Ricans flying in from the island in search of employment, opportunity, and full citizenship. It is this drama of a city undergoing massive changes in infrastructure and demographics, wrought out in personal lives, that was the foundation of *West Side Story*.

New York infused the making of the production and gave it much of its realness; it was the place of love and conflict, and the place to escape. Reviewers at the time picked up on the importance of the city to the story, describing the musical as portraying the "jungles of the city" or the film's opening as offering "the most remarkable shots ever taken of New York City from the air."[1] But the travels of the musical and film throughout the United States and then the world diminished the centrality of New York to the story. The further the production moved from its time and place of creation, the more it became a story of America and, then, a universal tale of youthful longing and conflict.

FIGURE 0.1 Visual research for the film, New York, ca. 1960. Jerome Robbins Dance Division, New York Public Library for the Performing Arts, Astor, Lennox, and Tilden Foundations.

Two specific images hint at how the streets of New York became transformed into a more abstracted vision of love across boundaries. Research for the film included the taking of photographs around the city, not only for location shots but also for a sense of place. One of those photographs caught a boy walking along a chain-link fence, looking through it to the camera. Lining the background are older tenement buildings, a neighborhood grocery store, a person looking out from a second-floor window. The frame of the photograph seems to be the window of a car or train; the scene is seen in passing, from the safety of a moving vehicle. A splotch, musty corner, and filmy haze add moodiness to the picture. It may be a Puerto Rican boy; it may be a picture of Spanish Harlem. The specifics of time and place were not recorded. But the photograph alludes to the spirals of life beyond those specifics—the wanderings of youth in the city; the searching, even beseeching, for something beyond a fence; the gaze between one and another, marked by both directness and distance.

The idea behind *West Side Story* was never to document life in New York. Instead, the creators took insight and inspiration from the

FIGURE 0.2 Rendering by Oliver Smith of a stage scene in the prologue of *West Side Story*, ca. 1957. © Rosaria Sinisi.

world around them, synthesized, stylized, and dramatized it. They heightened the emotional registers, tightened the action, and made the consequences extreme—but not unbelievable. It is the effort to connect the stage to the streets that set *West Side Story* apart from other Broadway and Hollywood musicals. How could a musical—a fantasy in song and dance—relate to the streets of Manhattan's west side?

The second image—a rendering of the stage set for the prologue of the musical by designer Oliver Smith—captures a different perspective on the creators' remaking of New York. Here, the background includes several city elements: the blanked-out windows of an apartment building, the arc of a bridge underpass, skeletal fire escapes on either side. The infrastructure dwarfs the pointed corner in the middle of the stage, lit by a lone streetlamp. A few stairs suggest the possibility of rising up, looking out over a chain-link fence. The edges of the proscenium box are black; shadows creep in from the sides. And the most prominent poster on the wall: July 4th. A street corner reaches out to a nation.

As much as this set transformed New York into a generalizable corner in the United States, it also left the stage bare for action: more specifically, for dance. One of the strengths of *West Side Story* was its evocation of a place that could be specific in one instance and general in another—a block on the west side of Manhattan that could be transferred to a contested desert in the West Bank. Dance was the channel that made that travel possible. It expressed bravura in the claiming of a block, longing in love, conflict in a rumble, joy in escape, and the brutality of prejudice. The story began with dance, in movement that defined the urgency of animosity, but ended without it, in a funeral march. The vitality that dance *is* in its very essence—as movement alive only in a moment—became the backbone of a story about death.

Dance—and the man who choreographed it—was central to the meaning and worldwide appeal of *West Side Story*. Following Jerome Robbins in the making of the musical and film uncovers the artistic, political, and personal struggles that gave shape to both productions. But much of the meaning of *West Side Story* arises not from its creation but from its reception, how it traveled the world and found resonance in places far from the west side of Manhattan. Following the production as it takes on a life of its own, beyond the creators' intentions, reveals the armature of the US cultural industry as much as the aspirations that the United States embodies for many.

This is a story, then, of a story (*West Side Story*) about a story (*Romeo and Juliet*). My story narrates the reimagining of one story into another, from Romeo and Juliet to Tony and Maria, from the Capulets and the Montagues to the Jets and the Sharks, from Verona to New York. It recounts the transformation of one form (a musical) into another (a film), and of one specific time and place (1950s New York) into a universal tale (somewhere). The power of stories—our need for them to give shape and meaning to our lives—has long been acknowledged. The power of *West Side Story* lies in how it realizes our attachment and belonging to different places—personal, city, national, global—and the ways in which we move between them.

∗ 1 ∗

"Have you heard the voice of my city"

1949–55

The choreographer Jerome Robbins and the actor Montgomery Clift overlapped in 1940s New York. Artistic, theatrical, sleeping with men and women, they might have met each other through a mutual friend or at a party or in an acting class. By 1946, they were lovers. They lived a block from one another in midtown on the east side and shared ambition, talent, and emerging fame.

They also shared an artistic challenge. Around 1948 an actor friend of Robbins, probably Clift, as the legend goes, was struggling to bring to life a monologue from William Shakespeare's *Romeo and Juliet*. Both Clift and Robbins were students of Method acting, which directed the actor to plunge into a character's background and emotions to fully inhabit the role. This immersion in character, Method taught, would ignite the belief of the audience; the electricity of live performance depended on personal conviction on both sides of the stage curtain. Such in-depth knowledge was hard enough to achieve in any situation, even when the topic was contemporary. How was a gay man in the mid-twentieth century to understand the iconic young heterosexual lovers caught up in family feuds in sixteenth-century Verona? How could an actor get to the emotional core of a character written so long ago, caught up in conflicts so distant from the contemporary moment?

Just a few years earlier, Robbins had burst onto the choreographic scene with *Fancy Free* (1944), a saucy tale of three sailors on leave that mixed pirouettes with bravado fist-pumps and competitive camaraderie. The piece captured the desperate need for relief in a war-weary city and revivified ballet by featuring everyday movement and scenarios that could be seen right outside the stage door. The challenge of enlivening *Romeo and Juliet* thus called on Robbins's strengths. He specialized in taking the ordinary and making it newly relevant. Robbins suggested that Clift place *Romeo and Juliet* in modern-day New York, to see the age-old story in the new day.

This insight prompted Robbins to dash off a cryptic scene outline, noting a street carnival as the setting for the star-crossed lovers' meeting, a mock marriage in a bridal shop, and a fight on a playground.[1] The development of the idea required compatriots. Robbins called upon the young composer Leonard Bernstein. Their first collaboration, *Fancy Free*, had created a splash for both of them and was followed by the musical *On the Town* (1944). With Bernstein on board, Robbins enlisted playwright Arthur Laurents, best known for the play *Home of the Brave*, which depicted how the army was ensnared in the underlying anti-Semitism of the era. (Bernstein and Laurents also cruised the homosexual arts scene of the city.)

The first meeting did not go well. Bernstein proclaimed the possibilities in the story. In it he could see the makings of a great American opera—a homegrown version of the classical European art form, which *Porgy and Bess* had moved toward ten years earlier. Bernstein's mix of classical and popular flavors in music had yet to sustain a full evening's performance. And then there was the opportunity to entwine dance and music with a brilliant partner. Laurents bristled. He did not want the music to outshine the story he would write. Neither he nor Bernstein saw himself playing second fiddle. "They did not get on!" Robbins remembered.[2] But Robbins was determined to focus on the idea—and what could come of the combination of these partners' talents.

The trio emerged quickly with a fuller scenario initially titled "Gang Bang," then "Romeo" and, eventually, "East Side Story."[3] The first crisp two-act outline set up the conflict on the Lower East Side between Jews and Italian Catholics at a street festival, possibly in Chinatown, and situated the famous balcony declarations of love between Romeo and Juliet on a fire escape. Even in this early version, the collaborators emphasized movement and space; a "stylized prologue" would show "the restlessness of the youths and indicat[e] the various areas in which they let off steam." Within a couple of weeks of the first meeting, the New York press proclaimed a new musical in production.[4]

It was January 1949. The musical did not debut until September 1957.

For the creators, fame and other projects intervened. So too did politics and a changing city. In the 1950s, New York was ascendant: home to the United Nations; to Abstract Expressionists, a school of poets, jazz, and rock 'n' roll; to a dizzying number of newspapers, magazines, radio shows, and television programs that broadcast all the action to the world. Swaths of the city were demolished and rebuilt with urban renewal funds and private investment; public housing projects and office high-rises sprouted, linked by networks of bridges, roads, and tunnels. While the city's total population remained largely stable in the postwar period, it was also in flux, with African Americans and Puerto Ricans claiming a larger presence; increased Puerto Rican migration in particular became a wedge that exposed questions of space, housing, and discrimination.

These changes in New York infused the creation and production of *West Side Story* and tied the musical to an evolving sense of place. A network of white gay men dominated much of the arts, particularly on Broadway, and created coded stories of longing, such as *West Side Story*'s update to *Romeo and Juliet*. But aligning the star-crossed lovers with 1950s New York street gangs instead of elite families in Verona shifted the meaning of the classic tale, raising the stakes of loving across lines. The gangs claimed turf in the city as part of their dogged fight to be full citizens, to be embraced as worthy individuals, to define the world they wanted rather than accept the one they were given. Fights over whose block, whose city, and whose nation

molded the fevered dancing, discordant sounds, and escalating conflict. Rather than the blinding power of love evoked by Shakespeare,
in 1950s New York the theme became the quest to find one's place, to
belong, in an ever-shifting city.[5]

This competition over "who belongs" makes up much of the history
of the United States. The country and its opportunities are rhetori-
cally and ideologically open to all, even as barriers have continually
been erected to deny some and embrace others. Once here, establishing a sense of *belonging*—and gaining recognition of the attendant
rights—has often remained a battle in the face of prejudice. The
contest is often an oppositional one: the Jets versus the Sharks. And
the fight becomes more material and clear when it is about belonging
some*where*, taking up and possessing a particular space. *West Side
Story* reveals this more fractured tale, in which prejudice mangles
opportunity, pierces communities, and dooms love in the bustling,
diverse, dense, and often bruising conditions of New York. The story
exposes the costs of the struggle played out every day on city streets,
rooftops, and playgrounds.

The battle over finding a place in the city brought together groups
separated by difference and prejudice—Puerto Ricans and those understood as white; men and women; old and young; gay and straight;
American and international. Prejudice and bigotry were the bywords
of the day, the language the creators used to describe the new twist
in the plot of *Romeo and Juliet*. These words reflected the common
belief of the era in the power of judgment, of changing preconceived
ideas of others. The language of *discrimination*, primarily modified
by the word "racial" in the case of civil rights, shifted the debate to
highlight actions that resulted from particular prejudice. (Now the
more common frame of reference is *justice*, to highlight lack of parity
and demands for retribution.) This distinction comes into focus in
looking at the complicated impact of the show on Puerto Ricans. The
production pointed out prejudice but may also have perpetuated it,
replicating stereotypes rather than ameliorating them or exploring
responses other than revenge. In the show, the resolution of strife
is incomplete. But it is this chastened portrayal of New York that

creates a believable place that still holds out hope that one day there will be "a place for us," a testament to the fragility of aspirations that encompass sustenance *and* challenge.

The creators of *West Side Story* knew personally of the struggle to define and realize a place in America, against the resistance and discrimination that shaped the country. Director and choreographer Jerome Robbins, composer Leonard Bernstein, and playwright Arthur Laurents were born within little more than a year of each other, in 1917 and 1918. (Stephen Sondheim, thirteen years younger, joined the team as lyricist years later.)[6] Robbins, Bernstein, and Laurents are part of what has been called the Greatest Generation—Americans who grew up in the Great Depression, fought in World War II, and rose from immigrant or lower-class backgrounds to middle-class status. This generation has come to exemplify the American dream of rising prosperity and opportunity. But just as *West Side Story* shifted the meaning of *Romeo and Juliet*, these men cast a new perspective on the Greatest Generation. Sons of Jewish immigrants, they leaned to the left politically, toward men sexually, and excelled in the arts, a realm far outside the norm of business or politics.

Their experience of World War II encapsulates their battle to define the America they believed in. Robbins received a formal exemption from service because of an asthmatic condition, although there is little evidence he had the illness, but also declared his homosexuality. (When Robbins admitted in his army interview that he had had homosexual encounters, the officer asked how recent. "Last night," Robbins reportedly announced.[7]) Bernstein also received formal dispensation because of chronic asthma but also probably because of his early prominence as a conductor and composer. Laurents served. He did not see active duty, instead using his talent to write radio scripts and propaganda. He used his experience as the basis for his first play.

West Side Story is largely these men's story—about the fragility of love, the power of prejudice, the betrayal of hope and opportunity, and, especially, the fight to be recognized as Americans. They battled against discrimination prompted by their Jewishness and homosexual inclinations and achieved rousing artistic success with a story

FIGURE 1.1 The final team of creators minus set designer Oliver Smith: lyricist Stephen Sondheim, playwright Arthur Laurents, producers Harold Prince and Robert Griffith (sitting), composer Leonard Bernstein, and choreographer and director Jerome Robbins, ca. 1957. Photofest.

that directly addressed prejudice and the ways it robbed people of their place in the United States. In telling it, they exposed the sacrifice and cost of their personal achievements in a society fraught with bigotry. They are a kind of Greatest Generation of the arts, with *West Side Story* as a pinnacle of artistic achievement for them personally and for the genre of musicals as well.

Robbins was the prime motivator of *West Side Story*. From his initial inspiration to set *Romeo and Juliet* in contemporary New York, he went on to choreograph and direct the production. Even more, though, the challenges of his life fueled the tragedy of the show. Born Jerome Wilson Rabinowitz on October 11, 1918, in New York City, Robbins was the son of Jewish immigrants from Poland and Belarus, lands then under Russian sovereignty. His parents achieved an immigrant success story, running a delicatessen on East 97th Street. They were devoted enough to their new homeland to give their son as a middle name the surname of the current president, Woodrow Wilson, who signed the armistice that ended World War I a month after Robbins's birth. Assimilation begun, the Rabinowitz family continued to move up and then out, from Manhattan to New Jersey, where they eventually settled in Weehawken.

For Robbins's father, part of a generation of immigrants also yearning to belong in America, leading a successful life here meant excelling in business. He left managing a deli in Manhattan to manage a corset factory in New Jersey. For Robbins's mother, success meant driving her daughter Sonia and son Jerry to expertise in the arts; Jerry showed early promise, playing piano and violin and writing poetry. Financial stability and accomplished children, then, defined the parents' quest. They provided opportunities but rarely displayed affection. After one incident, Robbins penned a poetic acrostic that began "Dear Mommy / I'm very SORRY . . ." His mother edited it, correcting the grammatical errors in red pencil.[8] His parents modeled the perfectionism that propelled Robbins throughout his life, but their distance, even disaffection, had perhaps more impact. It served to heighten his emotional acuity, which he used in his theater and dance work to give weight to movement and character. But the wounds it inflicted also affected his relationships, making him needy, caustic, and aggrieved. The search for love, and an embrace of who he was, became his quest.

Jerry found solace in the arts, eventually including dance. His sister Sonia had studied ballet with Michel Fokine and the nascent modern dance with followers of Isadora Duncan. The Russian Fokine expanded the balletic tradition by concentrating more on movement than on mime and elaborate costuming. The impresario Sergei Diaghilev persuaded Fokine to join the Ballets Russes in Paris, and he later founded a ballet school in New York City, which Sonia Robbins attended. Isadora Duncan moved dance away from ballet and toward expressive, natural movement that conveyed philosophical ideals. Like Fokine, Duncan was interested in bringing dance to new audiences, making it more central to and well regarded among the arts.

Robbins's mother thrust her children into these fertile creative grounds. Jerry followed Sonia into dance, though it wrestled for his attention with music, theater, writing, and poetry. All of the arts captivated him, though he had not yet conceived of them as a possible profession. Robbins graduated from Woodrow Wilson High School in 1935, in the midst of the Depression, with little idea of what to do. He spent a year at New York University, failing out of mathematics and French. Work at his father's struggling corset company seemed to be his future. Robbins resisted. He had some inkling that his way in America was not to be through business. He asked his parents for a year to explore other possibilities before settling into a job at the factory. They agreed.

With little work or hope to fuel his dreams, Robbins took the ferry from New Jersey to Manhattan daily, as if crossing and recrossing the river would churn up possibilities. It perhaps made him think of movement, as he turned more resolutely to dance. As before, Robbins followed his sister. Moving beyond Fokine and Duncan, well-established traditions by the 1930s, Sonia migrated to the Gluck Sandor Dance Center on the west side of Manhattan. There, Senya Gluck Sandor and his wife Felicia Sorel had built up an eclectic training program in dance and theater. Uninterested in constancy or purity of tradition, Gluck Sandor pulled from many genres, ranging from ballet, Spanish dance, and modern dance to tap and vaudeville, whatever might be most useful in expressing a theatrical intent. The key was to use whatever movement was necessary to expose character, a lesson that Robbins picked up and expanded. And Gluck Sandor saw talent in Robbins—creativity and ambition—and became his mentor.

Robbins entered a world of the arts bubbling with purpose. The economic uncertainty of the Depression inspired a search for meaning that artists sought to answer. Art mattered in these tremulous times, to define enduring values and project hope. And much of it centered on distinguishing the United States from Europe. Artists helped define American democratic ideals as the beacon of the future, in opposition to the growing fascism in Europe. The federal government's Works Progress Administration bolstered much of this with necessary cash and infrastructure. Artists became workers, paid an average weekly wage of approximately thirty dollars, alongside bridge builders and steelworkers. Choreographing dances, making plays, and painting murals across the country, in small towns and major cities, became part of the work of the nation, as necessary to its renewal as building post offices and planting trees.

Robbins waded into this creative maelstrom, pursuing both acting and dance. Artists in both realms were brewing with ideas of how to create plays and dances that not only featured American topics but also American ways of moving and acting. Playwrights such as Eugene O'Neill, for example, configured a new kind of realism that used vernacular language and tackled difficult contemporary topics such as US military involvement in Haiti (*The Emperor Jones*, 1920) and miscegenation (*All God's Chillun Got Wings*, 1924). Robbins, in fact, first got work in theater, through his mentor Gluck Sandor, who introduced him to the Group Theatre, the influential collective that brought the acting philosophies of Konstantin Stanislavsky to the American stage. In Russia, Stanislavsky had revolutionized acting technique, adding psychological depth and physical practice to build a character. His fame reached the United States, where artists endeavored to apply these techniques to the American theatrical tradition. The Group Theatre, formed by Harold Clurman, Lee Strasberg, and Cheryl Crawford, took up the challenge in a time ripe for the stark and emotional realism of Stanislavsky's approach. The Group Theatre put on some of the most celebrated plays of the decade, starting with Clifford Odets's *Waiting for Lefty*, a paean to unionism, in 1935. Gluck Sandor choreographed for the group, and Robbins served in the tech crew backstage.

To these lessons in theater, Robbins added classes in ballet with Ella Daganova, following Russian traditions. And to that he added classes in the latest modern dance techniques with Martha Graham and Charles Weidman, both crucial figures in codifying a new way of moving that utilized gravity, the torque and weight of the body. As a relatively young art form in America, dance sought to throw off the inherited balletic techniques of Europe, its pointe shoes, frothy costumes, and fantastical stories. These American dancers embraced bare feet, wore tubular dresses that revealed the action of the full body, and choreographed ideas that heaved with political intent. From modern dance Robbins also began to learn what it meant to choreograph, taking a class with Bessie Schönberg, a young teacher who embedded movement, and students, with purpose. Robbins soaked up the possibilities along with the techniques. Taking classes and working backstage in these fledgling endeavors was not yet a career, but he quickly left behind the idea of business and a more secure job at the corset factory for the creative, if uncertain, ferment of the arts.

Robbins's first professional appearance, in 1937, was in a performance of Gluck Sandor's company, sponsored by the Works Progress Administration. As was common in the theater, particularly among Jews, Senya Gluck Sandor had changed his name from Samuel Gluck or Glick. Robbins's sister followed suit, sloughing off Rabinowitz, first for "Robyns," then settling on "Robbins"—perhaps inspired by the Jewish character in the 1927 film *The Jazz Singer*, who changed his name from Jakie Rabinowitz to Jack Robin. Jerry again followed his sister's lead: Gluck Sandor's 1937 program marked the debut of "Gerald Robbins." He later dropped the Gerald to return to Jerome. In 1944, soon after his first choreographic successes, his parents too changed their names from Rabinowitz to Robbins. Names and naming would haunt Robbins throughout his life. The change from Rabinowitz to Robbins both exposed and attempted to cover up the struggle to assimilate, to belong, in America. From his first appearance onstage, Robbins sought a new way to define himself: in dance and with a different name.

Robbins continued to train in various dance forms and began using the Anglicized name offstage as well. He performed throughout the late 1930s, grooming his skills in dance and theater, then delved further into choreography in the summer camps in the Poconos to which New Yorkers escaped. Summers at the Tamiment resort introduced him to other soon-to-be stars such as Danny Kaye, Imogene Coca, and Carol Channing and dancers such as Dorothy Bird and Anita Alvarez. It also threw him directly into the practical challenges of production.

He learned the importance of timing, how to convey humor, and the need for clarity—all while on the deadline of a new revue each week. Tamiment proved to be an excellent training ground for the world of entertainment.

Back in New York, it was the world of Broadway that tantalized Robbins, not ballet or modern dance. Trying to get his first break as a dancer in a show, he failed audition after audition, but finally landed a role in the *Great Lady* (1938), which featured choreography by a little-known Russian-born ballet choreographer, George Balanchine. Balanchine began to choreograph his own story in dance when he arrived in New York in 1933, sponsored by the impresario Lincoln Kirstein. Balanchine and Kirstein had the same aim: to reshape ballet in American terms. But there were stops and starts on that long road; musical theater and movies provided steady income in the early days. In Rodgers and Hart's *On Your Toes* (1936), Balanchine proved he had musical theater chops with the sultry and dramatic "Slaughter on Tenth Avenue" ballet. He went on to choreograph other Rodgers and Hart musicals and a movie, proving the importance of dance to the action. Robbins imbibed the lesson and would further it in his own work in musical theater.

Jobs in musical theater came after *Great Lady*, but Robbins began to better his ballet technique and seek work directly in ballet. In 1940 he became a part of a new company, Ballet Theatre (later called American Ballet Theatre). With this company he danced ballets of the most prominent choreographers of the time, except Balanchine (who would soon start the company that would evolve into the New York City Ballet). Working with the choreographers Anthony Tudor, Michel Fokine, Eugene Loring, and Agnes de Mille, Robbins was at the forefront of the nascent American ballet. De Mille gave him a small but featured role in her *Three Virgins and a Devil* (1941). Taking a comic turn as a wily youth, he stole the show with a quick cameo that required complicated musical counting. More roles came his way from Loring and Fokine, and he was promoted to soloist. In a few short years, Robbins had emerged as a leading dancer in a company at the forefront of bringing ballet to America.

But this was not enough for Robbins. At the same time that he was mastering ballet technique, and learning and performing new roles, he was furiously writing scenarios for dances. On tour with Ballet Theatre to Mexico and around the States in the early 1940s, Robbins saw stories everywhere. He outlined ballets about an air raid and another populated with the comic book characters Superman and Little Orphan Annie. Most scenarios, however, focused on New York. As he began to think choreographically—to imagine stories told through movement—he continually turned to the city that was his home.

The idea of New York had long inspired artists, but Robbins shifted the emphasis in his scenarios. In ballets and musicals, the city often served as a backdrop rather than the basis for plot, theme, and meaning. More often than not, the show within a show—the musical *42nd Street* (1933) or Balanchine's "Slaughter on Tenth Avenue," for example—portrayed the city as the place and business of entertainment. (Naming productions for streets and avenues was also a way to key in to the specifics of the urban landscape.) Robbins looked away from the city as backdrop for show business and toward the ways in which people's lives were formed in interaction with the city. One scenario focused on "war babies," those in the slums of the city who were born in the First World War and headed to serve in the Second, claiming "this cockeyed city is THEIRS." Robbins identified the circumstances that defined his generation—enormous sacrifice and commitment to country—but also detected the new landscape within which their lives were being played. The United States had gone from a rural to an urban nation in the early twentieth century; the American dream was now tied to struggle and success in the city. Finding one's place in the city was the first step to finding one's place in the nation. In his stories, the city would become not a platform for entertainment or business but a foundation for relationships, between people and between people and their places.

Robbins tied his own search for a place in the world to New York. In this city, he could see glimmers of where he fit: in the arts, in the closeted but vibrant homosexual scene, and among other strivers claiming opportunities in America. One dance scenario he drafted described this battle for possession of the city, mindful of the contrasts that defined it. "My city lies between two rivers—on a small island," he began:

> My city is tall and jagged—with gold + slated towers. My city is honeycombed with worm tunnels of roads. My city is cut + recut + slashed by hard car filled streets. My city chokes on its breath, and sparkles with its false lights—and sleeps restlessly at night. My city is a lone man walking at night down an empty street watching his shadow grow longer as he passes the last lamp post, seeing no comfort in the blank dark windows, and hearing his footsteps echo against the building + fade away— . . . Have you heard the voice of my city fighting + hitting + hurt.[9]

This image of the city throbbed with loneliness, grief, and defiance. Robbins personified the city, moving from buildings and streets to breath, lights, sleep, a lone man, and, finally, a voice. The place was a character, living alongside the people who populated it.

The sense of desperation in the character of the city also weaved through Robbins's other scenarios about the aspirations of artists. "Four young people caught in the struggle for living in New York . . . live in two rooms in brwonstone [*sic*] in the west fifties the[y] don't worry about money cause they don't have it t[o] worry over." They look for "only a little step toward what they want."[10] Notes for a "Negro Ballet: South and North" contrasted a levee scene with one of Harlem. The most fleshed-out scenario, ". . . like a little town . . . ," tried out different scenes of misery: a homeless man roused ruthlessly by a cop; vacant souls on a subway that "swayed and rocked and leaned all together like a long line of twin puppets on one string"; a blind man shuffling through the crowds of Times Square; and a woman passing by men leaning against a building, "hands deep in their pockets and their pants pulled tight across their thighs," with eyes "that seared up and down her legs and thighs and buttocks."[11] Robbins played out his search for a place to belong through towns, regions, men, women,

African Americans, landing most often in a New York smoldering with alienation.

Robbins sought a kind of possession of the city as a way to belong to a place and forge an identity for himself—and his talent. He had been looking for a chance to choreograph for Ballet Theatre since soon after he joined the company, but his early scenarios had too much character, too much exposition, or were just too complicated. The trick was simplicity. Dance worked best when movement could convey the situation, mood, and meaning between people rather than depicting a complicated plot or serving only as decorous background. Charles Payne, an administrator at Ballet Theatre, pushed Robbins to create something on an American theme. But instead of the western themes that had proved successful for de Mille and Loring, Payne suggested that Robbins look to the city. Another friend recommended searching for a topic in Paul Cadmus's paintings, full of raunchy sailors vying for sex and adventure, with an undertow of homoeroticism that may have appealed to Robbins. Building off these suggestions, Robbins wrote the scenario for what would become *Fancy Free*.[12]

The scenario sparked interest at Ballet Theatre. The next hitch was to find a composer. Robbins wanted Marc Blitzstein, well known for *The Cradle Will Rock* (1937), or up-and-coming experimental composer Morton Gould. Neither was available or interested. Perhaps someone who could do something a little jazzy? Leonard Bernstein's name popped up. Young, brash, and just appointed assistant conductor of the New York Philharmonic, Bernstein seemed likely to appreciate the opportunity of a commission from the still-developing Ballet Theatre. Like Robbins, Bernstein was finding a place for himself in the music world by defining an American style. Here, then, was a chance to fuse an American approach to music with one in dance. It was an opportunity to mark a new kind of success in the arts, one not tied to European traditions but distinguished by melding classical techniques with more popular styles of music and dance.

This aim made Bernstein and Robbins artistic brothers, egging each other on through prodding, ego, sometimes even meanness, to achieve a distinctive vision. They were like brothers in other ways too.

Born just months apart, of Jewish parents who had other careers in mind for their offspring, each eventually preferred male over female lovers, and each had changed his name, in Bernstein's case, from Louis to Leonard. Bernstein, though, had a clearer path to the arts, having gone to Harvard and then the Curtis Institute in Philadelphia for musical training. His prodigious talents were apparent very early, as he migrated from playing the piano to conducting, and his charm eased his way directly into the upper echelons of the world of music.

The *Fancy Free* commission was a chance for Bernstein to distinguish himself in composing. Like dance, music was being reformed by composers and musicians experimenting with form and sound. Henry Cowell banged his forearms on the piano and plucked its strings; Roy Harris incorporated folk music into his symphonies. But it was Aaron Copland who was gaining the most notoriety at the time, with his open, clear tones that evoked the frame of a house on a prairie. Dancers turned to Copland too, as the aural accompaniment to their American-style movement. Copland had composed music for *Billy the Kid* (1938), Eugene Loring's ballet on the western legend; *Rodeo* (1942), Agnes de Mille's more playful western romp; and *Appalachian Spring* (1944), Martha Graham's pioneer drama. Like Copland, Bernstein longed to define an American voice in classical music and saw in dance a creative partner to do so. Like Robbins, Bernstein sought inspiration from a wide variety of sources, including folk music and, especially, jazz. When Bernstein and Robbins met to discuss working together, Bernstein played a passage from his unfinished symphony. Its syncopation, dissonance, and energy bowled Robbins over. He had met his match.

Fancy Free marked the beginning of a famously fruitful collaboration, one that quickly propelled Robbins and Bernstein to the forefront of the arts. But scheduling and competing demands almost defeated the collaboration at its outset. In November 1943, just as Bernstein began composing for Robbins, he was called at the last minute to substitute for an ailing Bruno Walter in conducting the New York Philharmonic. He became an overnight sensation, flooded with demands for interviews, rehearsals, more conducting.

The new fame bound Bernstein to New York while Robbins was on tour with Ballet Theatre, so their collaboration proceeded by mail. Robbins wrote a detailed scenario for Bernstein, even noting musical moods and tempos; Bernstein sent off a section as soon as he finished it, describing for Robbins the movement he saw in the music. Robbins suggested "sudden, loud, change of tempo and mood. Hot, boogie-woogie influence, which quiets down to being insistent with sudden hot loud licks." Bernstein rejoined: "The rhythm of your pas de deux is something startling—hard at first, but oh so danceable with the pelvis!"[13] This detailed back-and-forth, and confident assertion and comment on the other's genre, led to an unusual level of intimacy between music and dance. Balanchine, too, fused music and dance, but in more abstract ways; dance, in Balanchine's hands, was a way of "seeing music." Robbins and Bernstein instead used music and dance to create a livable, knowable world. The sailors' New York in *Fancy Free* was fixed to a particular moment, opening up a new way to see what was happening just outside the theater doors.

In this, *Fancy Free* reflected scenes of New York but also adjusted them. The effect was heightened by the set, designed by Oliver Smith. Part of this generational wave of gay white men in the arts, Smith was born six months after Arthur Laurents and just a few months before Bernstein and Robbins. Trained as a painter, he sought to use those talents on the stage, as a set designer for both Broadway and ballet. His set for *Saratoga* (1941), a ballet on horse racing by the Ballet Russe de Monte Carlo, led him to be picked for de Mille's *Rodeo* the following year. And so began a long association with American Ballet Theatre, where he became codirector, with Lucia Chase, in 1944. The overlapping worlds and talents led to Smith working on *Fancy Free*, the first of his collaborations with Robbins and Bernstein. He would work with Robbins again on *Interplay* (1945), with Laurents on his play *A Clearing in the Woods* (1957), and with Robbins, Bernstein, and Laurents on *West Side Story*.

A corner bar focused Smith's vision of New York in *Fancy Free*. The homey bar, though, stood against a cool backdrop "with a pattern of windows and hazy outlines of buildings forming a vague cubist

FIGURE 1.2 Oliver Smith's set design for *Fancy Free* (1944) creates a cozy corner amid a towering city. © Rosaria Sinisi. Photofest.

pattern," as Smith described it. Eager to point to the city but not locate it definitively, Smith used spray guns to "soften the contours of buildings on the drop, but keep them purely in a block form, without anyone being able to identify any special building."[14] The buildings hover over the corner bar, making it appear small and subject to their surveillance.[15] This more abstract, even haunting, image finds its parallel in the opening of the music. Shirley Bernstein, Leonard's sister, sang "Big Stuff" on the jukebox, evoking a bluesy intimacy, soon shaken by a bravado interruption.

Big stuff, in the form of three sailors on a short leave in the city, bursts onto the stage, the music pronouncing their arrival with drum and trumpets.[16] They are ready for excitement, fun, and adventure. Leaning against a lamppost outside the bar, they wait for the city to happen. A woman passes, and the action begins: the men ply their charms, one tires of the game, then another woman saunters by.

Competition grows as the three men pursue the two women, resulting in dueling solos. Specific, individual, different, each sailor has his
own mood, music, and movement. "They cannot be written about—
they must be danced," Robbins wrote to Bernstein. The third—the
role Robbins originally played—has "a feeling of Latin or Spanish
about him"; "his keynote is his intensity." "There are swift and sudden movements . . . a strong passion and violence . . . an attractive
quality of flashiness and smoldering."[17] The fight among the sailors
takes over, the women realize they have been forgotten and stride off,
and the men find themselves where they began: waiting for something to happen. A third woman saunters by.

Opening night stunned the young New York ballet world. *Fancy
Free* prompted over twenty curtain calls—and heralded the artistic
arrival of Robbins, Bernstein, and Smith. It signaled a new direction, which *West Side Story* would further. Perhaps most important, Robbins tied movement directly to character; the second solo,
for example, used movements to reveal someone "more naïve, lov-
able, there is more warmth, humor and almost a wistfulness about
him." Drawings Robbins made showcase the breadth and openness
of stance, the angularity that came from combining modern dance
and ballet.[18] He also integrated vernacular motions—somersaults,
shrugs—into classical dance vocabulary, making the movement
between a common and recognizable gesture slide into a more technical one. In the first solo, the sailor executes a double pirouette that
ends in a wide bent-knee stance. Looking at his friends at the bar, he
then pumps his fists in the air.

Music abetted this slide between forms. "I have written a musical double-take when the sailor sees girl #2;—has that ever been
done before?" Bernstein wrote to Robbins.[19] They continued the
long-standing pattern of drawing upon exotic others to register an
American quality; African American and Latino aesthetic traditions
supplied "the under-excitement and sexuality" of "negro fluidity
and suppleness."[20] The flow between music and movement evident
in the creative exchange between Robbins and Bernstein harmo-
nized mood, setting, and character. Robbins pleaded for simplicity,

FIGURE 1.3 Sketch for *Fancy Free* made by Jerome Robbins while on tour with Ballet Theatre, ca. 1943. The buoyancy and camaraderie of the piece comes through even in these sketches, with two sailors lifting a third and the puffed-out chests and wide, open stances. Courtesy of the Robbins Rights Trust; Jerome Robbins Dance Division, New York Public Library for the Performing Arts, Astor, Lennox, and Tilden Foundations.

to which Bernstein responded earnestly, if perhaps a tad disingenuously: "The score actually is very simple—only the rhythms have to be concentrated upon like fury. There's no simplifying the rhythms—they're there, + they're the essence + basis of the whole score—but the notes will be very easy."[21] The tussle between simplicity—perhaps clarity is the better word—and underlying complexity would be a hallmark of the Bernstein-Robbins collaboration.

Fancy Free exhibited the collaborators' ability to pick up on traces of the era and recalibrate the image for the stage. Making sailors enjoying the city the central characters reflected the prevalence of military men in uniform during World War II. The brimming sexuality of the dance and music reminded people of the joy and possibility in these sailors, rather than the harsh realities of wartime. While on tour, Robbins had witnessed sailors on leave "jitterbuggin like crazy" in Philadelphia, and he sought to translate in the dance their brief liberation from more intense duties.[22] The photograph by Alfred Eisenstaedt just a year later of the jubilant kiss between a sailor and a nurse in Times Square that has come to symbolize the Allied victory in World War II only confirms the relevance—and buoyancy—of *Fancy Free*.

The idea of *Fancy Free* transferred quickly to the Broadway stage, with the primary input from the original collaborators being the instigating concept—three sailors on leave in New York City—and Bernstein's music. *On the Town*, coproduced by Oliver Smith, opened by the end of the year, in late December 1944, and became well-known for its tunes by Adolph Comden and Betty Green, especially "New York, New York," "where the Bronx is up and the Battery's down." On-screen five years later, boasting Gene Kelly and Frank Sinatra, the story was depleted of its underlying tension. *On the Town*, the movie, presents a fun but ultimately frivolous view of the city. The sailors take the leisure of those in *Fancy Free* to a tourist extreme. They don't dance the city or even dance in the city; they just wander in wonder from sight to sight. The city had become a spectacle for visitors rather than a place full of contradictions, conflict, and passion.

While *Fancy Free* and *On the Town* displayed a New York for outsiders, the productions made Robbins and Bernstein insiders. Robbins quickly choreographed more ballets, such as *Interplay* (1945), that extended and formalized the play at the heart of *Fancy Free*, as well as shows in musical theater, such as *Look, Ma, I'm Dancin'!* (1948), a backstage story of love in the theater. Bernstein continued his conducting successes, becoming music director of the short-lived New York City Symphony Orchestra from 1945 to 1947 and traveling to Europe and Israel to make his conducting debuts abroad. The collaborators reunited to work on *Age of Anxiety* (1950) for the New York City Ballet, Robbins's new home. W. H. Auden's poem of the same name conveyed the existential questions of the postwar period in New York, which the ballet set against city-inspired scenery, again created by Oliver Smith. Spare, jagged skyscrapers in the background paralleled the dance's twitchy movement.

The initial ideas for *West Side Story* emerged between the extremes of *Fancy Free* and *Age of Anxiety*. Setting *Romeo and Juliet* in current-day New York meant instilling it with the hope of the postwar city in its economic and development bustle, the sauciness of *Fancy Free*. But it also meant confronting the global tensions that the war revealed and that were growing increasingly cold, the anguish of *Age of Anxiety*. *West Side Story* would fuse these characteristics into a passionate, humane portrayal of a troubled city of people searching for their place.

Updating *Romeo and Juliet* was challenge enough, even without these concerns. The story had been reimagined many times before, primarily as it was translated to new genres. *Romeo and Juliet* had served as a basis for a short film as early as 1908, a full-length spectacle by director George Cukor in 1936, and a full-length TV adaption in 1947. Musical interpretations abounded, from Berlioz, Tchaikovsky, and, most recently, Sergei Prokofiev, who had composed a new version debuted by the Kirov Ballet in 1938. The Russian ballerina Galina Ulanova made it her signature piece in 1940, and a film version that came out in 1954 played to huge audiences across the eastern bloc. Robbins-the-dancer had played Benvolio in a one-act version by Antony Tudor that premiered in 1943. And Robbins-the-choreographer had considered the realm of forbidden love in *The Guests* (1949), which, in Balanchine's charming speech, was about "the cluded—the included and the excluded."[23] Unlike *Romeo and Juliet*, *The Guests* conveys difference through a physical trait, those with a mark on their foreheads opposed to those without. A masked party allows lovers to meet and only later uncover that they are from different groups. They defy efforts to separate them, and boy carries girl offstage at the end.

Ideas of "the cluded" were clearly on Robbins's mind when he brought Bernstein and Laurents together for their first discussion. *The Guests* premiered January 20, 1949. Seven days later, the *New York Times* announced that an update of *Romeo and Juliet* in musical theater form would debut the following season. Headed by Robbins, Bernstein, Laurents, and Smith, the star team alone promised a hit. The turn on Shakespeare also built on the recent smash *Kiss Me, Kate* (1948), a rendering of Shakespeare's *Taming of the Shrew* by Cole Porter. The key elements were in place.

Neither *Romeo and Juliet* nor reimaginings of it were anything new, so the success of this revision, in a not-yet-tried genre, hinged on finding a fresh perspective on a familiar tale. What contemporary corollaries would resonate with family feuds in Verona? And how could this tragic story work in musical theater? Broadway shows most often trafficked in happy love stories. (*Carousel* [1945] and *South Pacific* [1949] were notable exceptions that contained bits of tragedy.) How could the entertaining song and dance that carried Broadway shows be utilized to convey tragedy? This was the challenge that intrigued Robbins and Bernstein. Here was a chance to conceive of musical theater as American opera, to give to the form a fuller emotional palette and artistic range. Gershwin's *Porgy and Bess* (1935) was a promising model, but Robbins and Bernstein wanted to push the form further, particularly in the synergy between music and dance. Robbins dashed off the skeletal scene outline, then turned over the idea to Laurents, with whom he had worked on *Look, Ma, I'm Dancin'!*, to flesh out the story.

Like his collaborators, Laurents, born to Jewish parents in Brooklyn in 1917, had changed his name, from Arthur Levine. Like Bernstein, he traveled up the educational ladder and attended Cornell University. Unlike Bernstein or Robbins, Laurents ended up in the army during World War II. There he wrote training films and propaganda scripts for radio and amassed evidence for his play excoriating anti-Semitism in the army, *Home of the Brave* (1945). The primary character, Peter Coen—nicknamed Coney, tying him to New York—struggles with insults, being marked as different, and the guilt of living after the battleground death of a friend. Coney charges that difference is imposed, not intrinsic: "You make us different, you dirty bastards!" Laurents revealed both the made-up character of prejudice and the social embeddedness that makes it so difficult to root out. (He transferred the same insight to *West Side Story*. Doc to the Jets: "You make this world lousy!" A Jet replies, "That's the way we found it, Doc.") In *Home of the Brave*, Laurents exposed the betrayal at the heart of military service for those asked to sacrifice their lives for a country that denied them full rights and the embrace of belonging.

Laurents's wrestling with prejudice and betrayal in *Home of the Brave* led Robbins and Bernstein to ask him to write the book for their *Romeo and Juliet* adaptation. Laurents's screenplay for Alfred Hitchcock's *Rope* (1948)—with homosexuality hiding behind murder—may also have attracted Robbins and Bernstein. Both stories reveal anguish underneath the bravado of the military or the polish of success. Laurents had brotherly affinities with Robbins and Bernstein in his slightly at-odds relation to the vast majority of their generation. Rising from an immigrant background, Laurents grew up through the Depression and military service, but never eschewed his homosexual inclinations. He knew he had to mark his own path.

After the initial contentious meeting with Robbins and Bernstein in January 1949, Laurents continued the work, fleshing out the outline with more description and plot turns. The next version still hewed closely to Shakespeare, with the double suicide at the end and attention to warring families rather than youths and gangs. But Laurents began to think through the dimensions of placing the story in

New York. He staged the conflict during the Easter/Passover season and put in bits that reflected current issues, such as suggesting that Romeo go to the druggist for a Wassermann test, a common way at the time to check for syphilis. The outline contained more details that would remain, particularly the love-at-first-sight meeting at a street carnival that isolates the lovers from the crowd. And Laurents began to wrest some control from Shakespeare, simplifying the plot by reducing the number of primary characters. (Paris—Juliet's intended—is left out because, according to Laurents, "forced marriage is too old-fashioned for these times." Paris thus "becomes useless."[24])

The New York setting then began to change the story. In one early draft, Juliet and her nurse arrive at the street carnival directly from the country and "are gaping at the city, the sights, the people." Juliet comes to see her relatives for Passover on the Lower East Side, prompting the possible name "East Side Story" for the musical. Juliet and the Capulets lived on Allen Street, Romeo and the Montagues on Mulberry.[25] Jewish immigrants from Eastern Europe had dominated the Lower East Side since the turn of the twentieth century. The dense neighborhood, populated with Yiddish signs and institutions such as the Yiddish theater and the Jewish newspaper *The Forward*, bordered Little Italy, where the Catholic Montagues would have lived, with Chinatown just blocks away for the street festival. Placing a Jewish-Catholic conflict in that part of New York seemed to make perfect sense—except that it did not reflect changes occurring at that moment. In the postwar years, Jews began to leave the Lower East Side for other parts of the city and the suburbs, and newer migrants started moving in, most noticeably a significant number of Puerto Ricans.

This early version imagined the dilemmas faced by the collaborators' parents' generation, not their own. The story was not yet personal or fused to the contemporary moment. The ballerina Nora Kaye, a close friend of Robbins and Laurents, declared it little more than a tragic version of the 1920s comedy *Abie's Irish Rose*. The trio lost interest; momentum drifted. Spurts of inspiration dotted these initial outlines, some of which would become central elements in the final version of *West Side Story*. But the difference with *Romeo and Juliet*—the relevance of the story here and now—was not yet convincing. And any collaboration such as musical theater is built through haphazard bursts of energy and innovation—and lots of plodding through to realization. No one at this point was willing to commit to plodding. Laurents was tied up in Hollywood, with an affair with actor Farley Granger and a screenplay for the film *Caught* (1949). Bernstein and Robbins were creating *Age of Anxiety*. Hopes for a *Romeo and Juliet* adaptation in 1949 faded. Perhaps belonging seemed less tenuous in the face of individual artistic accomplishments.

As years passed and successes accumulated, the men continued to cross paths and talk of working together. In 1955 Robbins stopped the drift and pushed Bernstein and Laurents to commit to a project. They considered an opera based on James M. Cain's novel *Serenade*, about an opera singer's dramatic love life, including a struggle with his homosexuality. Robbins, though, wanted to go back to the Romeo idea. Bernstein and Laurents talked about the possibilities that summer, hitting on the possibility of something about the "juvenile gang war news" that was "all over the papers every day." At this point, Laurents favored a nonspecific locale.[26]

Later that summer, though, the locale came into focus. Laurents and Bernstein talked again when they were both in Los Angeles, Bernstein conducting a five-concert series at the Hollywood Bowl called "Festival of the Americas," with music from the United States, Mexico, and Central and South America, and Laurents plying his skills writing screenplays. Newspaper headlines again caught their attention: stories of gang violence, particularly between Chicanos and whites. What about placing *Romeo and Juliet* in Los Angeles? That got something right—a volatile new ethnic conflict among youth rather than religious strife or family feuds—but Laurents claimed he knew nothing about LA.[27] They then transferred the idea back to their home in New York. Shifting the conflict from animus between Jews and Catholics to gang violence between whites and Puerto Ricans set minds whirring. Laurents promptly wrote a new outline,

FIGURE 1.4 Mexican American in driveway framed by a chain-link fence and flat vista, Los Angeles, ca. 1955. "Shades of L.A.," Mexican American Community Collection, Los Angeles Public Library.

now in three acts with some characters identified and named, such as Bernardo (Tybalt), Anita (a revision of Shakespeare's Nurse), and Doc ("possibly a Jew"), and with mambo and jitterbugging central to the action.[28]

The inspiration of Los Angeles stood behind the setting in New York. A city with overt Mexican influences, Los Angeles was also a city undergoing massive infrastructural changes, as highways expanded and diffused the urban core. Seeing New York from the perspective of Los Angeles highlighted the notable influx of Puerto Ricans that occurred in the 1940s and 1950s and the impact of urban renewal on the landscape of the city. Buildings in the Lower East Side

FIGURE 1.5 Looking north from Spring Street toward the San Gabriel Mountains, Los Angeles, 1955. Note the numerous parking lots that edge the roads. Herald-Examiner Collection, Los Angeles Public Library.

had been razed and replaced with high-rise public housing projects, nearly erasing the Jewish-centered neighborhoods and tenement life of the early twentieth century. And the impact of cars was becoming ever more noticeable, with the construction of a regional network of highways and a dramatic upsurge in parking lots in Manhattan itself.

Looking at New York with Los Angeles in mind, the latest and most extensive razing by master builder (and destroyer) Robert Moses stood out. In 1955, Moses declared almost fifty-three acres on eighteen city blocks on the west side of Manhattan between 60th and 65th Streets as blighted, thus eligible for Title 1 funds from the federal government. (Eventually the project decreased to fourteen city blocks, about forty-eight acres.)[29] This led to the dramatic transformation of a neighborhood known as San Juan Hill by some and Lincoln Square by others. In the place of two- to five-story brownstone buildings,

FIGURE 1.6   Looking southwest from around 65th Street, including the junction of Broadway and Amsterdam Avenue (on the left), the area called Lincoln Square, New York, 1950s. Photograph by Bob Serating.

small shops and local businesses, and a mix of low- and middle-income families would arise the largest performing arts complex in the world, high-rise apartment and office buildings, and a midtown campus for Fordham University. The replacement of religious conflict between Jews and Catholics on the Lower East Side with racial and ethnic conflict between whites and Puerto Ricans on the west side connected the story to contemporary social and political strife. It also placed the story in the rifts occurring in the specific landscape of New York.

The years between 1949, when the creators first discussed adapting *Romeo and Juliet*, and 1955, when they picked up the idea again, proved critical to *West Side Story*'s eventual innovation. Urban economies were adjusting to the relocation of industries, and with them, secure factory jobs, to the suburbs. Industries and the people who worked for them provided a robust tax base, which then moved outside city centers. And, more generally, it was unclear what would replace the hyped-up wartime production. This economic change devastated those already leading marginal lives in the city, particularly African Americans and Puerto Ricans. Urban renewal plans reinforced these economic and demographic trends. Highways, housing projects, and cultural complexes like Lincoln Center, just underway when the musical debuted in 1957, rebuilt cities in the postwar years with little attention to economic sustainability and residential stability for those struggling to make their way in the new America. For the world and the country had shifted too. In these years the Cold War flared, with the creation of two separate states in Germany after the Berlin airlift, the Korean standoff, and a budding space race to the moon. Domestic battles heightened as well, particularly African Americans' fight for civil rights: the Supreme Court decided *Brown v. Board of Education* in May 1954, Emmet Till was lynched in Mississippi in August 1955, and the forced integration of Little Rock Central High School in Arkansas would take place just days before *West Side Story*'s Broadway debut in September 1957.

These events were not just headlines in the newspapers for Robbins, Bernstein, and Laurents. They all were personally involved in questions of civil rights, as Jews, as gay men, and as liberals. All three had been attached to leftist activities. They added their names to protests against Franco's dictatorship in Spain and petitions for friendship with the Soviet Union. In the wave of anticommunism that began in earnest in the late 1940s, the FBI followed Bernstein and Robbins.[30] Artists and entertainers in film and radio were especially targeted, as these were seen as particularly effective forms of propaganda, a direct line of communication to wide swaths of the population. At the same time, as men who desired men, they must have watched with some alarm the firing of gay men and women from the national government in February 1950. A growing concern for national security fueled an intensive look for the enemy within, those liable to work with communists because of shared political interests or those vulnerable to blackmail.[31] Both Bernstein and Laurents were blacklisted in Hollywood, the State Department briefly refused to renew their passports, and they endured months of self-exile abroad during the worst years of the anticommunist purge led by Senator Joseph McCarthy in the early 1950s.

Robbins, though, suffered the contradictions of the era most acutely. In the spring of 1950, just months after putting the Romeo project on hold, he began receiving intimations that his loyalty was in question. Robbins was scheduled to appear on the highly popular Ed Sullivan television show *Toast of the Town*, a surefire endorsement of his talent and broad success. Sullivan was in close touch with the FBI and determined to make his show a ringing endorsement of American loyalty as well. Weeks before Robbins was supposed to appear on the show, Sullivan rescinded the invitation, accusing him of communist activities.

This was not an unfounded accusation. Robbins *had* been a member of the Communist Party, joining in 1943, the year before *Fancy Free*'s debut. He later claimed that he came to the party because of its fight against anti-Semitism—a more sympathetic way to defend his choice, perhaps, while also critiquing American society. He left the party in 1947, finding its fight against anti-Semitism mainly rhetorical. Still, like Bernstein, Laurents, and many others in the arts, he leaned left, continuing to attend events that had become identified as attracting communists, including the conference for world peace held at the Waldorf Astoria hotel in March 1949, which Bernstein and Laurents also attended. A year later, Sullivan refused to have Robbins on his show and threatened him even further. If Robbins did not provide the names of people at a party for Soviet-American friendship—given at his home but hosted by Lena Horne—Sullivan would expose not only Robbins's communism but also his homosexuality. An interview with an FBI agent shortly followed. Robbins squirmed but did not mention any names.

The interview granted him only a short reprieve. Robbins was summoned to testify before the House Un-American Activities committee in May 1953, where he admitted to being a party member and then named names. The names were well known; it was a brief performance laced with righteousness and pity. Anticommunism had peaked, and the testimony was a desperation-infused playing-out

FIGURE 1.7 Jerome Robbins appears before the House Un-American Activities Committee (HUAC), May 1953. Photofest.

of a show of loyalty, a perverse test of belonging. Robbins won high
praise from committee members for his honesty, and congressional
representatives commented on the Americanness of *Fancy Free* as
an indication of Robbins's true political alignment. "It's always been
identified everywhere it's played as a particularly American piece,
indigenous to America," Robbins explained to the committee. Another congressman asked him why he risked being called a stool pigeon by identifying other members of the party. "I think I made a
great mistake in entering the Communist Party," Robbins declared,
"and I feel that I am doing the right thing as an American."[32]

Despite this declaration, Robbins was tormented by the decision
to testify and by its ongoing impact on his life. It saved him from the
blacklist but provoked continuing doubt and accusations of betrayal.
Some saw his testimony as proof of a willingness to do anything to
advance his career, and specifically to keep open the possibility of

working in the movie industry, which was wracked by anticommunism more than ballet or Broadway. Others believed his affirmation of loyalty covered the perceived sin of homosexuality. His testimony blackened his relationships with others, particularly Laurents, who complained throughout his life that Robbins was a careerist who could not be trusted.[33] Laurents could not resist the opportunity to work with someone he considered an artistic genius, but he did not let Robbins forget his action and embedded a reminder in their work together. Early in *West Side Story* a gang member remarks on the "difference between bein' a stool pigeon and cooperatin' with the law." Robbins never commented on the line and there is no definitive evidence that Robbins was an inside informant for the FBI. But the line in the play stands as a reminder of what was at stake. The dramatic, personal, and tragic consequences of prejudice, politics, and love were apparent to these artists in immediate and pressing relief.

Robbins, Bernstein, and Laurents grew up and achieved success during decades scarred by a deep economic downturn, a necessary war, and the crippling specter of a new kind of enemy within. They grappled with markers of being different from the mainstream, in their Jewish background, homosexual desires, and need for creativity and expression. The arts provided a realm of real hope and opportunity to define their contribution and their bid for belonging, for full participation in the possibility and hope of America. New York was their place, their stage and home, the site of aspiration and need. The years between the frivolity of *Fancy Free* and the ideas for an updated *Romeo and Juliet* heightened the terms of the challenge. *West Side Story* was set to reveal the struggle to find a place, for its creators and then far beyond them.

* 2 *

"Make alive the Daily life"

1955–57

Robbins eagerly awaited an outline of the new story that changed the Montagues and Capulets to Puerto Ricans and white American gangs. Laurents wrote up a three-act scenario in which discrimination and prejudice were shown to warp the innocence of love and shape the relation between an individual and a group. The leader of the Puerto Rican gang and his girlfriend were named Bernardo and Anita. The scenario opened with members of the Puerto Rican gang trying to scar a member of Romeo's gang. Juliet sings in Spanish with her family, and after Romeo kills Bernardo, Anita berates Juliet, insisting that she "stick to your own kind."[1]

Robbins thought it all a "hell of a good job and very much on the right track"—but he already had severe reservations. The conflict of the story could not be sustained for three acts, he feared, allowing "the audience out of our grip for 2 intermissions." The story depended upon snakelike tension, everyone poised to strike. The character of Anita, written as older, knowing, and cynical, particularly bothered him. This characterization "falls into a terrible cliché," he argued.[2] Already Robbins recognized that the world they were creating held few adults. The passion of youth needed no knowing commentary; it was a world unto itself.

The heart of the show, though, was the effort to put on stage a dramatic rendering of what happened on the streets outside the theater.

One idea to link stage and street was "the reading of headlines . . . with references to the teen-age gangwar and murders."[3] This degree of literalness did not make it very far. The difficulty of finding a nuanced way to remake the streets onstage is perhaps most obvious when the question is put in terms of the primary elements of a musical: what do song and dance have to do with gang warfare? Robbins defied the contradiction and insisted—at this early stage and throughout the production process—that dance was key. He gave an ultimatum to his creative partners: the principal characters needed to be dancers. If they weren't, he argued, a noticeable separation would occur in the action and, even more, in the coherent intensity of the drama. "It's a sorry sight and a back-breaking effort, and usually an unsuccessful one, to build the numbers around some half-assed movements of a principal who can't move," Robbins stated baldly. "*Right*," Bernstein noted on the margins of Robbins's letter.[4]

The *role* of dance in the production would be more important than the dancing ability of the principal characters, however. Dance would be central to conveying the meaning of the story and realizing the city onstage. Robbins knew that movement defined space; a straight jump upward could fashion a sense of verticality, a leg splayed high and wide one of breadth. It could also define a place. Architecture, street design by grid or spoke, the clanging elevated railways or rumbling subways underneath the pavement: these were elements that typically evoked a city. These material elements, though, often did not include people, their interactions and inhabitations. Dance could capture the contradictions of passion, of a relentless drive to connect people to one another and to their place. In the long phase of creating the script and score, from 1955 to spring 1957, Robbins directed and revised Laurents's drafts of the script and Bernstein's of the score and kept a focus on the place—New York. The believability of the story, its evocation of real streets, demanded this specificity. In fixing the story first in words and music, Robbins kept tuning it to the street, to the city, and left a defining role for dance, even though it was the last theatrical element to be created. A musical that was tragic could only make sense if the city pulsed with emotions—desire, hatred, fear, longing. And the best way to relay the urgency and consequence of those drives was through movement that created character, of people and of the city itself.

Emotions charged through the plot. The story begins with gang rivalry, danced to a score that escalates from loping to menacing. The growing presence of the Puerto Rican Sharks prompts the white American Jets to force a confrontation: a rumble to decide who owns the block, once and for all. The Jets determine that the battle will take place after a dance at the gym that night. Riff, the leader of the Jets, knows he needs all men on board and seeks out his friend, Tony, who has recently lost interest in the gang. Tony agrees to come to the dance in support of Riff, and it is there that Tony first sees Maria, the younger sister of Bernardo, the head of the Sharks. The brief encounter rouses desire between Tony and Maria—and further inflames tensions between the gangs. After a declaration of love on a fire-escape-balcony, Tony agrees to Maria's request to halt the rumble. Blinded by love, he intervenes in the battle and costs Riff his life. Tony responds by charging at Bernardo, killing him. His world now shattered, Tony returns to Maria, pleading for her forgiveness. They plan to get away, somewhere. Anita, overhearing the plan, confronts Maria for loving the man who killed her brother, but Maria convinces her of the necessity of love in the midst of hate. When the police show up to question Maria, she engages Anita to deliver a message to Tony that she is delayed. Anita agrees. But the Jets bar her entry to where Tony is hiding out, harassing and assaulting her. In revenge, she spits out a lie—that Maria is dead. Hearing this, Tony goes to the street, seeking the gun of a Shark, to join Maria in death. On her way to him, Maria calls to Tony just as he is gunned down. As Tony dies in her arms, Maria exhorts the gangs to end their violence. The battle ends where it began, on the street.

Robbins's hunch was that the tragic love at the center of the plot was not enough to fill out a musical or to make it matter. It was the ground on which the battle played out that would add both realism and heightened impact. This was not just an isolated love story but one that would encompass the struggle over who belonged in New

York. Instead of being born into the Shakespearean houses of Capulet and Montague, gangs were chosen and gave youth a "sense of belonging to *something*," as Laurents avowed. Setting the story between Puerto Ricans and white Americans interlocked young love and bigotry; it was a story "about two young lovers destroyed by a violent world of prejudice," in Laurents's summary.[5] That prejudice not only shaped attitudes toward different groups of people but life in the city more generally.

New York had undergone vast changes during the creators' lives, especially after the war was won in 1945. Looking at the streets around them in 1955, they would have seen numerous construction projects, demolitions of blocks of three- and four-story buildings and the rise of skyscrapers, particularly in midtown Manhattan. Urban renewal plans sought to remake the city through massive building projects, primarily of public housing. Private construction, though, exceeded that sponsored by the government. From 1947 to 1960, Manhattan saw the rise of approximately 120 new office buildings and 400 new apartment buildings, most of them tall, sleek skyscrapers. Park Avenue became a canyon of steel and glass anchored by the Lever House (1952), designed by Skidmore, Owings and Merrill, and the Seagram Building, by Ludwig Mies van der Rohe (1958).[6] This new cycle of demolition and construction was not just in big towers or projects or in one area of the city. The shifting landscape encompassed most of the city. In 1957, just prior to the opening of the show, Laurents noted that the building in which the creative team's first meetings about the idea had occurred, in 1949, had come down—as had the building in which they revived the project in 1955. "Wreckage proceeds faster these days," he quipped.[7]

The new buildings gave sheen to the city. They pronounced the rising power of New York as a new global capital. But that sheen covered a roiling underbelly. Enduring segregation confined African Americans and Puerto Ricans to neighborhoods distant from the gleaming business districts of midtown Manhattan. Migrants flowed into parts of the city crumbling from the weight of density and poverty. From 1950 to 1960, approximately 470,000 migrants arrived from

FIGURE 2.1 Backdrop elevation for the prologue of *West Side Story*, ca. 1957. Set designer Oliver Smith evokes the strong verticality of the era through the wall-like structure, its blocked-out windows suggesting abandonment. He points to the importance of cars in the use of the bridge arch, and fences introduce the theme of barriers that will be picked up by other elements in the set. © Rosaria Sinisi.

Puerto Rico, the largest number in any decade of the twentieth century and over 300,000 more than the previous decade.[8] The migration occurred at a time of renewed attention to US control over the territory. Continued colonialism received heightened scrutiny at the newly formed United Nations, headquartered in New York. US domination of Puerto Rico was a too-close reminder of the United States' own involvement in colonization.

Puerto Ricans had been citizens of the United States since 1917 but with little control over their own governance and no voting rights in elections on the mainland. After World War II, Congress granted Puerto Ricans the right to elect their own government and adopt a constitution, which they did in 1952. But both the process and the results kept the island in a state of limbo. The constitution needed ratification by both Puerto Rico and the US Congress, and established the territory as a commonwealth, existing between full independence and statehood. As with states, the federal government maintained authority over military, judiciary, and international affairs. But

Puerto Ricans could not vote in national elections, a right given to residents of states, nor were they represented by a voting member in Congress. They were exempt from federal income taxes but subject to military conscription.

This political conundrum spawned unease, particularly in New York City, the place to which the vast majority of Puerto Rican migrants came: by 1960, Puerto Ricans represented 80 percent of the Latino/a population in New York.[9] The press dubbed this mass of difficult, entwined issues the "Puerto Rican problem," focusing primarily on the impact of the influx on jobs and housing. Soon competition for resources seeped into social issues—especially increased gang activity. Gangs combined the long-term troubles of continued segregation and inequality with the new trends of changing migration and demographics and the beginning of the postwar baby boom. Rebellious young people spilled across the media. Newspapers investigated the ominous threat presented by wayward teens. Movies spread the worry. In *Rebel without a Cause* (1955), James Dean wrapped the danger in charm, romanticizing the appeal of defiance. *Blackboard Jungle* (1955) placed the troubles directly in New York City, its portrayal of gangs in schools dramatizing the sense that youths were careening out of the control of parents and were increasingly in control of the streets.

Robbins, Laurents, and Bernstein dropped *Romeo and Juliet* into this volatility. The city's drastic changes rippled through the plot. People teetered on the edge of emotions, rebelling against strangers and contained by buildings that could be gone tomorrow. The instability—the underlying roiling—enlivened the old story, and young love uncovered the social and political forces threatening to rupture the city.

All of this operated at the edges and underneath the mechanics of working out the script and score through 1955 and 1956. Laurents and Bernstein gave incomplete attention to the task amid crushing schedules of other commitments. Bernstein soon realized that his duties at the New York Philharmonic and to another musical, *Candide*, made it necessary to turn over the lyrics to someone else. Laurents suggested Stephen Sondheim, a young, precocious composer and lyricist and protégé of Oscar Hammerstein. The ambitious Sondheim worried that he would become known only as a lyricist if he accepted the job. But Hammerstein convinced him of the benefits that would come from being part of such an auspicious team. After a quick meeting, Sondheim came on board, adding his considerable talent with words.

Laurents, Bernstein, and Sondheim batted around draft scripts, score, and lyrics, and Robbins edited, commented, and opined. If dance was to be central, it remained abstract and talked about rather than realized at this point. But that did not stop Robbins from scratching asides on scripts and scores, crossing out whole sections, and inserting piercing questions that kept the ideas clear. When Laurents had Riff indict members of the Jets for being caught by Sharks on their territory—"Lettin' yourself be lassoed in our own corral"— Robbins exclaimed in the margins: "? Turf!"[10] The city was the meaningful reference for the conflict, not a cliché tied to western lands.

Heeding Robbins's initial comments, Laurents narrowed the play to two acts and sought to develop characters that made sense of the neighborhoods of New York, bristling with new migrants and old tensions. Slowly the script focused in on the gangs, eventually stripping away most adults. Laurents merged Mercutio and Benvolio into one sidekick for Romeo (Riff), settled on the name Maria for Juliet, and moved from Tonio to Tony (and Italian to Polish) for Romeo.

Meanwhile, Bernstein listened to the sounds of the city. One day he missed an exit off the Henry Hudson Parkway and drove under a causeway around 125th street. All around him, "Puerto Rican kids were playing, with those typical New York City shouts and the New York raucousness," he remembered. It was in the contrast between that liveliness and the backdrop of the causeway, with its concrete pillars and Roman arches, that Bernstein found his theme: "contemporary content echoing a classic myth." "Suddenly I had the inspiration for the rhumba scene," he realized.[11] This awareness of the changing landscape of New York, which infused the production, was then tied to the continued destructive forces of prejudice. While Bernstein saw the merging of classic and contemporary myth in his

FIGURE 2.2 Cars become a central part of the urban core through the proliferation of parking lots, garages, and automotive repair shops. Parking lot in midtown Manhattan, 1941. Photograph by Arthur Rothstein, LC-USF34-024549-D, FSA/OWI Collection, Prints & Photographs Division, Library of Congress.

ride through Harlem, he heard the rumba, an African-Cuban music and dance style. Classic forms of architecture and music vied with newer infrastructure and cultural traditions.

The mix of the classic and contemporary clarified a primary motivation for the production for Bernstein, but it is telling that he got to that moment of inspiration in a *car*. Cars were forcing an update of the city itself. The building of roadways gave new primacy to circulation in, around, and out of the city. These changes in infrastructure accompanied a symbolic change, as cars became aligned with individual freedom and national pride. Not surprisingly, cars appeared in drafts of the script. In one version, a car provides adventure for Tony as he explains his unsettledness to Riff. "The other day, I did a kooky thing when I was making a delivery for Doc. I saw this car: long and low and all copper-bronze. Even the key the goon left in the ignition. I hopped in and drove off: zoom! . . . But the kick wasn't there.

FIGURE 2.3 Backdrop elevation for "The Rumble," ca. 1957. The highway underpass opens up spaces under cover but available for use. The stormy skyscape of the design suggests the possible drama of those uses. In the final version of the set, Smith added elements from the prologue—the fences, streetlamp, and angled perspective of a corner in the background—to the underbelly of the highway. (See figure 2.4.) Set design by Oliver Smith. © Rosaria Sinisi.

I brought it right back."[12] In another version, Riff wants a silver car with a big J (for Jets) in color, asserting both his and his gang's participation in the latest carriers of American freedom and prosperity.[13]

As the script evolved, cars became less obvious than the spaces of the city made necessary by cars. Streets, alleys, garages, highway ramps, and causeways—these are the places the characters of the play inhabit.[14] The detritus of the automotive era in the mid-twentieth-century city created the very stakes of the turf battle between the gangs. The setting for the peak of that conflict—the rumble—migrated in drafts from a playground to "Hangman's Hill" in a park, where the city remained firmly in the background and Tony could escape into trees.[15] Eventually, the park setting gave way to "under the highway." Here was a space that was unforgiving. Forgotten and abandoned, completely man-made with no respite of nature—the negative space of the highway was emblematic of the underbelly of urban renewal and the dominance of cars on the urban landscape.

FIGURE 2.4 Stage scene from "The Rumble," London, ca. 1958. George Chakiris played Riff (on the right) in the London production before playing Bernardo in the film. Set design by Oliver Smith. © Rosaria Sinisi. Photofest.

The causeway Bernstein saw became the set for the rumble. "My city is cut + recut + slashed by hard car filled streets," Robbins had written and would soon realize.[16]

Robbins looked over the scores and drafts closely and wrote up pages of notes on the characters, trying to understand their intentions and relationships. With that resonant name, Riff liked music, was "the tempo of N.Y." and a kind of father to other gang members, who he used "like an *orchestra*." Tony and Maria were idealists, Tony dreamier and Maria more practical: "Tony wants peace magically; Maria wants peace practically."[17]

Robbins, though, focused most on Bernardo. Injustice, anger, and defiance fueled the character. "Has been promised a dream + given shit," Robbins neatly summed up. Bernardo fights to be seen as an equal, not to be an American exactly but to be a Puerto Rican in America: "*I belong here*." While Robbins's notes suggest how well he knew this kind of burning defiance, he also calls Bernardo an "overly sensitive P.R." with a "chip on shoulder," "full of hatred," "very bigoted," "*proud*/satiric—bitter." Anita, in contrast, accepts "position society has placed her in—it's better than where she was she thinks—+ feels she's part of America." Bernardo does not envy Americans, and he cannot bear the position in which he finds himself. He's put down and fights for "his just place in world." More ominously, he wants "to make a ~~world~~ home of his own as exclusive as theirs."[18]

Robbins then describes what that world is: a war. "This is a play . . . about a square block on which there is a war. You can get everyone's character out of how they deal with it," a friend of Robbins's commented.[19] Maria and Tony seek to get beyond the "war area" altogether; A-Rab of the Jets loves the "theatrics of the war"; Anita initially ignores it. The fight is over possession of the street, a small slice of space that has grand symbolism and practical meaning: it is about the "need for each person to have some rightful place in the world." The city throws together "clans" and all are claiming a right to one part. The focus of a war on and about the street made clear the need—for a foothold.

While this made abstract, even emotional, sense, Robbins knew that the setting mattered to make the necessity and stakes of the fight believable. His charge was to "make alive / the Daily life— / the grouping + coexistence / the particular gathering places / the language / the food / dress—*the double sound* / the *poverty*" of the "City Area."[20] The setting did not just contain the war—it made it. The city instigated the action by forcing a confrontation that could not be ignored. The rolling lawns and amenities of the suburbs or the wide horizons of mountains or plains might have alleviated or at least deferred the conflict. Layered buildings preening to the sky and trapping residents offered no such possibility. The tragedy lay less in the fight itself than in its pent-up inevitability. "They are paying for so much that they didn't do," Robbins's friend wrote.[21]

If Robbins focused on the emotions at the core of the show, Laurents had to find language and dialogue to convey those passions.

The idea of war within a city block led to military allusions and metaphors, perhaps not surprisingly given Laurents's army experience in the recent world war. The Jets had ranks, with Riff as their commander, who expected soon to be hauled off to the army. The name of the gang itself referenced the new military might of airplanes, as well as the appeal and power of flight.[22] And these jets set their sights on a new target: the moon. "The jet's all set and the moon won't wait," Riff declares in a draft. Land had ceded to outer space in the brimming conflict between the United States and the Soviet Union. The new battleground appeared in an unused song called "Moon" that ruminated on how long it takes to fly to the "moonerooney."[23]

"I've crystal balled this. The raidin' parties are over; the cold war's hot; it's time to drop the bomb," Riff declares in one version of the script.[24] The race to space consumed headlines of the day and was another front, like anticommunism and the efforts of HUAC, in the Cold War. The Soviet Union won the first heat, launching its first Sputnik satellite only weeks after the debut of *West Side Story*. Not surprisingly, this cold war with its occasional eruptions shadowed the gang conflict of the story. Military metaphors and the escalation of weapons in preparation for the rumble localize the global conflict. And references to atomic warfare magnify the explosiveness of the fight. Riff begs Tony to take part in the rumble because, without him, "riga-tiga-tum, crock-o jacko—: Hiroshima!" in an early draft. A tabloid with a "screeching" title in the drugstore scene makes the connection to global politics explicit: "New Atomic Threat."[25]

Sondheim toyed with these ideas in another discarded song that overtly referred to the Cold War. "Atom Bomb Baby," a mambo for the dance hall scene, credited a hot, sexy woman with atomic explosiveness. This had been a common image during the war. Many fighter planes displayed pictures of women on the fuselage, including starlets such as the Latina Rita Hayworth, who added their wattage to military force. Sondheim pushed the analogy between female sexuality and atomic weapons even further. The "Atom Bomb Baby" starts a chain reaction, and "I go all out for her fallout." She motivates the fight: "She's my fission, she's my mission." And provides emotional cover for the devastating results: "Now my Atom Bomb Baby makes me feel so proud / That all day long I'm walkin' a mushroom-shaped cloud." Then: "Man alive, if I survive"—a rare recognition of the deathly endeavor—"I'll love just you, you, you, you two-thirty five," a reference to uranium-235, the unstable uranium isotope often used in nuclear weapons.[26] The over-the-top lyrics may have doomed the song. Or its explicit references to the perils of a newly fragile world may have proved too toxic for the story to contain. The Cold War simmered in the background of the script, with little direct mention in the final version of the play.

It is instead the volatile city that encompasses more and more of the tensions. New York became the place where conflict explodes. The final script was not explicit about the hostility of nation-states or even contrasting ideologies, but the aspirations of the characters in *West Side Story* stood as an analogy in their oppositional, high-stakes fight to claim their place in the city. Under the pressure of continuing prejudice, that claim became segmented into battles between groups of people. A wide variety of people settled in New York, and the compactness of its geography created inevitable collisions. It was a city famously open to the "huddled masses yearning to breathe free," as the poem by Emma Lazarus on the base of the Statue of Liberty proclaimed. The masses came and were often embroiled in a fierce competition for survival, one group pitted against another. The gangs of *West Side Story* enacted this battle in the midcentury city.

Membership in a gang was an active step into the fray. Groups formed to fight, protect, and defend their claims to the city. And one of the easiest ways to discount the rights of other groups was to label them as different and, ultimately, unworthy. When the creators moved the story away from a conflict between Jews and Catholics, Puerto Ricans stepped into the role of outsiders, the group marked as different. The production exhibited that difference through language, clothes, skin color, movement, and music. "Atom Bomb Baby," for example, reinforced a vision of women as sexual objects and tied that explosiveness to Puerto Ricans by making the song a mambo.

The creators explored just how to define that difference in multiple drafts of the scripts, songs, and lyrics. Laurents played most with the

use of Spanish. He even gave some of the Jets a Spanish word or two.
("Against the Sharks, we need every hombre we got," Riff declares in
one draft.[27]) Bernstein drew upon a variety of sounds in Latino cultures. He employed percussive instruments such as the claves and
güiro, essential to Latin American music, and the rhythms and style
of the mambo and rumba, popularized by musicians such as Machito
and Tito Puente in the 1940s and 1950s.[28] And Robbins used pounding
heels, swirling skirts, and matadorlike side bends with arms curving
high above the head to convey ethnic particularities. These elements
alluded in a diffuse, generalized way to Spanish-speaking cultures,
and not to that of Puerto Rico per se. In fact their generality betrayed
the creators' loose knowledge of Puerto Rican culture. Robbins traveled to Harlem to watch a Puerto Rican youth dance, and Bernstein
spent a week in Puerto Rico as he was composing. But Sondheim
may have been most honest when he reportedly quipped, "I've never
even known a Puerto Rican."[29] (Thrown-out lyrics for "I Feel Pretty"
reference Seville, Madrid, and bullfighting—exhibiting, perhaps, a
greater knowledge of Spain.[30])

   If the creators had only a vague sense of Puerto Rican culture, they
were aware of some of the political issues affecting Puerto Rico specifically. The press's attention to the "Puerto Rican problem" often conveyed the contradictions of colonial entanglement. An early scenario
made explicit the betrayal the Sharks feel because of their political
status: "Since Puerto Rico *is* part of the United States, the Sharks do
not understand why they are treated as foreigners, or why they do not
have a right to be in New York, in the neighborhood. And they use
their rivalry with the Jets as a release for the anger, the bitterness
inside them."[31] Sondheim, in particular, picked up on these contradictions. His early lyrics for the song "America" recognized the tense
issue of citizenship and statehood: "Soon or later America / Makes
us a state in America / When we're a state in America / Then we mi-
grate to America!"[32] Although this specific reference was excised, the
final lyrics pointedly declare that "Puerto Rico is in America now."
The production at least prompted another look at the Puerto Rican
"problem," this time from the vantage point of Puerto Ricans.

   Language became an obvious sign of difference that was utilized a great deal in the early scripts. Spanish filtered through the dialogue of Maria and her family and even snared Riff. Different language also became a way to hide more overt statements, as in Bernardo's reply, in Spanish, to Anita's claim that Maria is no longer a child—"But she's still a virgin." The peppering of Spanish in the drafts demonstrated Laurents's attempt to insert authenticity into the portrayal of Puerto Ricans; its absence in the final script indicated that authenticity had to bow to accessibility to the predominantly English-speaking audience. In his first outline of the story that included Puerto Ricans, Laurents even pleaded for no accents—"let us take the dramatic license of eliminating all accents" (a directive followed more in the musical than the film).[33] Laurents reduced Spanish to a few words in the final script, using it most noticeably as a sign of Tony's affection for Maria when he says both "buenas noches" and "te amo" in the balcony scene. It is a sign of his acceptance of her, rather than a binding trait among Puerto Ricans.

Other words conveyed the hatred behind prejudice. Sweet-tempered Tony even hurls insults at the worst perpetrator of discrimination, Sergeant Schrank. Swerving between ethnic insults, Tony calls him a Mick bastard in one draft and a Kraut bastard in another. Schrank returns the invective: Tony goes from Wop to Polack in his rantings, and he refers to a previous store of Doc's in Jewtown. The slinging of ethnic epithets demonstrated the prevalence of prejudice—there are so many stereotypes and insults to choose from!—and also blurred the particularities of discrimination. Most especially, ethnic distinctions and the struggles of Puerto Ricans were simplified to matters of racism based on skin color. The song "Mix," which served as an early declaration of war for the Jets, stressed this clearly and violently. The Jets look to "make a mess" of Puerto Ricans, saying that once they do, "there'll be less of 'em." And the song also named color as a distinction, calling Puerto Ricans "brown little bums."[34]

One speech in particular became the focus of the creators' efforts to show the prevalence of prejudice. Sargeant Schrank was the obvious messenger. Schrank comes into Doc's pharmacy knowing that a rumble is in the making. He wants to prevent that fight but cannot contain his disdain for both gangs. Still, he saves his most offensive vitriol for the Sharks, aligning with the Jets because of skin color. As he pulls out a cigarette to light, Schrank says, "I always make it a rule to smoke in the can. And what's a room with half-breeds in it, eh, Riff?"

> It's innaresting how they can carry their smell with 'em, and still leave enough behind to stink up a whole building . . . a neighborhood . . . a whole city if you don't stop 'em—and clear 'em out. Right, Action? Clear out, Spics. And don't, don't tell me how it's a free country and I ain't got the right. It's a country with laws. I *ain't* got the right. But I got the uniform and you got the skin. It's tough all over. Beat it![35]

Schrank snarls at Bernardo to "get your trash outta here." As Tony makes a move to follow the Sharks, Schrank stops him: "That's just for the colored folk, Tony." Schrank goes on to press the Jets for details on the rumble—he knows they will fight because "regular white Americans don't rub with coons otherwise."[36]

The gist of the passage remained the same in the final version. Schrank asserts shared allegiances with the Jets, which the Jets resist. But most of the specific comments about color and other inflammatory language were edited out. Schrank's remark to Tony became "That's just for brown bellies" and then, further de-colored, "That's just for them." Some insults became more specific: "coons" became "gold-teeth." This constant editing may have indicated discomfort with the direct use of blatantly racist epithets. Or concern about its potentially explosive effects. Or worry over a provocative portrayal of white ethnic police. Robbins, for one, consistently softened offensive epithets in his comments on the script, crossing out "brown bellies" in Schrank's speech, for instance.[37] And he noted the hypocrisy of the Jets' condemning the Sharks for their use of a language other than English by naming other white immigrant groups that used other languages, "Italian German Jew."[38] Robbins could not be accused of worrying about hurting others—he was too intent on protecting himself—but he could recognize offenses and insults. He knew how best to hurt someone, with precision rather than profusion.

The raw language was dulled, but the divisions between world-views were not. A hardened portrayal of Puerto Ricans and racism remained in the production, perhaps most prominently in the role of Bernardo. Robbins's notes on the character emphasize the injustice borne by Bernardo as driving his desire for revenge, but they also flesh out his unbending bitterness and pride.[39] Bernardo is defined by and acts out within a world of racism. The creators of *West Side Story* set out to expose this constraining bigotry, yet in their made-up world Puerto Ricans remain bound by stereotype. Men brandish switchblades, ever ready to fight; women are spitfires, tempestuous and sexy. Bernardo and Anita retained the names Laurents gave them in his initial draft, as other characters went through changes of name and personality. Ultimately, the creators found it easier to rely on stereotypes than to dispel them. They used Puerto Ricans to evoke more general tensions of difference and prejudice in the city, a choice that reinforced the racism of the era even as it purported to point out its injustice.[40]

The differences upon which bigotry is based ended up being displayed less through the inflammatory language of earlier drafts than through Latino-influenced music and movement. In the prologue, Jets and Sharks dance alike to music without a notable ethnic inflection. The scene introduces youth more broadly and the conflict over possession of turf. The dance at the gym draws out differences, as the gangs face off. The Sharks confront the Jets with a mambo, arms held aloft and framing the face, chest high, in a pose reminiscent of flamenco. The Jets respond with clucking heads and broad, gymnastic lunges to bluesy jazz. A restrained cha-cha, which becomes "almost a minuet," characterizes the first meeting of Tony and Maria, a blending of cultures representative of the hope of their love and the contemporary meeting the classic, as Bernstein wanted.[41]

The introduction of Latino elements in music and movement in the dance at the gym flowered fully in the song, lyrics, and movement of "America," which portrayed life in New York for Puerto Ricans. In the musical, Anita is pitted against another Shark woman in a debate over which city is better, Manhattan or San Juan. (In the film, the song pits the Shark women against the Shark men, adding sexual play and antagonism—as well as gendered dimensions of Puerto Rican experiences in New York.) Anita makes explicit criticisms of Puerto Rico, taunting Rosalia, who declares that she likes "the city of San Juan." "I know a boat you can get on," Anita responds. The lyrics play out aspirations of consumerism in the colonial relationship between the United States and Puerto Rico. Rosalia wants to bring a TV, a washing machine, and a Buick to San Juan; Anita extols the "Knobs on the doors in America / Wall-to wall floors in America!" Anita then summarizes the dilemma: "Nobody knows in America / Puerto Rico's in America!"

The music of "America" utilizes some of the most specific Latino influences in the score. Bernstein combines a huapango, a song of fast tempo and complex rhythms typical of Mexico, with a seis, a song type popular in Puerto Rico. The music opens with a knocking percussive sound from claves. But it is the wickedly complicated changing rhythms that distinguish the song. The rhythms propel the women to swish their skirts, turn tightly, and quickly kick their legs. The cutting movement is as bright and decisive as the stark difference in the attitudes of Anita and Rosalia toward the two places. This mash-up of Latino influences in music and dance diffuses differences among Spanish-speaking cultures while accentuating difference overall. And the biting wordplay and debate is overshadowed by the exaggerated pronunciation of "Amereeekka."

Heightening festive music and movement and dulling raw-worded insults diminished the threat of Puerto Ricans. But the playing out of the story in the context of the city reasserted their broader marginalization. The stage version of "America" takes place inside an apartment, but Robbins first wanted it to be performed in an alley—a leftover space for looked-over people. In his divided view of the city, Sargeant Schrank recognizes that rights and access to the city itself are at stake: the Sharks want "use of the playground . . . use of the

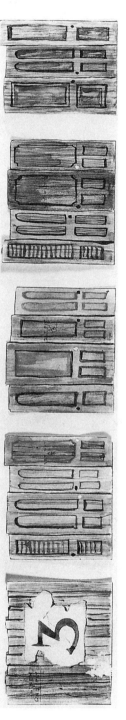

FIGURE 2.5 Doors units were used in "America" and as a prelude to "Somewhere," ca. 1957. They contributed to the theme of barriers, also conveyed by fences, bricked-up buildings, and the interrupting highway infrastructure. Set design by Oliver Smith. © Rosaria Sinisi.

FIGURE 2.6 Rendering of stage scene of "America," ca. 1957, by Oliver Smith. © Rosaria Sinisi.

gym . . . candystore . . . the streets."[42] An early draft of the argument between Maria and Anita over the limits of love names the differences Tony and Maria represent in spatial terms. "He is different; he's one of them! He lives on the Avenue, you on the side street—," Anita cries. "There's a corner between," Maria responds, a plea to see their spaces as joined.[43]

After the rumble, however, Tony and Maria realize that such intersections—and access to and freedom in the city—will never come for them. They have to imagine an altogether alternative world. The dream ballet "Somewhere" indicated that a different place is even more important than another time. This other place will be the opposite of the oppressive streets and concrete, tomblike setting of the rumble under the highway. Apartment and city walls fly away and the lovers find themselves in "a world of space and air and sun." Members of the gangs come onstage, now wearing "soft pastel versions of what they have worn before."[44]

Earlier versions of the song and the script make the dream world

FIGURE 2.7 Preliminary study for backdrop for "Somewhere," ca. 1957. Note the distant city skyline in the background. The final backdrop was more abstract, with more sky and clouds and no representation of the city (see figure 2.8). Backdrop study by Oliver Smith. © Rosaria Sinisi.

even more unlike a city. "We'll go someplace where there are no streets. . . . We'll go down the river, 'way down where it curves away and widens and the buildings turn into fields," Tony promises Maria.[45] Excised lines exhort them to dismantle the city—"Walls will be trees and streets will be streams"—and to make their way "to a place where the sky and the field and the trees aren't fenced."

> Some day, some day,
> We'll find a new kind of city,
> Peaceful and friendly and pretty,
> Somewhere, somewhere . . .
> There where it's green is the city
> 　we've seen in dreams
> And the walls there are all
> 　waterfalls and the streets are
> 　streams.[46]

FIGURE 2.8 Stage scene, "Somewhere," with Carol Lawrence and Larry Kert, ca. 1957. Photograph by Martha Swope/© Billy Rose Theatre Division, New York Public Library for the Performing Arts, Astor, Lennox and Tilden Foundations. Set design by Oliver Smith. © Rosaria Sinisi.

Robbins's notes for the choreography reinforce the freedom of this alternative world: "From the tight bent-knee, into-the-earth movement, the kids, using the light, air, sun, smell, and most of all the space and peace, open up and extend themselves in movements which are not out of character but suddenly released from the tensions of their realistic city problems." Tony and Maria dance a pas-de-deux that reenacts their meeting at the dance hall. Members of the gangs join them and all form a circle that covers the whole stage, where "each person has his own secure place."[47]

Reality returns, however. Buildings begin to reenter, "space becomes more limited," and groups are pushed together, jostled, "until finally the complete tempo and horrors of the cage of the city is upon them."[48] The dream world of fields and open air quickly evaporates as Tony and Maria plan to meet up at Doc's pharmacy and escape. Anita confronts Maria about her love and is persuaded to help the lovers.

It is the scene of Anita at the drugstore that haunts the entire pro-

FIGURE 2.9 Stage scene of Anita being taunted at the drugstore, with Anybodys (played by Lee Becker) looking away on the left, ca. 1957. Set design by Oliver Smith. © Rosaria Sinisi. Photofest.

duction and lays bare the price of prejudice. As she enters the shop to tell Tony that Maria is delayed, the jukebox plays a mambo. Against that background, the Jets tease Anita, at first with words. To Anita's "please," a Jet replies "por favor." "Will you let me pass," Anita asks. "She's too dark to pass," a Jet responds, a knowing and hurtful reference to the anguished reality of the color line in American society. Language dissolves into expletives—tramp, pig, Spic, gold-tooth, garlic mouth—and then movement overtakes words. Stripping Anita of her mantilla, the Jets begin to taunt her with it as if she were a bull, holding it just out of her reach and tossing her back and forth until, finally, she lands on the floor and they lift a Jet airborne to be put on top of her. Doc enters and yells a horrified "Stop it!" The Jets disassemble and Anita tells the lie—that Chino has killed Maria—that ensures Tony's death.

In this critical scene, differences of cultures—the mambo on the jukebox, Spanish phrases—become not just the background for but also the foundation of bigotry. Laurents believed the change he made here to Shakespeare's story made prejudice the clear theme of the show. It was not just a delayed messenger but one who was attacked. Discrimination begets revenge.[49] In the scene, movement embellishes what language and music have set up. Gestures take discrimination and hatred to its bitter extreme as the overdramatized actions of bullfighting devolve into shoves and harassment. Music and formalized movement stop in the production at the end of this scene. The world of the west side has become completely exposed.

This scene—and the betrayal of Anita at the heart of it—rips open the real tragedy of the story. Earlier in the show, Anita's less trenchant attitude toward racism allows her to see the opportunities of America. She even embraces the possibilities of love across lines when she is grieving for her own lover. But the taunting and attack force a complete reversal and confrontation with the implacability of the problems of urban life that can no longer be ignored.[50] Her understandable reaction to assault and prejudice make violence and destruction inevitable. Tony dies in the street where the conflict began—and where it will continue.

"Have you heard the voice of my city fighting + hitting + hurt," Robbins asked. *West Side Story* was his testimony to that part of New York and of American life. No longer able to celebrate the frivolity of sailors in New York, as in *Fancy Free*, the creators revealed a darker side of America in a portrayal of the city that made real and tragic the quest to belong.

Story set, now the challenge was to sell it. Could a musical whose first act ended with two dead bodies onstage get on Broadway?

* 3 *

"Comes from life itself"

1957

Two dead bodies onstage at intermission did not deter veteran Broadway producer Cheryl Crawford. Smart, connected, and a workhorse, Crawford knew talent and knew the complications involved in mounting any musical, much less one that did not fit the conventions of the genre. She had been producing Broadway shows since the early 1940s, with the hits *Brigadoon* (1947) and *Paint Your Wagon* (1951) on her résumé. So she knew just what a powerful combination the creative force of Robbins, Bernstein, Laurents, and newcomer Sondheim represented. Along with Roger Stevens, whose connections to New York real estate could open pockets, Crawford came on board in the spring of 1956. It would be "no cinch," she remarked. "It has very few of the customary Broadway values of comedy and splash with three killings and music leaning to opera and it must be cast brilliantly with no names which means the chance of big out of town losses and difficulty in getting benefits and a theatre."[1]

That challenge must have been part of the appeal for Crawford. She was fifteen years older than Robbins, Bernstein, and Laurents, and hardened by the backbreaking work of producing theater in America. She may have been attracted to the idea of *West Side Story* as she, too, struggled to belong, a lesbian in a male-dominated world. She had never wanted to be an actor; she wanted to make theater happen. Along with Harold Clurman and Lee Strasberg, she had fashioned the

Group Theatre in the 1930s, for which the young Robbins did some backstage work. In the 1940s, she founded the American Repertory Theater and, a year later, with Strasberg, the Actors Studio. The Actors Studio was a mecca of Method acting and a seeding ground for many of the era's most famous actors, including Marlon Brando and Paul Newman. Robbins took classes there, along with Montgomery Clift, and it's likely it was an acting class there that prompted the idea of staging *Romeo and Juliet* in a contemporary setting nearly a decade before its fruition as a musical.

With a large advance needed for the famous team of Robbins, Bernstein, and Laurents, Crawford quickly got an infusion of money from Stevens, a tycoon who was as deeply involved in the arts as he was in real estate. Stevens had been on the board of the Actors Studio and had begun backing Broadway shows in 1949. He provided the needed cash, but it was Crawford who did the work of producing—managing the creative team, finding talent, overseeing the many decisions involved in staging, casting, costuming, and set design. By June 1956, Crawford was as involved in the making of the show as the collaborators, although her primary contribution may have been prodding and worrying. She negotiated a hard deal with Robbins, Bernstein, Laurents, and Sondheim, using the unconventional parts of the show— the deaths, the operatic reach—to justify reduced authors' royalties.[2] That settled, she became anxious about possible competition. She was on the trail of a possible movie about teenage Puerto Rican gangs in Harlem who used expressions like "cool" and "rumble." "Essentially the story is a slice of life which I find rather pedantic. But it is worrisome to think that the milieu may be covered before *West Side Story* gets on."[3] Crawford also pressured Laurents to add more humor, back off from "invented slang," and do more research, spending a week "observing these kids at work and play."[4] Laurents balked, claiming that a "socioeconomic history of the neighborhood" was not needed: "I think the reality should be an emotional, not a factual one." He insisted that the rituals and experiences of gang life were more necessary to the show than specific causes and proposed solutions. "The point is prejudice and that is the background of the plot," he declared.[5] For Laurents, the musical's connection to the streets was in theme, not in a detailed description of the environment.

There was already a great deal about gangs and juvenile delinquency circulating in the media. The rebelliousness of youth was hardly new, but the shape of the problem had changed in the years after the war. The babies born in the boom years were growing up in an increasingly divided world; the existence of nuclear weapons only made the stakes of deviance and violence seem that much more consequential. Mass media heightened the drama. In addition to films such as *The Wild One* and *Rebel without a Cause*, journalists, politicians, and sociologists weighed in with articles, books, reports, and policy recommendations. In New York, the changing labor market as factories left for the suburbs, the rise of housing projects, and the migration of Puerto Ricans and African Americans all contributed to increased gang activity. The city responded by establishing the New York City Youth Board in 1947 and deploying a force of social workers offering recreation and social programs to lure young men away from gangs.[6]

Laurents understood what Crawford did not: that a story about juvenile delinquency on Broadway could not be an exegesis on social progress, on how a neighborhood went from middle class to poverty through successive waves of people moving in and then out, as she saw it.[7] That approach was already well covered in the press, and pedantic goals would likely result in leaden entertainment and artistry. What a musical might be able to reveal is the appeal of gangs, their behavior, camaraderie, and entrenchment in urban life, and how a gang secured for its members a place in the anxious world.

Crawford continued to hound Laurents about the script, but by early 1957, she turned her attention to raising money, scouring talent agencies for young dancers who could sing, and figuring out which cities would be best for the tryouts before coming to Broadway. She looked to the west coast, thinking San Francisco or Los Angeles might be welcoming settings for a different kind of musical. A theatrical producer in LA disabused her of the notion fast, suggesting that the work was too violent, with too much bad language, to get

past the "Catholics and Baptists who own the auditorium." She ruminated on possible cast members: Pat Stanley, who had been a hit
in the national tour of *The Pajama Game*; Chita Rivera; George Chakiris. (The latter two would make indelible contributions to the production, Rivera in the musical as Anita and Chakiris in the film as
Bernardo.)[8] For prospective investors, she used Bernstein's score to
pique interest: "It has more vigor and excitement than 'Wonderful
Town' with a mambo, tango, rock and roll, as well as ballads."[9]

Crawford had acute antennae for talent—and for trouble. Her
quibbles about the script only increased as she worried that there
was still not enough humor and not enough character to pull the audience through the more disturbing aspects of the story. And she still
wondered if the script hit hard enough on the issues of juvenile delinquency. In late March, she sent a draft to the director Elia Kazan, expressing her concern "about whether it is really there or not." Kazan
reportedly replied that the script was not realistic enough. And how,
he asked, could a musical convey the seriousness of the issue?[10]

Despite these worries, Crawford plodded on with gathering back-
ers. She arranged a presentation of the show on the evening of April
17 in the apartment of Beatrice Renfield, a Manhattan philanthropist
who lived at 10 Gracie Square, one of the most prestigious addresses
on the Upper East Side. Robbins presented a synopsis, Bernstein
played the score to which Chita Rivera and others sang—and the potential investors were not impressed.[11] Now Crawford balked. Just six
weeks before rehearsals were to begin, she pulled out (later calling it
one of a number of inevitable "errors and abortions").[12] To Robbins,
she claimed that she could not build the funding; to others, she complained about the script and its weakness in obscuring the causes of
juvenile delinquency. The difficulty in finding performers who could
sing, act, and dance—and who looked like teenagers—may also have
worn her down.[13] She called the team into her office and told them she
was bowing out.

Surprised and dejected, the collaborators left Crawford's office in
search of a drink, only to be rejected again at the Algonquin Hotel because Laurents was not dressed formally enough. They drowned their

artistic and fashion sorrows at the less fussy Iroquois next door. The loss of a powerful producer was damaging, but the difficult scheduling of people-in-demand made it likely that the show would die altogether. Bernstein had just agreed to become the codirector of the New York Philharmonic in the fall. If the show could not be put together in the next few months, it would likely fall apart.

Laurents made a desperate call to Roger Stevens, who was in Europe, and Stevens assured them that Crawford's decision was not his own. He still believed in the project. But his monetary investment could not cover all that was necessary from a producer. It was Sondheim who found a savior, somewhat by accident. The evening after Crawford backed out, Sondheim got a call from a friend, the fledging producer Harold Prince. Prince and his partner Robert Griffith had had a number of successes on Broadway, including *The Pajama Game* (1954) and *Damn Yankees* (1955). The *West Side Story* team had thought about approaching them before turning to the more experienced Crawford. On the phone, Sondheim explained their dilemma. Prince expressed interest but was caught up, in Boston, for the out-of-town tryouts of their latest show, *New Girl in Town*, which would open on Broadway just a few weeks later. As soon as they could, Prince and Griffith came down from Boston to talk to the collaborators and hear the score—and then quickly signed on.

Prince and Griffith had more appetite for risk and ability to persuade others that the risk was worthwhile, perhaps more for artistic invention than monetary gain. They raised $300,000 in a week, eventually putting together a list of nearly 175 investors, whose contributions ranged from $250 to $12,000, with most around $1,000—a fairly typical bunch of long-standing Broadway investors, as well as some personal connections, such as Robbins's parents.[14] They changed the name of the show to *Gangway* in early June, then back to *West Side Story* a month later because *Gangway* seemed "misleading."[15] Even more important, Prince and Griffith soothed egos and kept the show moving through auditions and rehearsals, to tryouts in Washington and Philadelphia and an opening in New York City in September, on time.

Much of their work involved moving Robbins. Robbins had long been researching the show—reading other Shakespeare plays, Kafka's *The Trial*, and recent books on juvenile delinquency and Puerto Rico, and attending an exhibit at the Museum of Modern Art on graffiti photographed by Brassaï, the Hungarian photographer.[16] His continuing courses in Method acting with Stella Adler proved more influential, however. Pushed to get firsthand experience with the world of New York gangs, Robbins left the dance studios of midtown Manhattan and wandered through the Puerto Rican section of Harlem. At a school dance there, he talked to young men who were gang members and looked closely at the dancing itself. Robbins saw movement he had never seen elsewhere. Partners rarely seemed to dance *with* each other, he noted. They started out together and then avoided contact for the rest of the song, although "I'm told that the partners know damn well who they're dancing with." A large sign proclaimed "NO GRINDING," denouncing the slow motion that connected pelvises. Trips to Brooklyn underscored the importance of dress at these dances: one gang in red, another in black. But what impressed him most about these teenagers "was the sense they gave you of containing their own world. Not arrogance, exactly; but a crazy kind of confidence. And there was always a sense of tension. At dances, you got the impression they were trying to exorcise their own tensions."[17]

Robbins approached this world as a kind of ethnographer, "by osmosis and infiltration," seeing its distinctiveness and figuring out its codes. He left his office on 74th Street and Lexington Avenue and walked twenty blocks north to a world where "the streets are darker, the signs are in Spanish, and the people lead their lives on the sidewalks." Gangs offered security and identity in this tense world-within-a-world, containing the violence, fear, and passion, even as they also caused eruptions.[18] It is "absolutely like going into a foreign country," Robbins wrote.[19] A journalist prodded him on the obvious contradiction: how insulated was he in his *own* world that he did not know about this growing part of the city? "But I hadn't really *seen* it," Robbins explained.[20] The repartee revealed the segregation that slashed the city into parts, one often hidden from another. Robbins

FIGURE 3.1 On the street in New York, ca. 1960. Visual research for the film captured these kinds of random moments of urban life. Jerome Robbins Dance Division, New York Public Library for the Performing Arts, Astor, Lennox and Tilden Foundations.

incorporated into the musical this exploration of how separate worlds could exist so close to one another, whether Puerto Rican and white or, by analogy, gay and straight, Jewish and Gentile, immigrant and self-fashioned American. The production exemplified the around-the-corner quality of life in New York: separated and yet inextricably connected.

Robbins brought these real-world revelations to auditions and rehearsals. His observations on dancers at auditions noted those who were Puerto Rican, calling them the "*real thing*."[21] But that authentic connection to experience rarely earned a dancer or actor a callback. Casting started almost a year before the show opened and went on month after month after month, going through over seven hundred actors and dancers. Well-known singers, such as Anna Maria Alberghetti and Jerry Orbach, were not good enough dancers or not able to convey the restlessness and credulity of youth. Others, such as Chita Rivera, were identified early and kept coming back, audition after audition, to prove their talent. Who would play the key roles of Maria and Tony was particularly vexing to the collaborators. They wanted an ingénue for Maria, someone unknown, but the singing alone demanded professional experience. Similarly, the actor playing Tony had to combine a kind of innocence with the war-weariness of a tired gang member. And whoever played Maria and Tony had to move well, if not dance spectacularly. Robbins stuck to the bar he had set at the beginning: dance was central to the production and all cast members had to have some comfort with it.

Eventually it was Carol Lawrence who projected the right balance of artfulness (talent) and artlessness (naivety) for Maria—if not the appropriate ethnic background. A native of Chicago, Lawrence dropped out of college to find her place in New York. She had played a few roles, most recently in the *Ziegfeld Follies*, but had not yet had a starring one. The multiple auditions for *West Side Story* almost broke her, though. She showed up at the first audition with excessive makeup to convince the collaborators she could be Puerto Rican. Robbins told her to "take a shower and come back."[22] The creators were not especially interested in ethnic authenticity in this role (onstage or, later, in the movie). Ideas of romantic attachment across racial and ethnic lines may have been easier to imagine in storytelling than to realize in casting. And the demands of the role often served as believable excuses, perhaps to the creators themselves as well as many others. Lawrence had taken dance, but it was her singing voice and acting that most suited her for Maria. It was a voice that was neither grand nor showy; its "not too schooled" quality appealed even to Bernstein, who knew that an opera-star voice would doom the believability of the character. Finally, after thirteen auditions (which now would violate union rules), Lawrence received the score to three songs to take home with her and study. "I remember how wonderful the score sheet felt under my arm as I rode on the subway," home to her apartment in Gramercy Park.[23]

Larry Kert, eventually picked for Tony, also kept coming back for auditions, each time for a different role or the chorus and then primarily to test for Riff. He never fit any ideal vision of a character, whether a Jet or a Shark, and certainly not Tony. He was less than six feet tall, dark haired, and Jewish, with a baritone voice, trying out for a role described as needing someone six feet tall, blond, Polish, and a tenor.[24] What convinced the collaborators was the audition with both Lawrence and Kert. Robbins told Lawrence to hide; he then told Kert to find her, simulating the balcony love scene that defined both *Romeo and Juliet* and *West Side Story*. Lawrence hid high up on scaffolding on the side of the stage. Kert was dogged in his pursuit, conveying all the pent-up excitement of newfound passion in his scramble up the scaffolding to get to her—and then act the balcony scene.[25] The collaborators had found their dewy-eyed, tenacious young lovers.

Just as casting and financing settled, though, Robbins delivered another blow. At a meeting with his collaborators and Prince and Griffith, Robbins declared that he would be too busy directing the show to do the choreography. It was a surprise to everyone, perhaps no one more than the newly signed-on producers counting on the distinguished creative team. With the aplomb that led him to succeed in the ego-driven world of Broadway, Prince told Robbins that he and Griffith had come to the production largely because of Robbins's talents and would need to consider backing out if he did not do the choreography. The strong parry surprised Robbins. He backtracked. Then he threw out other demands—eight weeks of rehearsal instead of the usual four, an assistant choreographer, and three or four rehearsal pianists. Prince said they would consider all of these requests (and delivered on the longer rehearsal time and assistant choreographer but drew the line at so many pianists).[26] Robbins had been handled.

Rehearsals started in late June in the Chester Hale Studio. It was a fitting space in the reconfigured city: a dance studio above a garage on 56th Street near Carnegie Hall. Laurents's script was basically done and Bernstein's score largely finished, with a resonant tritone that appeared throughout much of the music to tie together such disparate songs as "Cool" and "Maria."[27] Sondheim fiddled with the lyrics up until the last minute. The primary tasks that remained were choreographing the dances and staging the action. Peter Gennaro, a budding choreographer, created much of "America," although

FIGURE 3.2 Carol Lawrence and Larry Kert in the famous balcony scene on a fire escape, ca. 1957. Photograph by Fred Fehl, courtesy of Gabriel Pinski. Set design by Oliver Smith. © Rosaria Sinisi.

FIGURE 3.3 Jerome Robbins in rehearsal, 1957. The signs of popular and ethnic dance moves, with their isolation of body parts, can be seen in the swagger of hips pushed to one side and topped by a nonchalant torso. Photograph by Martha Swope/© Jerome Robbins Dance Division, New York Public Library for the Performing Arts.

Robbins staged it, and Gerald Freeman and Donald MacKayle provided general assistance to Robbins.

Robbins, though, took control. Instilling many of the lessons of Method acting, he created a world onto itself, starting in rehearsals. He had dancers write out backgrounds for their characters and would randomly ask someone in the midst of the rehearsal a question about his parents, meaning the *character's* parents. The psychological quest merged with contextual research including postings of newspaper articles about Puerto Rico, juvenile delinquents, and general struggles in the city, such as rent disputes. Robbins wanted the cast members to absorb the challenges, tensions, and details of life on the edge in the city. One day every member of the Sharks came to rehearsal with a strip of wool around his or her wrist, a made-up sign of their gang membership.[28]

Robbins even instituted a policy of referring to everyone by character name and refusing to let members of one gang speak to those in

FIGURE 3.4 Chita Rivera in rehearsal, 1957. Here Rivera highlights the distinctive elements of Anita's movement with the frame of the uplifted arm, one shoulder askew and forward, all embellished by the swirl of the skirt. Photograph by Martha Swope/© Jerome Robbins Dance Division, New York Public Library for the Performing Arts.

the other on breaks. This way of viewing others became so ingrained that when Tony Mordente, a Jet, began dating Chita Rivera, a Shark, the other Jets did not speak to him for a week. Robbins was relentless in his demands. He pushed the cast often to the point of tears and breakdowns. He demanded a great deal from everyone but reserved a high degree of venom for a few. Larry Kert, playing Tony, and Mickey Callin, as Riff, were the primary targets of his wrath. He seemed intent upon terrorizing them into anger, taunting them, shaming them in front of others, including, in some accounts, calling them effeminate and "faggots." (Kert was open about his homosexuality.) Following the precepts of Method acting, Robbins told Callin to find somebody to hate. Soon enough, Callin started muttering under his breath that he hated Jerry Robbins.[29]

While the actors playing the roles of Tony and Riff seemed to have been special targets for Robbins's persecution, the character of Anybodys crystallized the isolation and longing in the play that Robbins may have felt more generally. Lee Becker, who played Anybodys, found herself alone during breaks in rehearsal, belonging neither to Jets or Sharks. The persistent exclusion became increasingly difficult and *personal*. "Look, maybe you like Lee Becker. But forget that. Just remember that she's like a mosquito," Robbins reportedly told the cast. Becker quickly became depressed. Although she claimed to have overcome the backstage isolation as the rehearsals, and eventually performances, went on, Becker still waited every night for the brief moment when a Jet appreciates her help in finding Tony after the rumble—"You did good, Buddy Boy." "She's a character who just wants to belong and never can. She could be anybody," Becker declared.[30] (This feeling may have been exacerbated by Becker's and Robbins's affair—and the fact that he was also having an affair with Tommy Abbott, another dancer in the company, at the same time.[31])

Anybodys was a misfit. With short hair, wearing clothes similar to what the men in the show wore and markedly different from the swirling, form-flattering dresses of the other women, she pushes against stereotypes that keep her from being an acknowledged member of a gang. She was a woman attempting to fit into a man's role in a gang—as a fighter rather than a clinging girlfriend. There was also recognition of sexual domination and abuse that Anybodys—and women in general—might have experienced. "Pants is protection," Anybodys claims in a draft of the script in response to fellow Jets taunting her for not wearing skirts.[32]

Anybodys's predicament may have been closest to the creators' struggle to find their own place in society. Even more than her difference in just being a woman, Anybodys suggests the social conundrum of homosexuality. Her role as a woman attempting to be a part of a man's world played off a common understanding of homosexuality as inversion: men acting like women and women acting like men. Given the sexual orientation of the collaborators, homosexuality would have been a familiar subject of prejudice and ostracism. There was much to draw from the reality of gay life in the 1950s amid entrenched ideas about sexual perversion and difference that interfered with establishing one's place in the world.[33] In fact, the collaborators toyed with more references to homosexuality in the various drafts of the script, particularly in the relationship between Tony and Riff. The initial scene between the two characters kept shifting settings: at times a playground, where Tony could swing, at other times in the drugstore, and in one draft, in a bedroom. Riff lives with Tony because of his own family's dysfunction, and their tie is like that of brothers—from "sperm to worm" or "womb to tomb."[34] It is Bernardo who points to the homoeroticism of their relationship in one draft. Riff and another Jet prevent Tony from fighting in the rumble, and Bernardo spits, "I can just about guess what pretty boy does for the two of you." Tony stops. "And I was worried for Maria!" Bernardo continues. The Jets expect Tony to begin slugging, but he resists.[35]

These suggestions quickly disappear in the drafts, however, leaving Anybodys to stand in for difference in sexuality as a girl who wants to be a gang member, and who is neither sexually interested in men nor willing to draw their sexual attention. In research for the film, co-director Robert Wise found a real-life version of the character at the LaGuardia Settlement House on the Upper East Side, noting that the "local Anybodys" was "really Nobodys— . . . always twitching, moving, smoking, gaffing, laughing—full of hell."[36] An Anybodys who is nobody seeking to be somebody. The very name conveyed her isolation, invisibility, and lack of particularity. She uses this to hide in the shadows and overhear crucial conversations, such as the Sharks discussing that Chino has a gun and is on the hunt for Tony. But ultimately, she wants to be part of the Jets, defined solely by herself rather than her sexual attachment to someone else.

Membership in a gang served as one test—and way—of belonging, and the creators considered revealing more of the needs that gangs fulfilled late in the rehearsal period. "Like Everybody Else," an abandoned song, brought together the misfits of the Jets—A-Rab, the shortest; Baby John, the youngest; and Anybodys, the only woman. A-Rab laments being a "shrimp," who should "get refunds for all of the scenes that I miss" in parades and movies. "Nobody listens to no one who swears with a squeak," Baby John mourns. "Girls ain't good for anything," Anybodys sang, "No good for nothing but wiggling and giggling around." Anybodys fits into neither groups of men nor of women: "With boys I'm the strangest freak on earth. / With girls, I'm an accident of birth." They all desire to be "like everybody else"— perhaps the clarion call of adolescent culture overall.[37] Despite the clarity of the idea and the appeal of the song, Laurents deemed that it pitched the show closer to musical comedy than the lyric theater they were trying to achieve. Others agreed, and the song was dropped.

Two other songs that conveyed more of what was at stake for the gangs were thrown out as well. "Mix" was a "war cry" from the Jets, a rousing call to violence, with racist taunts of the Sharks as "spics" and "brown little bums." "This Turf Is Ours" put the dispute with the Sharks in territorial terms: "East to the Avenue . . . And west to the Drive . . . South to the parkin' lot . . . And north to the Five and Ten."[38] These songs, along with "Like Everybody Else," carry much of the thematic foundations of the production upon which the story of forbidden love rests. Marginalization and prejudice play out over the space of the city. But it's telling that the songs themselves were not included. Instead, as the famous anecdote goes, months of drafts, revisions, and rehearsals into the musical, Robbins told his collaborators that he could do the opening, the setup of the whole production, better in dance.[39] And he did.

But it took him awhile to get around to it. An initial run-through about three weeks into rehearsal proved "disastrous," according to Prince. "The show was slow, lugubrious, somewhat self-conscious, IMPORTANT. Too much introspection, no impulse, no energy."[40] When Robbins pushed beyond Method to movement, the show found its mark. The earlier attention to character and background, though, fueled the movement so that a sequence like the prologue would work—both as foundation for the story and as a riveting piece of dance and music. Movement carries the stories and meanings of the show; it forms the structure and language of the gangs. From the opening depiction of growing aggression between the Sharks and the Jets to the competition of the dance hall and the rumble, these characters dance their moods, intentions, and tragic ends.

The prologue conveys this in less than five minutes. The curtain rises on a gang of young men already in possession of the stage. The music sets the tension from the beginning with four loud sustained chords progressing to hushed, stealthy notes. Then the snapping begins. This distinctive, sharp sound of fingers slapping against palms suggests the control, unity, and growing power of the gang. With this small gesture, Robbins drew attention to bodies as instruments and voices beyond speaking. He created a distinctive way for one person to move—a sweep of the arms, a hop forward—that then joined with others to become a physical crescendo.

The gangs form quickly so as to taunt. The intrusion on the Jets' possession of the stage—of their turf—begins slowly, first with one Shark and then another, and another, to mimic the wave of migration into a neighborhood. At first solidly outnumbered, the Sharks have little chance of retaliating against the Jets. But as their numbers increase, so does their boldness. The confinement of the stage—its defined parameters—accentuates the desperation of fighting over limited territory. The music and dance shift back and forth between easy lyricism and sharp attack. A few words puncture the increasingly rapid rhythm and motion ("beat it," "hey," "c'mon, c'mon") as the fury seethes. The prologue ends with the merge of dancing into brawling, as Bernardo wounds A-Rab on what has been the Jets' turf.

This dramatic beginning set out the conflict at the root of the story—and the new storytelling that marked the show's innovation. Dance could carry not only character but also plot and tragedy, and an old story could be remade in the conditions of the contemporary city. The first full rehearsal in front of an audience hinted at the success to come. Before the production left town for tryouts, in Washington and Philadelphia, the company put on a so-called gypsy run-through in New York for Broadway professionals, presenting the complete show but without full orchestration, costumes, or scenery. Hal Prince awaited this moment with high anticipation, favoring it over the formal opening night because "the audiences are sophisticated, predisposed in favor of friends in the cast, and unprepared."[41]

That combination proved to be magical for this run-through. The show stunned the audience: Lauren Bacall, tears coming down her face, could not move; bursts of applause thundered from others.[42] This audience might have better appreciated just what had been accomplished in terms of talent—that of both the creators and the performers—but, even so, the reaction indicated the surprise of the show, its unexpected impact and resonance.

The buildup in the press then began to shape its opening. Stories featured large-spread photographs of the leading actors and the dance. Other articles focused on the story behind the story, particularly how the famous creators came up with the idea. Laurents penned an early narrative of the show's creation in "The Growth of an Idea," first published in early August, which dramatized the shift from a conflict between a Jewish girl and a Catholic Romeo on the Lower East Side to juvenile delinquents, a Puerto Rican gang and a "polymorphous self-style 'American' gang," on the west side. The relevance to headlines captured journalists' attention. Robbins's visits to settlement houses authenticated the story and, in an even tighter parallel, one article noted that policemen in midtown were "having a spot of trouble trying to decide which passing youths are juvenile delinquents and which are merely singers and dancers on their way to rehearsals."[43]

The press attention and laudatory audience of the gypsy run-through buoyed the cast as they set off for Washington in early August. There, in the hot humid days of high summer, the creators continued to fidget with the production. Tony needed more motivation early on; Bernstein and Sondheim wrote "Something's Coming." Sets made in New York did not fit the stage of the National Theater in Washington so either had to be redone (Laurents remembers Robbins attacking the scenery with a saw himself) or numbers restaged. Robbins then went after Bernstein's lush orchestration at the end of the dream ballet, cutting it down to a simpler transition. Tensions raged, particularly between Robbins and everyone else. Expectations kept climbing.

On August 19, the show opened its out-of-town previews at the National Theater to an audience primed for drama. The curtain dropped to silence—and then an explosion of applause. Reviewers raved and the AP wire carried the news around the country. Some Washington critics took the opportunity of being a tryout town to make suggestions—slim down the dream ballet, move "Gee, Officer Krupke" to an earlier point in the show—but, in general, they praised the music, the dance, the cast, and the surprising eloquence on a difficult subject.[44] "Despite its throb of violence and passion, *West Side Story* has a becomingly diverting vitality," one writer decided.[45] Another picked up Cheryl's Crawford's concern: one would not learn much about "the causes of juvenile delinquency." More important than causes, though, were consequences—what Laurents had rebutted to Crawford. The show would make you "feel a great deal more deeply its effects," and the score, in particular, "articulates what the juvenile offender cannot say of his compulsions by showing what he does as a result of them."[46]

For their effectiveness in making a musical out of juvenile delinquency, Bernstein, Robbins, and Laurents received a gold key to the city. Already, though, the creators were backtracking from the idea that they had set out to solve the problem of youth rebellion. Instead, they wanted to show the discrimination and alienation that put violence in motion. In taking the key, Bernstein put the focus on the "racial and national frictions that provide the seed ground for juvenile delinquency and gang warfare" rather than on the behavior of youths themselves.[47]

Gold key in hand, the creators and cast moved on to Philadelphia for another tryout. Eyes really turned to Broadway, however. Within a few days of its opening in Washington, the show had sold out weekend dates all through October, November, and December in New York. And, despite the suggestions of some critics in Washington and Philadelphia, little changed. Robbins toyed with the dream ballet, Bernstein added a few notes to "One Hand One Heart," and Laurents cut the book a bit.[48] All while the publicity mill churned. *Life* magazine carried a photographic spread and added to the drama of the opening by noting that two Spanish-language publications had denounced the show already. The *New Yorker* featured a story on gangs in Brooklyn the week of the Broadway debut, replete with an organized social dance at the YMCA, a rumble, and hanging out at a candy store. The caricaturist Al Hirschfeld created one of his signature drawings of Broadway productions with kneeling lovers in front of knife-wielding men and leaping dancers. And an article about the difficulty in casting the show—including Robbins's failed search for authentic amateurs—added another act to the evolving story about the story that tied the production to the streets and artistic quality at the same time.[49]

On the night of September 26 at the Winter Garden theater on Broadway, gangs danced—and were seen to be wounded, if still threatening, members of society. A young man and woman saw each other and fell deeply, immediately, in love—and were believed to be genuine and sympathetic. The curtain closed at intermission on two dead bodies onstage—and the audience returned for a second act that ended with yet another death. A cast of little-known performers danced, sang, and acted—and received warm reviews. And Robbins, Bernstein, Laurents, and Sondheim stopped arguing (for the moment) and reveled in the praise. (Bernstein's fictitious log of the creation of the show, which appeared in the evening's *Playbill*, cast the collaboration in a warm glow, with no indication of the disagreement and haranguing.)

The cast partied afterward at Sardi's and then in the hotel room at the Ambassador of producer Roger Stevens, waiting for the reviews. Brooks Atkinson, in the *New York Times*, endorsed the revelation that had occurred onstage. Walter Kerr, of the *Herald Tribune*, chastened the glow with biting cuts of disapproval, calling the action an "onstage threshing machine."[50] But little could calm the general hubbub that the opening had excited.[51]

Exactly what kind of triumph the show was confounded many reviewers. Some thought it was the dance that made it a spectacle, others the music, still others the blend of all the theatrical elements. But few failed to comment on just what an oddity it was to set a story about juvenile delinquency to music and dance. Atkinson had a hard time getting around the "horrifying material," even though the "workmanship is admirable." In a second review ten days later, he tried to figure out more precisely the pull of the show and determined that it was the contrast between the "beauty" of the love that Tony and Maria find and the gangs "whose speech is acrid and ugly and whose conduct is neurotic and savage." The setting in the "jungles of the city" provided the meaning—and ultimately the success—of the production. The gangs reveal "the hideousness that lives under the scabby surface of the city," and the love of Tony and Maria is "purer" because of the "treachery and violence that swirl around it." This love "gives two young people a hopeless glimpse of how ecstatic and cleansing life could be in a decent neighborhood," a simplistic rendering of the ease with which the problems of the city might be solved.[52]

In fact, the vision of the city hooked most critics: "The stage is not a stage, but this fascinating and fearful town of Manhattan."[53] Set designer Oliver Smith had effectively created a kind of "serious modern painting," as he himself described it: "Nothing is more beautiful to me than a row of doors, nailed up to hide a vacant lot; a solitary 'El' column, rusted and deep red and blotched with turquoise black; dark red fire escapes, and brick buildings the color of dried blood; a sudden flash of brilliant blue fence; black and green doorways with multicolored halls beyond."[54] The city was ugly, frightening, and sordid but with enough bits of allure that shone through the grit. The show conveyed both the hard truth of the city and its persistent potential. It "came right out of urban America, out of the venom generated between races jammed festeringly together," one review testified. "It said frankly that back alley people can do little more than hate because hatred is all they can feel and love is a thing that has hardly a chance to be born. It scoffed at our era's patented psychology and chromium-plated panaceas and it scorned the over-educated ignoramuses professing to offer cures for the eroding evils of poverty and racism."[55] The realities of urban life show that "these young people are cramped, stifled, crazed by the walls around them," Marya Mannes wrote.[56] In another article, she honed in on the demographic changes of the city alongside its building frenzy: "The people of this great city are turning dark while the buildings are turning light." Gleaming skyscrapers, "relentlessly bright and cheap," do not hide the entrenched poverty and discrimination.[57] The musical thrived *in spite* of this disheartening picture not only because of the moments of love and hope that peeked through, but also because of the artistry of its creators. "Here we breed evil in our cities, but here we also parade a Bernstein and a Robbins."[58] The city, the place in which Jets and Sharks fought to belong, became one of the complicated stars of the show.

Neither the truthful portrayal of the city nor the talents of its creators persuaded everyone, however, especially those with ties to Puerto Rico. Many felt that the lyrics to "America" were only the most obvious example of a more general negative view of the island and its migratory inhabitants. The New York Spanish-language papers *La Prensa* and *El Diario* advocated an effort to picket the show in New York soon after it opened in Washington, although a boycott never materialized. They protested the denigrating view of Puerto Ricans as caught up in crime and disdainful of their home island.

This initial objection among Puerto Rican communities spread wider when an article in the *Times* bolstered their protest. A doctor took Sondheim to task for describing the island as full of "tropical diseases." Not only was this inaccurate, Dr. Howard Rusk wrote, but it denigrated the effective work in recent years in reducing deaths from malaria, diarrhea, and tuberculosis. "Would that we in New York City could find as effective measures to control our social blight of juvenile delinquency as Puerto Rico, island of tropical breezes, has found in controlling its 'tropical diseases,'" he concluded.[59] Puerto Rican papers spread this criticism and endorsed the condemnation by Rusk, who they identified as a prominent theater critic.[60]

The Spanish-language newspapers in New York and in Puerto Rico then tracked the views of Puerto Rican public officials who had seen the show, in particular Governor Luis Muñoz Marin and former health commissioner Antonio Fernos Isern. Isern came under swift indictment by *La Prensa* in New York and *El Mundo* in San Juan when they noted that he did not condemn the lyrics. Isern felt compelled to correct the record, writing in *El Mundo* that the press had not reported his full statement, which included a plea to strike the remarks about a diseased island.[61] Muñoz Marin, on the other hand, shifted the inquiry in an interview, suggesting that the problem of juvenile delinquency was New York's and not at all specific to Puerto Ricans. The story could have worked just as well with any two other groups, even the original Jews and Catholics, he claimed. The show's value was in what it revealed about New York, not Puerto Rico.[62]

West Side Story presented a difficult challenge for Puerto Ricans. It cast a rare spotlight on them, even highlighting the "tragic intolerance that Puerto Rican migrants face in New York," as an article in *El Mundo* put it.[63] Yet it perpetuated negative stereotypes, whether of men wielding knives or diseases of the tropics. And although the show featured very few Puerto Rican actors, there were two with links to the island in key roles: Chita Rivera (born in Washington, DC, to a Puerto Rican father) as Anita and Jaime Sanchez (born in Rincón) as Chino. Both actors pleaded with Puerto Ricans that they not be swayed by the negative appraisals. They insisted that they would leave the show if the roles were truly derogatory. Sanchez even pointed to the character of Maria, usually passed over in critics' view of Puerto Ricans in the show, as humble and pure.[64]

Belonging, then, was skewered by various prejudices. Puerto Ricans in New York looked at the show differently than those in San Juan, for instance. New York papers were more likely to denounce the show; San Juan papers found ways to praise it. The portrayal of lives lived, rather than imagined, may have pushed Puerto Ricans in New York to pessimistic judgment. Even the highly racialized world of New York appeared more overtly in discussion of the play in New York. When the critic John Chapman, writing in the *Daily News*, described the love story as between a "white young man and a Puerto Rican girl," the New York-based *El Diario* was quick to correct the implication that Puerto Ricans were not white. "Hundreds of thousands of Puerto Ricans are whiter than Mr. Chapman, and they can be as black as anybody," the newspaper declared. "Those of color are as proud and deserving as the white ones. Among black and white Boricuas there is neither discrimination nor tension. But characterizing all Puerto Ricans as people of color is Mr. Chapman's mistake."[65] The editorial predicted that the show would cause disruptions for the Puerto Rican community in New York. No slight went unnoticed when any notice was so rare. More important, New York–based Puerto Ricans knew more acutely how the color of one's skin mattered on the mainland.

The San Juan newspaper *El Imparcial* tried to resolve the dilemma by taking the question to theatergoers themselves. A journalist for the paper asked people as they exited the Winter Garden what impression of Puerto Rico the show had conveyed to them. All good, they responded unanimously. The lyric regarding tropical diseases had passed "unnoticed," while the music, dance, and overall verve of the show relayed only positive associations of the island. "There is nothing wrong with Puerto Rico; Puerto Rico is a beautiful country and I like it a lot," a theatergoing priest insisted.[66]

To an unusual degree, *West Side Story* prompted discussion about the relation of a stage show to the streets outside the theater and beyond the tight circle of theater critics and the generally homogenous Broadway audience. Its relation to Puerto Ricans was challenged and debated most among Puerto Ricans themselves, but the show's acuity on juvenile delinquency generated even wider debate. *West Side Story* became linked to an ongoing issue that filled the papers

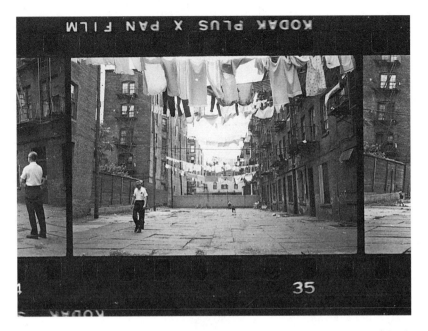

FIGURE 3.5 Hanging laundry was a common city scene captured in photographs of the alleys and backyards that connected residential buildings. Jerome Robbins Dance Division, New York Public Library for the Performing Arts, Astor, Lennox and Tilden Foundations.

and frightened many city residents. As Robbins began rehearsals, he was thinking about a recent stabbing in the Bronx over gangs' contested possession of Orchard Beach. Another brutal gang killing, in Washington Heights, part of a dispute over who controlled the pool in Highbridge Park in northern Manhattan, occurred just six weeks before the show opened. *West Side Story* highlighted the ethnic basis of discrimination and violence at a time when most portrayals of juvenile delinquency focused on a kind of youth rebellion that had little basis in social conditions of race or class. The production sat between the confident liberalism of the 1950s, which censured individuals for egregious behavior, and the grim structuralism of the 1960s, which uncovered deeply embedded racialized stratification and oppression.[67]

The showstopper "Gee, Officer Krupke" dramatized the inadequate and stagnant approaches to juvenile delinquency of the late

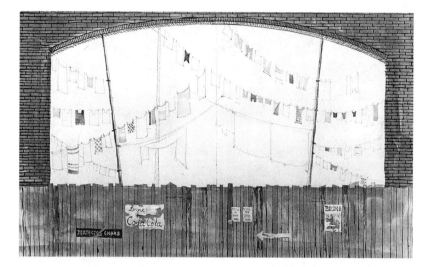

FIGURE 3.6 Oliver Smith picks up on the ubiquity of hanging laundry in his rendering of the set design for "Gee, Officer Krupke," ca. 1957. © Rosaria Sinisi.

1950s. The Jets mock psychiatrists, social workers, police officers, and judges, in both words and action. The one playing a psychiatrist mimics a German accent when he determines that juvenile delinquency is a "social disease"; another, playing a social worker, declares, "He's no good," in a tinny voice. The Jets thus caricature the people and the system that created an unending cycle of fixes that shuttle youths from courts to settlement houses, to the psychiatrist's couch, and to prison. Most pointedly, however, the problem lay with the self-fashioned white American gang. The Sharks' violence was prompted by their experience of prejudice—or perhaps an assumed innate predilection to violence. Where exactly the Jets' restlessness came from was far more difficult to nail down.

Perhaps most important, the song showed how young men themselves played the system. Different explanations are offered up to different authority figures, creating a closed social loop with no end. One explanation is parental deprivation ("I'm depraved on account I'm deprived!"); another is lack of worthwhile employment ("They say go earn a buck, / Like be a soda jerker, / Which means like be a schmuck"). As in other parts of the story, though, the underlying

FIGURE 3.7 Stage scene, "Gee, Officer Krupke," ca. 1957. All the action takes place in front a fence, which blocks and contains movement. Photograph by Fred Fehl, courtesy of Gabriel Pinski. Set by Oliver Smith. © Rosaria Sinisi.

result of the multiple reasons for misbehavior is an absence, an ache in the heart from being left out of a wider world. Sondheim made this explicit in a set of lyrics he eventually dropped: "Society don't love us, / We just don't seem to fit."[68] Not belonging was not enough to explain the rash of violence, the increase in numbers of gangs, and the newly perceived conflict between youth and their parents or authority figures. But this feeling of not being accepted and the desire to be part of something bigger at least stood in for a growing unease about societal and city changes. The Jets satirized the painful and confusing situation of juvenile delinquency—provoking laughs as well as awareness of a lack of surety about the future and the place of brash young men in it.

The question of juvenile delinquency attracted a variety of commentary, from theater critics to journalists and even a minister who ran a television show about contemporary theater and religion. The show provided another way to think through the problem. Most reviewers saw it as a condemnation of an approach that only looked at explanations of "'insufficient housing' and 'broken homes.'" That neglected "the vacuum which these teen-agers feel obliged to fill with cool and fierce bravado."[69] But others found the portrayal—and the song "Gee, Officer Krupke"—an overly simplistic rendering of a complex problem. Harold Clurman, one of the founders of the Group Theatre in the 1930s, now turned critic, articulated this perspective in a biting critique. The song exposes "the hollowness of everything we see" in the show, and is only the most vivid example of "the intellectual slumming by sophisticates for purposes of popular showmanship." The creators had talent indeed, he summed up, but they lack "true moral-artistic perception." *West Side Story* mixes "the pain of a real problem, penny sociology, liberal 19-thirtyish propaganda, Betty Comdem–Adolphe Green fun and the best of the advanced but already accepted musical comedy techniques into an amalgam which eliminates what is supposed to be the heart of the matter." It was no *Threepenny Opera*.[70]

Clurman's review in particular, and the perspective it reflected more generally, rankled the musical's creators, especially Robbins. All of them often defended the show by reminding critics that it was really about love, a remaking of *Romeo and Juliet*. This defense, though, was disingenuous given the seriousness of their intentions to convey the city with its injustices intact. In an appearance on the television show *Look Up and Live*, about contemporary theater and religion, the host, Reverend Sidney Lanier, asked Robbins what could be done about the violence and hatred consuming young people. *West Side Story* did not propose to solve the problem, Robbins replied, but to understand it. In halting words, always a bit hesitant when speaking rather than moving, Robbins explained the world with which these youths had to contend:

> a world which threatens them constantly and gives them no security. A world in which hydrogen bomb and total destruction is bandied about all the time. A world in which, through public investigations etc. there seems to be corruption everywhere. On the other hand dangled in front of their eyes is a

great big giveaway, shows and freedoms and they don't know where to turn. I don't think that one can do something. I think they are like a plant. The seeds have been planted long ago, the growth is there, you can't suddenly expect it to be a fir tree when it's an elm.[71]

West Side Story was a plea for understanding and tolerance in an altered world.

Robbins revealed his own demons in this defense of the show, as well as those of the United States in the late 1950s—"public investigations" hinted at HUAC. Solutions were beyond most, and even what was proposed often failed to comprehend the deep roots of problems, like the extent to which the discrimination Puerto Ricans faced was built on the legacy of slavery and the intransigent ideology of racism. Clurman and other deriders exposed the oddity, even pretentiousness, of serious social issues masquerading on the Broadway musical stage. But they missed the effectiveness of the mask in revealing a more empathetic view of maligned teenagers, lambasted in the press as the scourge of the city and a generation. It was a story of youth more broadly, not just Puerto Ricans or those in the United States, with strong yearnings that "*can't wait*," as Cheryl Crawford put it.[72]

Teenagers themselves recognized the reaching out, the attempt to understand them and their worlds. Hal Prince followed through on this connection between the onstage story and the one playing out on the streets by giving free tickets to social work agencies to bring young people to the show.[73] George Young, a social worker at the University Settlement House on the Lower East Side, brought six young men—four second-generation Italians, one Puerto Rican, and one African American—to a Wednesday matinee in early 1958 with the tickets Prince provided. They created a bit of a stir among the mainly female audience. (Young estimated that there were not more than a hundred men in the entire audience. As one of the teenagers put it, there were "many ladies from the bridge clubs.") "Gee you boys look like you should be on stage," an usher commented as she led them to their seats in the orchestra section. Young thought that the teenag-

STAGE AN

'Story' Acts as J. D. Deterrent

By JOHN McCLAIN

WITHOUT any fuss or fanfare, Bobby Griffith and Hal Prince, producers of "West Side Story," have for the past year been involved in a rewarding experiment. If you haven't seen the show I can tell you it's a dazzling and rampaging musical which translates the violent Montague-Capulet feud from "Romeo and Juliet" into terms of New York juvenile gang warfare.

So it occurred to them that maybe it ought to be seen by the very kids who make up the gangs in town today.

Charles Cook, director of the University Settlement House, down in Rivington st., on the lower East Side, was brought into the picture and said he liked it fine. He said he didn't think any of the tough kids in his neighborhood had ever been inside a real theatre.

Selfless Gesture

In any event Griffith-

AFTER THE SHOW . . . Gang members sit down with youth worker George Young and discuss "West Side Story," the musical hit at the Winter Garden.

FIGURE 3.8 Producers distributed tickets to young people regarded as juvenile delinquents, inviting them to a Broadway show about them and blurring the line between stage and street. Whether the show in fact served as a deterrent is unclear. *New York Journal American* (2 November 1958); Harry Ransom Center, University of Texas at Austin.

ers, most of whom were sixteen or seventeen, were not offended by the comment; "they were kind of proud." They seemed to know that people eyed them as related to the show, the real players behind the actors on the stage. As they discussed the show at intermission, other audience members listened to *them*.

Young recorded an interview with the teenagers after the show, back at the settlement house, and launched immediately into the issue, was it real or just funny? The young men insisted that it was real, "very real, comes from life itself." They went on to quibble with some aspects that were not quite so real—the actors' hair was far too long; their dress was overdone—and then honed in on details closer to their lives. They made clear that a war councilor (someone who negotiated the terms of a fight and checked for weapons) was distinct from the president of a gang, unlike in the show, where the heads of the gangs played both roles. The young women seemed "too open," and one teen in particular thought there was no way that Maria would have continued to love Tony after he killed her brother. Perhaps the largest divergence from reality was that the cops had far less power and presence onstage than did those in their own lives. Where were the police after two people died in a rumble? In their world, if a fight involved two hundred kids and even one of them died, all two hundred would be picked up, one explained.

Then Young asked whether the reasons for fighting, some serious and some funny, were accurate. They were, most initially replied. But then they protested that "Gee, Officer Krupke" exaggerated their situation and, especially, degraded their parents. They conceded that a rumble could happen in their neighborhood, into which Puerto Ricans were also moving. They needed to protect "their girls" and the Puerto Ricans were taking over more and more of the neighborhood; we "don't want to keep moving." In the old days, one explained, when everyone was of the "same race," fighting occurred one-on-one. Now, with "Spanish people, Jewish people," fighting goes beyond individuals and involves gangs. People born here are "more mature, not more mature like, but they're born here": they get "more culture, more understanding, more schooling and everything." Puerto Ricans, on the other hand, are just "becoming Americans." It takes a while. They remember Puerto Rico, but, after a while, "they will be the same [as us]." The conversation was an awkward analysis of the existing tension and a hope for the end of it at the same time.

Eventually, the young men turned the interview around to ask Young himself a question: do you consider us delinquents? Young evaded the question, remarking that some of them had been in trouble but "I don't think this neighborhood is a delinquent neighborhood." "I'm not saying the neighborhood," the young man followed up. This emboldened another to suggest that the show made them out to be murderers. Another reasoned that it was "stupid" to fight over a "Spanish girl and American guy in love." "It started before that," another responded. "It had nothing to do with that. It's about them taking over." Their extended discussion of the play proved what one had said earlier: "I think the people around here should be the critics. I mean, the people who live in it. Not the people who live on 5th Avenue and just see it."

After the young men left the discussion, Young continued to talk to the head of the settlement house about the experience. He described them in more depth, saying that the Puerto Rican teen identified with the Italians and generally had agreed with everything that had been said against the Puerto Ricans; the African American member seemed fully integrated into the gang. The teenagers were less interested in the love scenes, as was the case when they watched movies, and there had been a comment or two about the dancing not being "manly enough for them." A visit backstage after the show again brought up the question of the actors' manliness, as they saw them take off their costumes and makeup. But Young noted that they had not called them "fags," as they usually would.

Despite this slight unease about dancing and manliness, Young noted that the young men had been riveted by the movement of the show and were intensely interested in meeting the actors. "We're going to invite some of these guys to our rumble so we can teach them a few things," one wryly remarked on the way to the dressing room. The desire to compare themselves with the actors reflected the identification they felt, although the illusion may have been broken once they arrived backstage, Young noted. There they realized that the actors were not fellow gang members; they were different from the roles they played, and differed from the visiting teens in the rouge they put on to perform and in the casualness with which they changed from their costumes in front of people.

The discussion after the show, though, revealed the extent to which the teenagers understood the story of *West Side Story* as theirs, despite its unduly negative portrayals of parents and errors in depicting war councils and police.[74] Their possession of the story marked the kernel of truth in it about their lives. Compared to long explanations in newspapers series or short snapshots that highlighted the violent episodes of their lives, the show was a more complete picture. It added color and vibrancy, misunderstanding and betrayal, to what was typically conveyed as just rage. The show magnified their lives on the streets and gave it new meaning onstage.

If Robbins saw the show as highlighting a world in which juvenile delinquency was just one small part, the young men from the Lower East Side brought that broad view back to the streets of the city. The show succeeded partly because it could be read—and hold meaning—from either perspective, that of an artistic master reflecting on global events or that of teenagers surviving on the city streets. The interview with these young men, too, brought the show back to its roots in the Lower East Side, reflecting the changes then occurring in Harlem, Brooklyn, the Bronx, and the west side of Manhattan. Cheryl Crawford may have judged that the show did not reveal enough about a neighborhood or the causes of juvenile delinquency. Puerto Ricans may have been angered by the perpetuation of stereotypes. And politicians may have wanted more solutions than the show provided. But the range of reactions indicated that the show had found its own place in these debates. It became a touchstone, around the world, for discussions of the yearnings of youth to belong.

* 4 *

"Get cool, boy"

1958–59

Before: Juvenile delinquency was an isolated issue blamed on troubled teenagers themselves. Puerto Ricans were a problem. Carol Lawrence was a struggling actress. Robbins, Bernstein, and Laurents looked over their shoulders for FBI informants. Broadway was a place of fanciful, funny stories.

After: Books and articles on juvenile delinquency invoked the Jets and the Sharks to explain the issues. The problem associated with Puerto Ricans was increasingly the discrimination they faced. Carol Lawrence was feted and proclaimed the next big star. Robbins, Bernstein, Laurents, and Sondheim were lauded for a full integration of dance, music, and book in the genre of a musical. Editorialists and writers of letters to the editor debated whether comedy was necessary to musicals.

Musicals do not change the world, but they do shape how we see it. *West Side Story* offered a new way to see New York, Puerto Ricans, youth, and American ideals. Success was immediate in the worlds of music, dance, and Broadway—even if not all the critics' reviews were ecstatic. But the impact of the show reached beyond the theater. The collaborators created a moral rather than a political story; given the contemporary setting, morality and politics could not be so easily separated, however. The onstage murders suggested not only the weakness of domestic policy to combat juvenile delinquency and dis-

94

crimination but also the absence of a political ideology robust enough to avert a more global tragedy. The production became an artifact in a global conversation about juvenile delinquency. Instead of a story about belonging in New York, it became a more general set piece depicting rebellious youth and, even more broadly, inflamed rivalry. And, for many, gang warfare between the Jets and the Sharks symbolized the global conflict between the United States and the Soviet Union.

Rhetoric about nuclear warfare, and the Cold War in general, infused *West Side Story* and responses to it. The musical itself was drawn into the strained exchanges between the two countries. Traveling Soviet dancers flocked to the show and pushed for it to tour their country. The producers sought State Department sponsorship. In the first years after the show's debut, the international volley of conversation about it exposed the fragility of cultural diplomacy of the era. The musical was too hot—in popularity, explosiveness, and critique—for a cool world.

The first reviews predicted this: "The radioactive fallout from *West Side Story* must still be descending on Broadway this morning," Walter Kerr began his opening-night review.[1] It was a mixed review. Kerr saw brilliance in the parts but little emotional wallop overall; the clear exception, as he wrote in a second review, was the dance: "the sense of seething pressure and detonating release is extraordinary."[2] Dance was the focus of many of the analogies to war. Another critic declared that Robbins's dances "advance the action with the momentum of an inter-continental missile."[3] Robbins himself promoted this connection, seeing the gang members as living in "pressure cookers": "I think they have a sense of having been born into one of the worst worlds possible—fall-out, hydrogen bombs. You get the feeling that they think they have to live their lives now—without delay."[4] An issue of *Life* that appeared just before the Broadway debut placed the rise of gangs and crime alongside an article about US missiles; the next issue featured photographs of the soon-to-open *West Side Story*.[5] The show fused with the moment.

This was true not just for critics but for audience members as well.

"The two warring groups, the terrible weapons to be used only if the other fellow proves untrustworthy, and the tragedy that faces the world if this deadly division is not stopped," wrote one in a letter to the editor of the *Washington Post*. "Can we see our own giant follies clearly enough, to understand that all of us are participating in developments toward the biggest rumble ever, and are we smart enough to call a halt?"[6] Critic Henry Hewes, writing in the *Saturday Review*, concurred: "Later, when the rival gang leaders agree to have a war council, their terse summation 'no jazz before then' is a capsule Cold War. And the discussion of weapons they will use in their forthcoming rumble is as ridiculous and at the same time terrifying as are most disarmament conferences." "The Cool Generation," Hewes argued, grew up in a vacuum of policy that ignored housing problems and family disintegration. Why wouldn't teenagers fill that vacuum with "cool and fierce bravado," the kind modeled for them by the United States and the Soviet Union on the international stage?[7]

As hot and explosive as the show was, though, it promoted "Cool." This signature song and dance built on the style of jazz musicians such as Lester Young, who combined intense expression and individuality with a relaxed confidence. African Americans were the embodiment of cool in the city, projecting a practiced nonchalance in the face of continuing discrimination and provocation.[8] *West Side Story*'s version appropriated that attitude—the Jets take on the style in a story that excludes African Americans even as it turns on prejudice. Tamping down anger and revenge in the gang then paralleled the theory of containment and deliberative diplomatic parry between the United States and the Soviet Union.

"You wanna live?" Riff asks, as setup to the number, which came before the rumble in the musical. His answer: "You play it cool." With a "rocket in your pocket," the song and dance allied nuclear frisson with sexual explosion and bravado. The eruptions of movement echoed the violent undercurrent of the coming war between gangs, and possibly between nations. Few words set the scene that music and dance dominate. Starting with snapping fingers to cohere the group, as in the prologue, Riff calls out to different Jets as they lose

FIGURE 4.1 In "Cool," the Jets charge forward, with Anybodys dancing with the men, 1957. Photograph by Fred Fehl, courtesy of Gabriel Pinski. Set by Oliver Smith. © Rosaria Sinisi.

their cool and "jump out of [their] skin," as one of the dancers put it.[9] The snapping fingers bring them back. And then the music begins to spiral tighter, building contrapuntal lines until trumpets blast the melody in full force. The movement goes vertical. Jets shoot straight up, tightening their bodies into coiled rods. Hands and legs dart out and up; tight turns end on the ground only for the dancers to spring off the ground into action again. Bernstein's music for the number is his most jazzed, his most dissonant, with swing lines by the brass and volume contrasts that propel a call-and-response. Groups of three or five move into and out of the action, advancing then retreating. And then there is the offensive charge of the whole group. Humped backs over bent knees, stomachs hollowed-out and fingers snapping, the Jets run and leap in a frontal attack toward the audience. The buildup reaches its peak as dancers spiral from spinning on their toes to sprawling on the ground in one motion, from desperate containment to grateful release. Pressure popped, they are ready to face the Sharks.

Even more so than the music or the few words, the dance makes clear that cool masks hot. Just below snapping fingers lie bodies primed to explode. "Dancing is not used as a release from tension but as a vivid symbol of it, as a desperate, sometimes evil and sometimes hopeful voice speaking through the body," a dance critic explained.[10] In fact, many reviewers focused on the dance, perhaps as a way to move off the content of the story. The challenging story line—of prejudice, murder, sexual assault, failures of policy and intervention— made it difficult to provide glowing reviews that did not take seriously the reprimand of the story. "*West Side Story* is a tough evening," one noted.[11] "It's hardly a pleasant show," commented *Variety*, in a calculation of its commercial impact. "Bits of the seemingly realistic gutter dialog will disturb a few showgoers, and at least one near rape scene in which members of the American juve gang corner and rough up the Puerto Rican gang leader's girl, will probably shock others." But, in the twisted ways of capitalist ventures, those very elements "may also attract business."[12] The spectacular, "frenzied" dancing provided a way into—and out of—the more difficult subject matter.[13]

It also provided a meaningful analogy to the dangerous global politics of the moment. Whipping turns mimicked the askew world. Just below the polite, careful diplomacy between the United States and the USSR lay hot tempers and nuclear weapons. This became clear when Soviet premier Nikita Khrushchev visited the United Nations in New York in the fall of 1960. He burst into anger at various times when countries criticized the Soviet Union's actions, even banging his shoe on a desk at one point. In a speech, British prime minister Harold Macmillan, who had become a mediator between the USSR and the US, quoted the song's lyrics, urging Khrushchev to "get cool, boy."[14]

Despite Khrushchev's antics at the UN, relations between the United States and the USSR had warmed slightly following the death of Stalin in 1953. Diplomatic niceties and cultural exchanges increased, even as actions in Eastern Europe, Latin America, and

Southeast Asia continued to fuel animosities. Beginning in the mid-1950s, Eisenhower used presidential emergency funds to support tours of dance, theater, music, and sports abroad. One of the first major successes was a European tour of *Porgy and Bess* that added shows in Moscow, Leningrad, and Stalingrad. (The State Department financially supported the European, Middle Eastern, and South American stops on the tour, but not those in the Soviet Union, Poland, and Czechoslovakia. US diplomats recognized the game they were playing and worried about the proselytizing potential of Soviet performers and troupes appearing in America. No government-sponsored shows in the East bloc meant that Soviet-sponsored performances were less likely in the United States.[15])

Cultural exchanges, though, seemed a good first step in a thaw. They were a soft approach, with little at stake: let us find out about and appreciate the other so that we may build a better foundation for larger compromise and negotiation. A visit of Moscow's Moiseyev Dance Company to New York in April 1958 acted on the idea. Such exchanges put on a show—literally—of diplomacy and rapprochement. The Moiseyev troupe appeared as a part of a carefully crafted narrative masterminded by impresario Sol Hurok, himself a Russian émigré. The production required months of deliberation and even changes to legislation that required fingerprinting of all foreign visitors. (The Soviet artists refused to accede to such police-procedural transactions in a cultural exchange.) Then a last-minute snafu nearly ended the visit before it began. The Soviets wanted to transport the dancers in jets; the Americans saw aggression in that kind of arrival that was not appropriate to an artistic journey. The Soviets finally relented, using commercial airliners. The dancers arrived in New York in April, garnering sold-out audiences and critical praise in their three weeks of performances at the Metropolitan Opera House.[16]

West Side Story entered the staged rapprochement when the Moiseyev dancers attended a matinee. Their leader, Igor Moiseyev, then urged the Soviet embassy to invite the musical to tour Russia.[17] A few months later, Soviet students visiting the United Nations chose seeing *West Side Story* over the play *Look Homeward, Angel*, three to one.[18] With this kind of attention from Soviets in New York, producer Hal Prince followed up on Moiseyev's suggestion with Hurok. Prince also solicited the help of the influential newspaper publisher Alicia Patterson, who had joined Adlai Stevenson on a trip to Moscow in July 1958 and had upper-echelon connections in both Moscow and Washington. She also became determined to arrange a tour of *West Side Story* in Russia.[19] The effort ended in frustration. The State Department viewed the production as fodder for anti-Americanism, with its stark portrayal of discrimination and juvenile delinquency, and tarnished take on the American ideal of opportunity for all.

The following spring, however, the visit of the Bolshoi Ballet reignited the campaign. The Bolshoi dancers announced on arrival that *West Side Story* was the show they most wanted to see, having heard exclamations by the Moiseyev dancers. The Bolshoi visit to the show prompted even more publicity, with a backstage photo shoot of ballet and Broadway dancers exchanging steps. A Jet taught a Bolshoi ballerina the mambo; a Bolshoi dancer hoisted Carol Lawrence, still playing Maria, into a high lift. "More cheers and laughter burst forth, and the Russian threw Miss Lawrence into the air again, this time with exuberance."[20]

The publicity gambit drove Prince to pressure diplomats again.[21] Support for exchanges had strengthened; Hurok's wheeling and dealing the year before had led to a more concrete cultural diplomacy program with very precise tit-for-tat exchanges: orchestra for ballet, folk dance for military marching band.[22] Music and dance dominated the exchanges because of the absence of language barriers. While other tours were possible, they still all had to go through heavily handled diplomatic channels.

Prince pushed the possibilities. He traveled to Washington to converse with the US diplomat who had negotiated the new cultural agreement with Russia. The diplomat held out little hope of US government support and urged Prince not to organize an independent tour. He even declared that the Russians were not that interested in the production. "Moiseyev is in the doghouse because he liked *West Side Story* too much," Prince reported to Robbins, Laurents,

FLYING HIGH: Carol Lawrence, star of "West Side Story," gets a soaring example of the Russian ballet lift from Viktor Smirnov, of the Bolshoi Ballet. Looking
on are members of the Bolshoi company and her colleagues in the musical show.
Half of the Russian company witnessed yesterday's matinee perforance of "West
Side Story" at the Broadway Theater, a nd then went backstage to meet the cast.

FIGURE 4.2 Carol Lawrence is held aloft by a Bolshoi Ballet dancer after the Russian company attended a matinee in April 1959. Jerome Robbins Dance Division, New York Public
Library for the Performing Arts, Astor, Lennox and Tilden Foundations.

Bernstein, and Sondheim. "So the Russians sent their Cultural Minister, Zaroubin, to see *West Side Story* so that he could report back that it wasn't so hot after all. His lukewarm reaction has been widely publicized." The American diplomat went on to suggest that if the Russians did agree to host the production, it would probably be because they planned to use it in an anti-American propaganda campaign. "Now I am convinced that we cannot take this chance," Prince concluded.[23] (Visiting New York a year later, Khrushchev called the city "repulsive" and a demonstration of the "ugliness and degeneracy of capitalism." It is not hard to imagine a touring production of the show garnering a similarly anti-American response.[24])

Prince, though, did not give up just yet. Performing in the Soviet Union would, he realized, give the show a global political impact to which few musicals could even aspire. In July 1959 he traveled to the Soviet Union himself to "see how I thought they would take the play." After two weeks there, he came back "fortified in the notion that it would do far more good than bad."[25] He believed that the aesthetic quality and innovation would withstand any propagandizing against it. He was sure the show's artistic merit would not permit an interpretation of the story as a literal rendering of American life.

Nonetheless, Prince dropped his effort to get the show to the USSR in the face of intransigent State Department disapproval. There were already plans for a privately sponsored tour in Israel and Western Europe that were far more concrete. But then—just a couple of months after Prince's visit to the USSR—a tiny squib in the *New York Times* fired up the question again. The Soviet minister of culture announced that three American plays were to be produced in the USSR that season: Arthur Miller's *Death of a Salesman*, James Lee's *Career*, and Arthur Laurents's *West Side Story*.[26] Infuriated, Prince fired off a letter to a Soviet diplomat insisting on the licensing rights necessary for any production. "I have no doubt," he demurred, "that you have always intended to respect the legal obligations to the authors and producers of *West Side Story* and that the newspaper announcement is somewhat premature."[27]

Rumors then began to come from Russia itself about the plans for a production. Bernstein, traveling with the Philharmonic there, heard about it from a woman at a party who claimed to be working with the Vakhtangov Theatre in Moscow on the adaption. Surprised, Bernstein asked if permission had been granted. (Each of the creators held the right to veto permission for licensing rights.) She replied that permission was not necessary since there was no copyright agreement between the two countries, a legally true if ethically questionable response. Bernstein pressed for more specifics. How had they gotten the music? They had composers of their own, she insisted. Who was in charge of the dance? What dancing, she asked?[28]

By December 1959, the Soviets clarified that they were making their own presentation of the musical, with little music or dance. ("Sounds as if they were about to discover the telephone—again," responded Robbins.[29]) Prince reprimanded the State Department for their role in this artistic scandal in the making. "It seems to me lethal propaganda without these artistic elements [the music and dance]. It is disappointing that something which is not *West Side Story*, but merely a devastating account of life in New York City, should be presented to the Russian people, when they might have seen the original, which was lyrical and totally stylized." A few months later, Prince received assurances from the State Department that the production was not going forward.[30] (In fact, a translation of the play appeared in a Soviet theater journal in 1959, complete with lyrics to the songs. Although the preface to the translation mentions that work on a production was under way at the Moscow Theatre, there is no evidence that one occurred at that time.[31])

Prince used the incident to press his agenda: can we reopen negotiations regarding sending an American tour of the musical to the Soviet Union, he inquired?[32] The State Department remained unsupportive. The first discussions of the Drama Advisory Panel in the International Cultural Exchange Service of the State Department, in February 1958, had voiced the underlying concerns about the show. "Gore, bloodshed and mayhem would add to the poor opinion of America that Europeans already have." Moreover, the panelists added, the show might burden embassy officials, who would have to explain away the critique of the United States; and a tour would be impractical because its sets and large cast were expensive. Ultimately, artistic excellence was not enough to counter the belief that "the theme does not show the best face of America to set before the world."[33]

Advocates for the production did not stop bringing up the possibility, however. A year later, panelists discussed the Soviet envoy who attended the show and claimed that he would not support a tour to the Soviet Union because he did not want "to present . . . American friends in this light." Another panelist countered that the Soviets refused jazz too, but the "real reason is that they are afraid of this great freedom of expression." The panel urged the State Department to consult its overseas officers, including those in Russia, about possible repercussions of sending the production to their regions. Then they recommended *Kiss Me, Kate* for South America, *My Fair Lady* for Europe, and "if *West Side Story* cannot go to Russia, then send it all over Europe."[34]

Despite the panel's recommendation, the State Department continued to withhold its support. The back-and-forth butted up against bureaucratic wrangling. The producers gave up again and sought private sponsorship for a production abroad. Perhaps they could launch a tour with a run at the World's Fair in Brussels in 1958, then move on to Paris and London? Plans kept shifting as requests for productions flooded in—from American embassies in Hamburg, Vienna, and Belgrade; impresarios in Israel; festivals in Berlin and Salzburg. There were multiple inquiries from Italy and Paris, others from Germany, Denmark, Holland, and Austria.

Musicals, though, presented a challenge abroad. They were indisputably American, a genre not quite like other forms of performance. Music and acting were fundamental, as in opera, but musicals utilized more popular kinds of music and added far more dance to the spectacle. These distinctions made musicals an obvious art form to export as Cold War propaganda: energetic, overflowing with sound, movement, and story, and indomitably American. But some of these same characteristics also created challenges. Agnes de Mille, the choreographer and mastermind behind *Oklahoma!*, believed musicals to be too idiomatic to travel well. They trafficked in linguistic informal-

ity and humor, she argued with her colleagues on the State Department panel, and the genre's sunny bounciness could seem particularly foreign to audiences outside the United States. They also cost a
great deal to produce and tour. State Department backing, then, was
often necessary—support that reinforced the underlying ideological
thrust of the endeavor. DeMille made a rare exception, however, in
supporting a tour for *West Side Story*. She thought it had a greater
chance of success because of the dominance of song and dance—and
perhaps its tragic look at American life as well.[35]

The producers Prince and Griffith believed it would work, and first
considered London or Paris. Exchanges between Broadway and the
West End theater district in London occurred often, although more
shows went from New York to London during this era than went the
other way. (The 1980s reversed the trend, with the mega-spectacles
of Andrew Lloyd Webber, such as *Cats* and *Phantom of the Opera*,
originating from London and fueling Broadway with new energy.)
Paris presented more technical difficulties; its theater lighting was
less sophisticated, as were its orchestras. ("We could not risk an all
French orchestra, particularly since it takes about a week before the
orchestra begins to play the score acceptably," Prince remarked.[36])

Worse, Parisian audiences were notably unimpressed by American
musicals, while *My Fair Lady*, *Kiss Me, Kate*, and *Damn Yankees* had
played well in London. London, then, was the better place to start,
Prince and Griffith decided. The common language with British audiences assured that the script and songs would be accessible to all.
One-upping Shakespeare might backfire, though. Others had transformed Shakespeare, of course, but usually it was a matter of a new
setting for an old, treasured story. *West Side Story* changed *Romeo
and Juliet*. It did not just transport the story to the west side of Manhattan but altered major plot points, perhaps most obviously in the
ending. Toying with an icon might provoke nativistic claims and
complaints of inauthenticity. There was a chance too, though, that
the charms of American song and dance might just upstage the plot
and words of the Bard himself.

Key to the London production was the American cast. The producers fought for an exception to British Actors Equity rules that insisted

upon British actors for productions from abroad—and won, the first exception since *Oklahoma!* crossed the pond in 1947. The unique dancing demands made the case. The creators also claimed that the subject matter required American voices, dialect, and experiences to be believable. British Equity granted them the exception with the stipulation that British actors replace American actors over time, as they learned the specifics of the production.[37] Having won that battle, the producers convinced Chita Rivera to lead the London cast and others from the Broadway show to go with her.

The producers began fishing around for directors, assuming Robbins would be too busy with his new company, Ballets:USA. Robbins took offense immediately. Griffith quickly began mending fences—"Naturally, we want you to direct the London company, the Paris company, the one in Italy, Moscow, Shanghai and Alaska"—and figuring out the complicated scheduling that ensued.[38]

Tending to Robbins's ego remained a constant task. As the show began moving beyond Broadway, Robbins tightened his tie to it. He demanded additional credit: not only as director and choreographer but also as the person who *conceived* it. This sparked ongoing animosity between Robbins and Laurents, who felt Robbins's initial idea would have had no legs without the words and structure he provided. The battle escalated, with each enlisting lawyers and Robbins insisting upon a special box on each poster and program saying he alone had conceived the idea. Laurents made a personal appeal, noting Bernstein's generosity in giving Sondheim complete credit for the lyrics soon after the opening of the show. Robbins only became more defiant. He insisted on that special box—and instructed his lawyer to be vigilant in protecting its size and placement atop other credits—for the rest of his life.[39]

Battles of egos such as these prompted Prince and Griffith to give up on organizing the tour of the show beyond London. (The creators then worked directly with the licensing agency Music Theatre International.) But, for London, they ensured that the Broadway version, as close as possible, would premiere in the West End. There were quirks of the script that had to be changed, though. The Sharks leave the "war council" in Doc's store, after Lieutenant Schrank's discriminatory routing of them, whistling "My Country 'Tis of Thee," flaunting the hypocrisy of the "sweet land of liberty." The same melody in England, however, was its national anthem, "God Save the Queen." Instead of attempting to translate the irony—and perhaps implicating England in hypocrisy along with the United States—the Sharks whistled "The Star Spangled Banner."[40] (Other confusions remained: Doc's white coat placed him as a barman or waiter rather than pharmacist in many European cities.[41])

The producers also fed stories to the press of the long rehearsals that often featured Chita Rivera and Tony Mordente, who by then had married. As a Shark and a Jet, Rivera and Mordente presented a living example of love across gang lines, but Rivera, of Puerto Rican descent, and Mordente, of Italian, also represented the American mix of ethnicities. With the personal and professional story lines blending, London was primed for the spectacle of West Side Story. The cast of thirty-two flew to London in November and had tryouts in Manchester before opening at Her Majesty's Theatre on December 12.

A telegram on opening night raised the stakes: "The Montagues and Capulets of the Old Vic salute the Jets and Sharks."[42] The endorsement of the Old Vic, the theater of Shakespeare, proved auspicious. The cast received twelve curtain calls on opening night and woke up the next morning to rave reviews. The critics swooned. Despite the somber, harsh, and "elusively alien" content, the show succeeded because of its "intense vitality," "requisite in any art."[43] Press in the United States passed along the adulation, almost berating New York critics for any ambivalence they may have shown about the musical.[44] Even Princess Margaret and her sister, Queen Elizabeth, endorsed the show. "On the whole the English audiences are more demonstrative and absorbed than the American audiences. Even diamond-wearing audiences of peers and peeresses have stamped their feet and gone crazy," producer Bobby Griffith declared.[45] The comeuppance was complete when British critics voted 17–1 to name West Side Story the best new foreign musical after US critics had given the Tony Award for Best Musical to The Music Man.[46]

The cast and critics believed the show resonated because the issues of juvenile delinquency and urban unrest did. A Broadway show like *Damn Yankees*—all baseball and dreams of bootstrapped success—failed in the United Kingdom because it was too idiomatic. *My Fair Lady* was a bit too familiar, British audiences resisting a British play reset in an American genre. *West Side Story* worked because it was neither too American nor too foreign. It was based on a Shakespeare play but did not merely mimic it. And the Jets and Sharks resembled Teddy boys, a designation for young men in exaggerated Edwardian dress (Teddy being a shortening of Edward). Much like zoot-suiters in the US, Teddy boys—with their roomy single-breasted jackets and double-breasted waistcoats over narrow trousers—were a fashion statement fused with a social one: young, largely lower-class and immigrant youth looking to define themselves and their place in society.[47] The Teddy boy was a "rather nasty stereotype which has grown up among us, a peculiarly dressed young fog with a cycle chain or flick-knife, sexually promiscuous, affluent with spending money, dazzled by gang ideology, licentious, violent, and destructive . . . living among us in a sort of nightmare West side story," a British social worker wrote.[48]

Robbins guessed that the social problems in the show that caused discomfort in the United States seemed remote to the British. "In London . . . the audience just took the show for what it is," he claimed.[49] As he had done in the US, particularly with the media, Robbins pressed on the show's theme of forbidden love rather than its rendering of societal issues. Others, though, saw those issues as more important to the London success: the audiences understood and related to the problems of delinquency and discrimination because they existed there too. Leo Kharibian, a Shark in the London cast, noted that it was only the occasional matinee performance—with its "out-of-town audience"—that did not connect.[50]

Perhaps the resonance of the issues was due to both the familiarity of the problem and the distancing of having it represented in New York—because London did indeed have similar difficulties. There was a growing immigrant population, particularly from former colo-

FIGURE 4.3 Long coats, pompadours, and constant smoking marked these young men as Teddy boys, but the insouciant attitude may have been even more indicative. Teddy boys in the street in Derbyshire Village, Sandiacre, England, 1950s. Rex USA.

nies in the Caribbean, Africa, and Asia, and an urban environment that showed the wear of economic constraints and social tensions. Riots publicized as a clash between recent West Indian immigrants and Teddy boys in the Notting Hill section of London occurred just months prior to the opening of *West Side Story*. (As in the United States, the press often distorted clashes into ethnic conflicts that were rarely that clearly defined.) The production could serve as a way in which to see those issues highlighted elsewhere, similar to but not exactly the same. The show prompted empathy and attention because of the ocean in between.

The London success buoyed hopes for a tour to the major cities of Europe, perhaps even Israel and Japan. Back on Broadway, though, ticket sales were slumping. Excerpts appeared on the television programs *Look Up and Live* and the *Ed Sullivan Show* in 1958. (*West Side Story*'s appearance on the latter was an indication of the diminishing valence of anticommunism, given Sullivan's earlier hounding of Robbins.) Tickets were discounted, and a flurry of sales after the announcement of the closing in June 1959 indicated that, perhaps, the show could have stayed open longer. By then, though, the producers and collaborators had moved on to arranging a domestic tour.

The show appeared in eleven major US cities, many of which had similar unrest, but these tours provoked more discussion of the show's American ideals than of its urban specifics. One character provided a wise perspective on these ideals. Doc was the only kindly adult in the show, the one to whom the gang members have some relationship—even if it is to tell him "you was never one of us" and accuse him (and his generation) of handing them a rotten world. He is the father figure for troubled-family kids, the boss of jobless young men, and the adult on the block who provides a home even if he is not always happy to do so. His character was based on that of the priest in *Romeo and Juliet*, but Doc is far less intrusive in the plot than the priest, who proposes the twisted plot to Romeo of faking death for love to flourish. In *West Side Story*, Doc plays a more passive role. He is a foil to the younger generation who is not as easy to dismiss as the oafish Officer Krupke or naïve social worker Glad Hand or cantankerous Sergeant Schrank. It is Doc who tries to help Tony but ends up passing on the lie that Maria is dead, causing Tony to seek out his assassin, Chino.

Laurents fleshed out the character of Doc along with Bernardo and Anita early on in the drafting of the script. If Bernardo and Anita appeared more fully and quickly because of reliance on stereotype, Doc was the character the most similar to Robbins, Laurents, and Bernstein—older, a bit wise and resigned, and subtly Jewish if not specifically so in the final version. (Initial versions of Schrank's monologue in the drugstore railing against the Jets included an aside to Doc about how a drugstore in "Jewtown" succumbed to gang violence.[51]) The character conveyed a general tolerance for others, those younger and different from him. And, key to the plot and the drama, he stopped the Jets from going through with a gang rape of Anita. His outraged shock paralleled that of the audience as prejudice wound toward tragedy.

In many ways, Doc was a liberal, a political stance associated with the belief in government intervention to expand democracy, equality, and civil rights. By the late 1940s, liberals were also increasingly attached to anticommunism, particularly in the international sphere. They did not embrace the radicalism of Joseph McCarthy, who led the effort to root out communists in the government and in Hollywood, but liberals such as George Kennan and Arthur Schlesinger articulated an aggressive foreign policy that sought to keep communism from settling into more countries. Doc, then, knew enough not to believe in peace but hoped to keep fighting at bay—to intervene to let love survive hate, if possible. He also understood the difficulty of migration and harm caused by discrimination, a Jew's recognition of the plight of Puerto Ricans.

Art Smith, the original Doc onstage, was older than Robbins, Bernstein, and Laurents by almost twenty years. As a member of the Group Theatre, he was already established in the theater world that Robbins entered as a teenager. Smith went on to star in films in the 1940s, but the anticommunist purge that ensnared the creators trapped Smith more tightly. Film director Elia Kazan named Smith before the House Un-American Activities Committee in April 1952, and the Hollywood blacklist prevented him from appearing on film after that. He returned to success on the stage as Doc, knowing well the limits of tolerance and liberalism.

Smith's replacement on Broadway, in April 1958, knew these limitations too. Albert Ottenheimer was five years younger than Smith, born of German Jewish parents, and was also caught up in the anticommunist wave that swept the nation. A longtime actor, director, and playwright, Ottenheimer had helped establish a permanent theater in Seattle, first called the Playhouse and later the Seattle Repertory Theater. It was known for putting on plays of social content (such as Clifford Odets's *Waiting for Lefty*) but also propaganda shows for the War Department in the 1940s. Ottenheimer taught acting at a labor school and had some association with the Brotherhood of Locomotive Engineers, both presumed links to communists during the 1930s.[52] In 1948, the Canwell Committee, the Washington state version of HUAC, questioned Ottenheimer on whether or not he was or had been a member of the Communist Party. He refused to answer the question, citing both his First Amendment rights to freedom of expression and his Fifth Amendment right not to incriminate himself. He was charged with contempt of court and served a month in prison.

The accusation and eventual conviction pushed Ottenheimer out of Seattle. Unable to find a job, he moved to Chicago, where he worked for the railroad union. Hoping to work in theater again, he moved to New York in 1951 and found jobs in radio and on TV. His success in New York was short-lived, however. An article about "reds" in New York radio and TV appeared in January 1953 in the *American Legion Magazine* and included his name. The jobs evaporated. "The first year I was in NY (a ten-month period, really)," Ottenheimer recalled in 1958, "I worked nearly 80 times on radio and TV; the next year about 85 times. From that point it began to toboggan, until it reached, a few years ago, absolute zero."[53] Exclusion from radio and TV did not prevent him from getting jobs on and off Broadway, though, nor did it stop him from signing a resolution against the blacklist in 1954. The latter action prompted yet another appearance before HUAC during its hearings on Actors Equity and the New York theater in August 1955. As before, Ottenheimer declined to answer specific questions. Instead, he fired a riposte: "I have never committed espionage or sabotage, and I have never knowingly used or advocated the use of force and violence for the overthrow of my government or for any other reason; but on the contrary, I have always been deeply and unswervingly loyal to the land of my birth."[54]

As with Art Smith, Oppenheimer's vindication was the role of Doc. The role provided financial stability and a new creative outlet. Given that Doc had relatively few lines, Oppenheimer spent a lot of time backstage watching others. He ended up writing an article about how musicians in the pit of a Broadway show filled their not-playing moments that ran in the *New Yorker* in August 1959. "Life in the Gutter" listed the books read, the music scores studied, the horses bet on, and the letters written. Ottenheimer himself finished *War and Peace* and caught up on "a rather voluminous correspondence for only the second time" in his adult life.[55] The surprising success of the article prompted him to propose other writing projects—first a book, or maybe just an article, about the domestic tour of *West Side Story*, then a book about the international tour of the show. In painstakingly typed entries, he wrote long descriptions of the challenges the company faced abroad and the reception they received. (The long descriptions may have daunted publishers, as no book came to be.)

The domestic tour stretched across the continent, starting in Denver in July 1959 and moving west to Los Angeles, up the coast to San Francisco, and on to Chicago, Detroit, Cincinnati, Cleveland, Baltimore, Boston, Philadelphia, and Washington. Ottenheimer racked up the anecdotes:

> Item: The oxygen tanks that had to be provided backstage in Denver for the dancers, to compensate for the thinness of the mile-high atmosphere; one or two of them blacked out during the show, as it was.

> Item: Author Arthur Laurents' opening-night wire to the company in LA: "Good luck, and don't be nervous. You have nothing at stake but your entire future in pictures."

> Item: The young man in S[an] F[rancisco] who, because of the impossibility of obtaining tickets, passed himself off as a newspaper reporter and was happily perched on an off-stage stool, making "notes," until the company manager investigated and threw him out.[56]

The items accumulated, ranging from backstage to life on the road. Long train rides started a knitting craze, in which the males "not only out-numbered but out-knitted the women." The gang members on-stage still confused the police offstage; "one of our stage hoodlums—a married man, at that—was twice during the tour picked up by the police on suspicion of vagrancy: once on Nob Hill in San Francisco, and again at a station stop in New Mexico. On both occasions he won his release by persuading the detaining officer of his solvency by displaying his Diners' Club card."[57]

In most cities, the show sold out and received rave reviews, despite recognition that the streets outside the theater in most cities were not jammed with Puerto Ricans or immigrants or masses of juvenile delinquents. "All I know is we don't have rumbles in Des Moines," one audience member had pronounced after seeing the show on Broadway.[58] Larry Kert, still playing Tony, claimed that San Francisco audiences, for instance, did not understand the show. "There are no such problems as racial gangs in the Golden Gate city, since the minority Chinese youths are exceptionally well behaved. People just couldn't see what was world-shaking about a girl from Puerto Rico falling in love with a boy whose parents came from Poland."[59] Arthur Laurents and Hal Prince believed that the enthusiastic reception across the country was abetted by this lack of knowledge of Puerto Rican migration, which kept fear at bay.[60] In Chicago, the crowds stayed home, much to the consternation of the producers and even the Chicago critic, perhaps for reasons that had little to do with the content and more to do with a certain raggedness that had crept into the show. (Robbins came "quietly" into town to whip the cast back into shape.) *West Side Story* closed after fourteen weeks at the Erlanger Theater in Chicago, while *The Music Man* continued on in its forty-fourth week.[61]

The production returned to Broadway and the Winter Garden in late April 1960. *Times* reviewer Brooks Atkinson was by now fully convinced that the show was a "major achievement of the American musical theater." He still gave most credit to the music and, especially, the dances: "They are sharp. They boil with animosity. But they also overflow with natural high spirits of young people who would like to stand tiptoe on the threshold of a joyous world."[62]

As *West Side Story* wowed New York again, plans sped up for its broader dissemination around the world and in a new form. A young production company formed by brothers Walter, Marvin, and Harold Mirisch fetched the film rights in August 1959, and intense conversations began about the transfer from stage to screen in early 1960. Summer stock theaters began performing the show in 1960 as well—in Cohasset, Massachusetts, Highland Park, Illinois, and Westbury, Long Island. The first international showing outside of London took place in Melbourne, Australia, in October 1960, with a cast of Americans and Australians, and after three months there, went on to Sydney. By fall 1960, Israeli impresarios had begun promotion for an international tour of the Broadway company, which took off first to Israel in January 1961 and traveled in Scandinavia and elsewhere in Europe through 1962.

Domestic and international politics fueled the show's creation and shaped its travels across the globe, and the production embodied the contradictions of the era. Doc spoke of tolerance, but the actors who played the role had suffered the consequences of anticommunist purges. The FBI kept its eye on Robbins, Bernstein, and Ottenheimer throughout the 1950s even as McCarthyism waned and restrictions lifted. The FBI closed its case on Bernstein in August 1956 and gave up on getting any more information out of Robbins by 1955. After his move to New York, Ottenheimer was active in a civil liberties committee that raised money for legal fees for those accused of communist activity. The FBI reported on these activities in 1958 and 1959 as Ottenheimer collected money for the cause among the cast of *West Side Story*. But in his August 1958 passport application, he did not answer the questions regarding Communist Party affiliation and still received the passport a month later. He renewed without issue in September 1960, a few months before setting off on the international tour.

Weary Doc held out little hope for making the world right. Battered by anticommunism at home and the shoe-banging invective of Khrushchev on the the global front, Doc-the-liberal was more resigned to the rotten world than capable of changing it. He is from an older world, an older immigrant group, belonging to the city more through mere age and squatters' rights than any particular battle over possession. Arthur Schlesinger, one of the noted defenders of liberalism at the time, called it a realistic philosophy, with little mystique and limited objectives. Doc in *West Side Story* played out the ineffectiveness of good intentions in a new world fueled by prejudice and battles for power under an atomic cloud.

5

"Camera and choreography"

1960–61

Cold War tensions prevented the musical from touring with government sponsorship, but the story soon found ways of leaping over the barriers of cultural diplomacy. Commercial productions had little trouble moving around the world, particularly in the medium of film. With different channels of distribution, movies had a wide reach. Here was an American export that did not need the endorsement of the US government and that traveled easily and, potentially, quite far.

That reach appealed to Robbins, who had long wanted to direct a film. The dance sequences he had done for *The King and I* (1951) only heightened his resolve, but the anxiety-fraught HUAC testimony may have made it even more necessary that he realize this ambition. His mastery of the material and the centrality of dance to the production swayed the Mirisch brothers, who held the movie rights to the story, to hire him as director, even though he had little direct experience in film. To assuage their concerns, the Mirisches also sought out Robert Wise, a film studio veteran who had moved up from editing—*Citizen Kane* (1941) was his greatest accomplishment—to directing. (*West Side Story* would be his first major success, followed soon after by *The Sound of Music* [1965] and eventually by *Star Trek* [1979].) Wise was well known for his workmanlike style. He brought in films on time, within budget, and managed the drama of the stars. He seemed like just the partner to keep Robbins in line. (The Mirisch brothers bypassed Laurents for the screenplay in favor of well-tested screen-writer Ernest Lehman; Bernstein composed some additional music for the film but turned over the orchestral scoring to Hollywood veteran Johnny Green.) Signing codirectors, of course, assured a battle.

When he conceived the musical, Robbins knew that the old story of *Romeo and Juliet* needed to be renewed by connecting it to the "city area." Onstage that meant attending to a script and song lyrics that evoked the contemporary tensions of the city in its migrations of people, and using dance to make visible the battle over space. The sets of Oliver Smith helped create the feel and sense of urban life, reminiscent of New York but also of a general city block. And the dream ballet "Somewhere" made clear the stark contrast between the grimy, violent, and bounded life of the streets and that of sunny, open, limitless space. On-screen, New York itself was the set—its actual streets and those places remade on the soundstages. The place was even more specific in the film, and so too was the battle over this block, this rooftop, this playground. Belonging, then, was specific too. Jets and Sharks fought to claim New York's west side.

The distinctness of that place made it impossible to create a "somewhere else." After numerous tries, the filmmakers dropped the idea of the dream ballet altogether. Instead of an imagined elsewhere, the film caught the city in flux. By 1960, when shooting took place, urban renewal and private construction had remade much of the island of Manhattan. Three- to four-story brownstone buildings had been bulldozed and replaced with gleaming glass skyscrapers in midtown; the edges of the island had become part of a network of roadways into and out of the city; and largely low-income people had been moved from small-scale buildings into large-scale housing projects. Robbins unwittingly summed up the fragility of these places—and the people who inhabit them—in an offhand remark while making preliminary tests for the film in March 1960: "We're pretty sure that the backgrounds we've photographed around here will still be standing [when shooting for the film begins], but who can tell?"[1]

Starting in early 1960, Wise and Robbins began an involved discussion regarding the transition from stage to screen. Robbins credited the success of the stage production to "the way it was told" rather than the accomplishments of any particular part, whether dancing, music, or book. The challenge for the film was to find a similar "approach," one not about cinematic technique per se but about the unique poetic qualities of cinematic conventions. He set out the arguments for abstraction. Wise seemingly concurred, saying that a "documentary approach" would not suffice and must even be cautioned against. He and Lehman had decided to stop "first hand research"—talking to "real west side kids and finding out about the gangs and their problems"— for "fear of finding ourselves wanting to change 'West Side Story' so much that the special quality that made it so exciting and unusual would be lost."[2] Nonetheless, debate ensued over how to represent New York on film. Those pushing for realism saw the grittiness and tension of the street as necessary to the drama. Those who valorized abstraction argued for the need to make the banal poetic, to see glory and tragedy rather than grime and blood. What followed was research and debate about how to conceptualize New York and build a resonant vision of it.

The theater had created particular parameters for blurring real and abstract: a proscenium arch literally framed the action, delimiting another world. The rituals of performing in three hours events that occurred over two days added to the otherworldliness of theatrical stylization. While hand-washed and beaten jeans and moving sets of bedrooms and cast-iron fire escapes created ties to real places, issues, and action, the ritual of theater set off these images as heightened versions of reality, dramatic analogues to what one might see on the streets outside the theater.

Moving to film, however, changed the parameters of real and abstract. Film created a hyperreality, a concreteness of the image that was solid, material, immortal. The transition, then, turned on the question of just what were the lines between real and unreal in a story that ran parallel to headline news but was filled with song and dance. For the stage, Robbins recognized "the problem of translating the reality of back street gang life . . . into the illusion of the theater." For the screen, the challenge was reversed: to translate the illusion of the stage into the "realistic medium of the cinema."[3]

Robbins's fixation on the *unreal* came from his belief in the "balletic approach" that had structured the musical, a "time-free, space-free, image-evocative method," poetic "in its use of all the theater arts." To capture the magic of the show, an analogous approach must be found that would use all the "*creative* film arts." To focus on the realness of the medium—the ability of film to depict in startling detail and depth what *is*—was to kill the story. It would be a "very tough, possibly moving, straight story-telling job, but let's all hold our breath whenever anybody sings," he implored, begging Wise to work against the realistic documentation of film.[4] Wise agreed, and did his own thinking about how the elements of film could create a distinct approach. The seasoned filmmaker wrote notes on photography and color, "the problems of style," and the particular challenges of musicals on film. Most films presented song and dance numbers in realistic settings, making them "often embarrassing," Wise conceded. *West Side Story* created an even more complex dilemma in that it was musical *drama*, not a comedy, with a story based on a serious contemporary social problem.[5]

Robbins and Wise agreed that highly theatrical treatment worked for the musical onstage but would not likely work in film, but they had yet to articulate what could work. In thinking about locations, for instance, Robbins thought that dance numbers should *not* be placed on actual streets. To do so would create expectations of realness that would always be at odds with song and dance.[6] To combat this, Robbins worked with the designer Saul Bass, hired as a visual consultant, to define a new approach. Their proposal consisted of a collage of pictures that set the danced story of rivalry in the prologue against abstracted images of the city. They shot dancers dressed in basic white T-shirts and khakis on a stage set, then put those photographs against backgrounds as diverse as a splash of paint reminiscent of Abstract Expressionism and brick walls with blown-out windows. The photo collages, numbering about twenty-five and evocative of the Photoshop-era to come, narrated the battle over turf between the Jets and Sharks in an other-world made up of fragments of a recognizable one.[7] The goal, Robbins and Bass argued, was to create a break with reality from the beginning. The mash-up of real and abstracted

FIGURE 5.1 Jets in khakis and white T-shirts, with Bernardo in a plaid shirt, rehearsing on soundstage, ca. 1960. Jerome Robbins Dance Division, New York Public Library for the Performing Arts, Astor, Lennox and Tilden Foundations.

bits would settle viewers into the unreal world of song and dance that followed.

Wise and the Mirisch brothers rejected the idea.[8] They were not unsympathetic to the problems a musical on film posed—Wise was bound up thinking through the conundrum as well—but they entreated Bass to come up with other possibilities. Bass returned again to the prologue. He sought to find a middle way between the polarities of abstract and real, a way of seeing the city that magnified the street-level fight over space and belonging. Taking some of the ideas he and Robbins had proposed, Bass's "visual interpretation" kept the abstraction and softened the stage-set collage: "We open on a series of highly stylized 'abstract-real' shots beginning, perhaps, with a direct overhead aerial view of the lower two-thirds of Manhattan."[9] His interpretation focused on patterns created by urban elements, such as an "'abstract real' handling of blinking, traveling, Times Square

FIGURE 5.2 Soundstage photo of Jets and Sharks taped onto location image of a gutted building, ca. 1960. Jerome Robbins Dance Division, New York Public Library for the Performing Arts, Astor, Lennox and Tilden Foundations.

lights," "direct overhead shot of the pattern of two streams of people flowing in opposite directions," and a "closeup of night shot showing safety gates drawn across entire front of store through which we see night-light on inside shop (entire screen becomes pattern)." With this visual introduction to city life, the images would then hone in on the west side, depicting the "Anglo" world before the arrival of Puerto Ricans. Visual suggestions of Puerto Ricans arriving included a moving van, a "se habla español" sign in a fruit and vegetable market, and an "abstract pattern of strange colorful exotic Puerto Rican fruits and vegetables; mangos, peppers, etc."[10]

Dancers would enter the frame only after this beginning, starting with snapping fingers and then moving more and more into a "semi-balletic manner." Bass suggested maintaining a consistent direction of movement for the Jets and the opposite for the Sharks. Fragments of patterned backgrounds—"the gas tank superstructure, the wire of the playground, the chalked boarding, the brick wall covered with layers of peeling posters, the red setting sun seen through the metal structures, etc."—would be interspersed with the movement of dancers. "These two images (the dancers and the backgrounds) are *not* in real conjunction with each other," he cautioned. The two sets of images should be shot differently, perhaps one in a straight-on view and another in an aerial or worm's-eye view.[11] Rather than creating one collage of both images, Bass suggested holding each world—that of aesthetic images and patterns of the real city and that of the dancers—apart, to be seen in succession, building to when they would be linked in words and dialogue.

A storyboard of the prologue Bass developed gives little indication of the differing camera angles but does show the reliance on abstracted backgrounds such as enlarged street signs (No Left Turn, One Way, Detour, Keep Out), walls covered with graffiti and scratchings with the word "Jets" visible, and patterns made from iron fire escapes. The confrontational encounters between Jets and Sharks increased toward the end of the storyboard and "supered over this would be a pulsating red orb which would quicken its pulse to the tempo of the action and cuts until an intense impressionistic war is on."[12]

This approach did not quell Robbins's qualms about location shots. He still feared that such direct use of the real city would undermine acceptance of music and dance as believable parts of the story. His uneasiness about actual locations may also have indicated a view of urban life that depended less on actual streets and more on the tense interaction of people. Countering Bass's storyboard suggestions, Robbins railed against starting the film "with wonderful shots of New York." The film should start with that which made it distinct—not New York, but music and singing and dancing. "This frame . . . is what the rest of the story fits within and instead of going from the realistic to the fantastic we should think of the magical parts of the picture leading to the realistic," Robbins urged.[13] Using song and dance to stylize the hardship of urban life, Robbins looked toward achieving not wonder but human drama.

Robbins, Wise, Bass, and art director Boris Leven continued this sparring throughout the first months of 1960. They also began searching for specific shooting locations in New York. Robbins and Wise scoured places in February, conducting tests in film as well as still photography. The location list ranged from playgrounds and alleys to warehouses, parking lots, and pools, most on the far west side, between 9th and 12th Avenues, and 24th and 134th Streets, with a few scattered on the Upper East Side. Restricted to large open spaces adequate for shooting dance, the locations indicated the real of the city in that they focused on workplaces—a slaughterhouse on 41st Street between 11th and 12th Avenues; a warehouse at 59th Street and 12th Avenue. These places also offered abstract elements, such as the "bricked arches" of the warehouse and the "painted wall" near a bus station that emphasized aesthetics rather than function.[14] A prominent image throughout the location search was of a large gas tank, a recurring feature that put the spotlight on the city's often-overlooked infrastructure. Robbins's notes for the tests continued the ongoing debate, daring convention: "Try shot from car following kids on street and then zooming in and out." He wanted to unbalance the reality and create a world unto itself: "Can places (like H&H [the warehouse for Horn & Hardart, which operated automats throughout the city]) be dressed with real elements—cars—people—light poles—signs—details that read real—and so make up our own *active* life *on* the turf and not be confined to warehouse, back alleys and walls. Then we create out of real elements an unreal."[15]

Wise did not dismiss Robbins's ideas. He even asked why the sky needed to remain blue in an article published in the midst of shooting; "Suppose you were to see it as orange, or lavender? It might shock your sense of realism, but it also might tell you that we are semi-abstracting an idea and you get into the mood of the piece that much faster."[16] Wise's quip indicates how much was being rethought for the film, but it also suggests an adventurousness that Robbins advocated more than Wise. Nearly the same day Robbins penned hopes for the "magical parts" of film, Wise began scheduling shooting in New York for early August that followed the Bass approach for the prologue.[17]

FIGURE 5.3 Location shot, New York, with gas tank in background, ca. 1960. Jerome Robbins Dance Division, New York Public Library for the Performing Arts, Astor, Lennox and Tilden Foundations.

With specific locations in mind, Bass created an outline for the prologue that matched dance moves to background shots, camera angles, and techniques. Jets enjoying their territory exhibited the "sailing step"—arms and one leg opening from front to side in a survey and command of the street—against shots of broken concrete, a "Jackson Pollock splash," and a brick building with windows and a floundering geranium. Reality shots included the confrontation between the Jets and Bernardo. When Bernardo and the Puerto Ricans begin to claim their right to the turf, they move against "detour and slow sign," "large arrow 'right,'" and a "cleaning sign." "Guerilla warfare," the direct skirmishes between the gang members, plays out against "burlesque lights" in and out of focus and, finally, "way out of focus."[18]

FIGURE 5.4 Location shot, New York, ca. 1960. Notice the line of doors in the background, reminiscent of the doors that Oliver Smith designed for the stage version (see figure 2.5). Jerome Robbins Dance Division, New York Public Library for the Performing Arts, Astor, Lennox and Tilden Foundations.

The Bass approach was not fully realized frame-by-frame in the prologue, but the play between real and abstract created much of its style. It also encapsulated much of the debate about how to visualize the city, as either a broad canvas upon which humans appear as symbols or a collection of up-close portraits of people moving that builds to a human-centered action environment. Robbins remained anxious. "We're trying to combine successfully this kind of startling material with real backgrounds, and we're hoping that some sort of style will occur," he pronounced—resignation clear.[19]

After compromising on the prologue, Robbins and Wise turned to thinking about the art direction of the film overall. One of the ways to lure a movie audience into an altered world was a specific and detailed use of color and light, elements more central to screen than stage. In a theater performance, "the design is held together by the geometry of the stage itself," explained Robbins.[20] Color, light, and camera angle provided that kind of framing for film. As art director, Leven played a large role in creating the style that melded a real and abstract city.[21] Using the streets of New York for location shooting concerned Leven as it did Robbins—it was a concrete rendition of urban life that could easily drain the tension of the tragic love at stake. To step up the stylization of the streets and reconcile the oddity of song and dance on them, Leven advocated shooting each locale "as a stage setting, as a drop." This involved selecting locations for their "color, shape and mood" rather than criteria of authenticity. Then "each locale—real as real can be" needed to be photographed simply, without obvious artifice, so that it was literally the background. A brownstone stoop, for example, "should be photographed straight on, preferably in shadow, so that it will appear as a backdrop," rather than at an odd angle or brightly lit. Any additional people are "there but they are part of architecture; they sit or stand, or move about, but they do not react to what takes place in the foreground." The primary actors, by contrast, work "in the foreground. They are in light." This contrast, in place and lighting, was to convey the idea that "this is their world, others just exist."[22] The filmic city, then, was built by layers of people, of light and shadow, so that even a tight view of a block encompassed the world beyond.

Visual research by Leven, Robbins, and Wise honed choices around color, light, and design of camera shots that relayed specific aspects of urban life. Leven and Wise collected photographs of locations and visited the homes of Puerto Ricans in their neighborhoods on the west side and in Spanish Harlem. Robbins gathered pictures of Latino men on the street—such as two suited men caught in mid-stride walking before a row of garbage cans with the sun creating a brownish glow. In keeping with his focus on aesthetic elements, though, Robbins more often filed away photos that captured formal

FIGURE 5.5 Visual research for the film, New York, ca. 1960. Jerome Robbins Dance Division, New York Public Library for the Performing Arts, Astor, Lennox and Tilden Foundations.

juxtapositions without people: the dark underbelly of a truck chassis against the lightened street behind it; a conglomeration of rooftop chimney pipes bronzed in the sun; the view out a store window with letters in high relief and a blurry man across the street in the background. These pictures stilled the jostling of elements that defined urban life.

Wise collected general articles on New York, including two from the February 1958 issue of *Look* magazine titled "This Is New York." Stories featured the daily life of a businessman and that of a dog and followed young tourists on their honeymoon in the city. But the contrast of two side-by-side stories paralleled the perspective underlying the *West Side Story* visual research. "The Changing Face of New York" presented the dramatic building under way in the city with a foldout picture of construction scaffolding against a backdrop of skyscrapers. The "new horizons," the copy noted, were a result of

FIGURE 5.6 View through the undercarriage of a heavy truck of a parked car across the street, ca. 1960. Jerome Robbins Dance Division, New York Public Library for the Performing Arts, Astor, Lennox and Tilden Foundations.

over two billion dollars invested in new buildings since 1947; "day and night," "Manhattan's tireless builders" provide "an endless, exciting panorama." The very next story burnished the gleam. "Behind New York's Façade: Slums and Segregation" detailed Manhattan's changing demographics, with a map that showed the persistent residential segregation of Puerto Ricans and African Americans. Slums were "growing as fast as they are being cleared, and . . . minority groups are multiplying faster than they are being integrated." A picture of children mostly barred behind a fence, with a few climbing up and two teetering on top, anchored the essay.[23]

   Both the formal aesthetic images collected by Robbins and the reportorial stories gathered by Wise focused on the contrast between aspiration and limitation that the city embodied. Pictures of globules of light, whether from traffic signals or signs, blare out in yellow

FIGURE 5.7 View of street from the interior of a shop, ca. 1960. Jerome Robbins Dance Division, New York Public Library for the Performing Arts, Astor, Lennox and Tilden Foundations.

and red. One-way signs sit atop the red of a traffic light in one photograph. In another, birds fly in an orange sunset sky above the black outline of rooftop paraphernalia. Poles and wires stretch across the foreground of a gray cloudy view of the sun rising next to the Empire State Building. A window with shade drawn breaks out of a stark wall of brick with potted plants on the sill, struggling to thrive. And in a literal blending of abstract and real, a woman, cut off at the shoulders, is caught about to step into a puddle that reflects the rise of a skyscraper downward. The most common images are of chain-link fences: close-ups of the interlocking diamonds that allow vision but obstruct movement; playgrounds ringed by such fences; people behind them.

Leven blurred the line between real and abstract to turn these themes of confinement and yearning—the aspirations restless youth of the moment symbolized—into color and light. He understood that

FIGURE 5.8 Close-up view of a one-way street sign with traffic light, ca. 1960. Jerome Robbins Dance Division, New York Public Library for the Performing Arts, Astor, Lennox and Tilden Foundations.

the credibility of a specific world was crucial to any rendering of the story and specified how to do this in film, through "the size, form and shape of sets . . . their color or lack of it, and of course the way they are used, lighted and photographed."[24] This highly controlled approach worked best on a set, of course, and most of the film utilized soundstages. Since much of the story took place at night or indoors, though, there was more chance that highly controlled soundstages could simulate real-world locations.

Leven's storyboards create continuity through color and composition: they portray people against buildings with windows bricked up; gang members who look out the open, lit windows of a demolished building; the warm orange of a rooftop that makes pipes and lattice glow. The bold red truck of "Ramonita Movers" and the blues and reds of storefronts mark the presence of Puerto Rican inhabitants. Perhaps the most abstract is a play of reds, yellows, blues, and whites that depicts a basement scene with a bright beam shining in from one side, a study in color and light. Like the shots developed following the Bass approach, the storyboard images rarely come across complete in

FIGURE 5.9 Brick wall with window and flowerpots on the sill, reminiscent of the gutted building in the collage with dancers on a soundstage (figure 5.2), ca. 1960. Jerome Robbins Dance Division, New York Public Library for the Performing Arts, Astor, Lennox and Tilden Foundations.

the film, but they guided the overall color schemes and design composition of the sets that dominated the picture and complemented the street scenes in the prologue.

In the midst of setting these aesthetic elements, Robbins and Wise also began the arduous process of casting the film. Since the success of the Broadway show was well known, stars began lining up. Elvis Presley, Marlon Brando, Warren Beatty, Anthony Perkins—all considered, all dismissed. Too old, or their fame too distracting from the innocence and naivety of young love. Then there were the actors who had become stars because of the stage version—Carol Lawrence, Larry Kert, and Chita Rivera. All dismissed. They were deemed either too old or better suited to the far-away illusion of the stage than the close-up reality of the screen. Then the cattle-call auditions around the country—hundreds upon hundreds of aspiring dancers turned

FIGURE 5.10 Ramonita Restaurant, visual research for the film, ca. 1960. Art director
Boris Leven applied the name of this restaurant to a moving van (Ramonita Movers) in an-
other storyboard. Robert Wise Collection, Cinematic Arts Library, University of Southern
California.

out for a chance to become a Jet or Shark, to be immortalized by Robbins's choreography on celluloid.

The auditions for the film were endless, just as they had been for
the stage musical. Dancers got called back time and again, let go
suddenly, or called back to try for different roles. This time around,
though, there was little attempt to be authentic by going to settlement
houses or into Puerto Rican neighborhoods on a hunt for amateur
singers and dancers. The directors went directly to seasoned professionals. In fact, they ended up hiring mainly dancers from the Broadway and London companies. Carole D'Andrea, who created the Jet

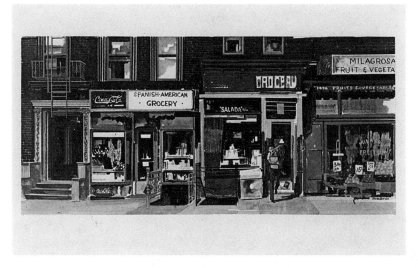

FIGURE 5.11 This storyboard by Boris Leven, ca. 1960, picks up on the storefronts in the visual research photo shown in figure 5.10. Courtesy of MGM Media Licensing; Jerome Robbins Dance Division, New York Public Library for the Performing Arts, Astor, Lennox and Tilden Foundations.

girl Velma onstage, traveled in State Department–sponsored tours in the months after leaving *West Side Story*. When she returned, Robbins called her immediately, asking where she had been and saying he had been looking for her for months. She needed to come to Hollywood immediately to be either Anybodys or Velma in the film. (She remained Velma.)[25]

When D'Andrea got to California, she entered into a battle between east coast and west coast dancers that rivaled the animosity of the Jets and the Sharks. New York dancers outnumbered those from Los Angeles, and most had already been in one of the *West Side Story* companies. Dancers from Los Angeles viewed them as high-handed, uppity, overconfident. They, after all, knew how to dance for the camera. The new rivalry—it was no longer Jets and Sharks not talking to one another—reflected the increasing professional nature of the production. The directors were less interested in the naivety of youth and more in the technical mastery of the actors and dancers who would be caught by the relentless, close-up, immortalizing glare of the camera.

FIGURE 5.12 Rooftop, visual research for the film. Jerome Robbins Dance Division, New York Public Library for the Performing Arts, Astor, Lennox and Tilden Foundations.

The long list of concerns—screen savvy and appeal, singing, dancing, acting, youth, beauty—made the search for the primary roles even more difficult. Anita was the easiest. Chita Rivera had been electrifying onstage but she was not considered for the film, possibly because her wizened face would read as too knowing and older on film. Robbins quickly sought out Rita Moreno, with whom he had worked on *The King and I* and whom he had encouraged to audition for the stage version. She was terrified by the idea at that point. Both the necessary dancing prowess and the immediacy of the stage frightened her.

But she jumped at the chance for the part in the movie. By 1957, when the musical debuted, Moreno had a spotty but relatively long career in film. Born in 1931 as Rosa Delores Alverío in Humacao, Puerto Rico, Moreno moved to the Bronx when she was five. Amid Jews, Italians, and Swedes, she felt "hunted." She found a more comfortable environment when the family moved to Washington Heights, where

FIGURE 5.13 Storyboard by Boris Leven, ca. 1960, showing a rooftop as leftover space to be claimed. The rendering picks up on the photo in figure 5.12 but leaves room for dance. Courtesy of MGM Media Licensing; Jerome Robbins Dance Division, New York Public Library for the Performing Arts, Astor, Lennox and Tilden Foundations.

they were surrounded by more Puerto Ricans and looked out onto the George Washington Bridge, born the same year she was.[26] Settling in, she learned Spanish dance from Paco Cansino, the teacher and uncle of Rita Hayworth, and capitalized on the Carmen Miranda craze by performing at bar mitzvahs, wedding halls, and the USO. At the age of seventeen, she debuted in *So Young So Bad* (1950), a movie about a reform school for girls. MGM quickly signed her to a seven-year contract, thinking they had found a Latina Elizabeth Taylor. She had a small speaking role in *Singing in the Rain* (1952), as a showgirl but not an ethnic one. Her rise ended abruptly, though, when MGM dropped her.

Moreno's career as Latina sexual siren continued, even as bit parts in B movies became the norm. She did a photo spread for *Life* in 1954, the same year she met Marlon Brando, the bad boy of Hollywood. Her affair with Brando was an open Hollywood secret, as was his attachment to other women. The torment of the love affair haunted her, even in the midst of filming *West Side Story*. And perhaps some of that experience of conflict in romance filtered into the character Anita, whose devotion to love crosses so many boundaries.

It was the Puerto Rican background of the character that mattered most to Moreno, however. Tired of playing random ethnicities—Thai in *The King and I*, Tahitian in *Pagan Love Song* (1950), Native American in *The Yellow Tomahawk* (1954)—and every generic Latina in a series of westerns, Moreno jumped at a chance to be a Puerto Rican on-screen. "Anita was real! She was Puerto Rican, and she was fighting for her rights. She had plenty to say about what was wrong in America—and in the world. At this point, I'd never been given the opportunity to play the part of the woman who stood up for herself. Her suffering, her anger, were *my* suffering, *my* anger. Becoming Anita was a personal mission for me. I had fled down those mean streets in fear of the gangs, chased and hunted by that awful hiss: '*Spic!*'"[27] That passion motivated her to work for the part. She worried about her dancing abilities, in particular, and asked a dancer in the show to help her prepare for the audition. Given her hard work, her Puerto Rican background, and her sexy starlet image, signing on Moreno was an easy decision.

The other main parts—Riff, Bernardo, Tony, and Maria—required much tougher decisions. The directors wanted strong dancers for Riff and Bernardo and looked to the existing leads in the London and touring companies. George Chakiris played Riff in London and was asked to Los Angeles for a screen test. He came away with the role of Bernardo. The directors then looked beyond the current and past casts and asked Russ Tamblyn to read for the parts of Tony and Riff. Tamblyn had gained fame in *Seven Brides for Seven Brothers* (1954), which showed off his gymnastic training, and was getting consistent roles in film even after being drafted into the army in the late 1950s. The role of Tony appealed to him. He was more boyish than dangerous, more starry-eyed lover than revenge-seeking gang leader, and he worried that the dancing required of Riff would be too difficult for him. But the directors slotted him in for Riff and continued to hunt for a Tony. A recent teen idol seemed appropriate. Richard Beymer had won attention from that key market with his appearance in *The*

Diary of Anne Frank (1959) as the love interest of the young Anne. Swarthy, pouty-lipped, earnest: this was Tony. (Critics would disagree.)

As it had been for the stage, filling the role of Maria was tricky. An ingénue who could sing, dance, and act—there were not many. Suzanne Pleshette, Jill St. John, Anna Maria Alberghetti (again!), Audrey Hepburn (before she became pregnant), Jane Fonda, and Angie Dickinson were all seen as possibilities and then dismissed.[28] Again, no effort appears to have been made to find a Puerto Rican or Latina actress for this crucial role; an affected accent and dark hair would suffice. When the dancers gathered in Los Angeles in early summer, the role had not yet been assigned, so even Carole D'Andrea was asked to read for the part. Finally, Wise and Robbins found their way to Natalie Wood, twenty-two, a beauty, and already a Hollywood veteran. Born of Russian immigrants, Wood had her first major role on-screen in *Miracle on 34th Street* (1947) at the age of eight. She received an introduction to the contemporary issues of teenagers as one herself in *Rebel without a Cause*, for which she earned her first Academy Award nomination. Wood lobbied for the role and, perhaps most important, captivated Robbins. She was "a fawn in the forest," as Robert Relyea, the first assistant director on the film, remembered.[29] (Robbins's earlier devotion to the ballet dancer Tanaquil LeClerq inspired his *Afternoon of a Faun* [1953], so the metaphor of Wood as a fawn may have been a knowing allusion to this history.) As with the role of Tony, naivety and beauty seemed to be the key elements the directors were seeking. Neither Beymer nor Wood had stellar dancing or singing skills, but they did have starlike glamor and good looks. Dubbing songs was common, and Robbins knew how to work around limited movement. He just had to be convinced that it was worth it. And, for Wood, it was.

Rehearsals began in the summer of 1960 at the Samuel Goldwyn studios at the corner of Santa Monica Boulevard and Formosa Avenue in West Hollywood. The Mirisch brothers took over the lot, the *Los Angeles Times* reported, and "turned it into a vast slum city, complete with the girders of an East River bridge" (thus mixing the east and west sides of Manhattan).[30] As usual, Robbins's demands caused terror among the cast. Relyea claimed never to have seen so many wounded cast members, with "scrapes, burns, shin splints, sprained ankles, torn ligaments, dehydration, hepatitis, pneumonia."[31] Dancers in "Cool," with its knee-grinding floor turns, held a ritualistic burning of their kneepads in front of Robbins's office when filming concluded for the scene. But the hurry-up-and-wait reality of filming also allowed for more pranks. Dancers scrambled up and rode the chariots being used for *Spartacus* on the adjacent soundstage, causing a ruckus that got them expelled from the set for the rest of the day. A "rain dance" in New York when shooting the prologue brought a day of rest. The laughter provided needed relief from the pent-up tension of the story itself, the anxiety induced by Robbins-the-perfectionist, and the inevitable clash of minds among the large team of people on the set.

The antics of the dancers worried Robbins less than the myriad challenges in filming dance. Even with his preference for abstraction, he took the rehearsals to the streets of Los Angeles to test light and movement against real backgrounds. Rehearsing on a soundstage unsettled him. The cavernous space overwhelmed him. "Nothing I did seem to fill it and, on the other hand, I felt that I *had* to fill it," he wrote a friend.[32]

The visual possibilities of film were dramatically different from those of the stage, with its proscenium frame that was always visible, delimiting both space and time. Film extended space. From helicopter panorama shots to intricately created stage sets, its materials and methods allowed for compression, lengthening, or simultaneity. "The concentration of the stage version, the sense of backstreet claustrophobia which summarized slum life at once and which led to the dream ballet about a place 'somewhere' with enough space for everyone, all this was obviously in danger of being lost," wrote one critic, anticipating the thematic ramifications of a change in medium.[33] "In the theater we tried to tell our story through music, dance, and dialogue equally," Robbins summarized. "In the film you add to those three the camera—that's the real difference."[34]

That addition—the nearly infinite possibilities of the eye of the camera—challenged Robbins. Dance, he believed, needed "a reference—that is, a limitation of space, a frame, in three dimensions." Movies had not yet conveyed the force of dance because of this. They had captured "sex, charm, and daring, but not the genuine energy that dance should have." He needed to combine "camera and choreography" to match the sense of ownership of turf that could be conveyed with choreography alone on a stage.[35] As much as he was learning about cameras and filming, though, he felt constantly hemmed in by Hollywood convention. "Rather than my teaching them how to make the camera dance it's possible that I'm being taught the limitations of imagination and lack of daring," he wrote in the middle of filming.[36]

"Cool" was his answer. Thinking through how to *limit* space for this key dance—now moved to later in the script, after the rumble—Robbins suggested to the screenwriter Lehman that they set it in a garage.[37] The infiltration of car culture into urban life made it an appropriate setting thematically, but the structural qualities of a garage also fit the piece—dark, buried, functional, shorn of any amenity. Robbins asked for one built with low ceilings but, "true to Hollywood standards," he was given a "super garage"—shallow in height but cavernous. "I seem to be spending most of my energy pushing walls closer to each other," metaphorically if not literally, Robbins complained.[38] But it worked. The filming increased the tension of the song with propulsive movement that exploded off the floor, nearly hitting the ceiling. Film also allowed dancers to keep moving forward—to keep the propulsion moving into the camera, in contrast to the stage, where they had to take two steps forward and two back to keep from diving into the footlights.[39] Headlights framed the Jets as caught and bound, even as they push, kick, and punch against these constraints. The low ceilings "made us feel the weight of the world on our shoulders," dancer Robert Banas remembered. "We felt contained, cramped, restricted, and asphyxiated, which certainly mentally and physically enhance the choreography. We really wanted to bust out and explode to destroy ourselves."[40] Harvey Evans, another

Jet, described it as "dancing in hell"—claustrophobic, hot lights throwing off intense heat, Robbins asking for take after take after take, always from the top so as to not miss the explosive momentum of the movement itself—and no place to escape.[41]

Filming "Cool" in a garage solved Robbins's dance problem. There and elsewhere, the use of cars, so prominent in the urban landscape, exemplified the way realistic elements—bathed in a subtle play of light and shadow—could convey the theme of confinement that dominated the visual research for the film. Highway ramps in Los Angeles provided the lead-up to the rumble in the quintet "Tonight," with the gangs moving through these concrete tunnels, empty and suspenseful at night but with strands of light breaking the dark. In transition scenes, oncoming headlights caught people running, marking them as hunted.

It was another set, though—Maria's bedroom, with its door with colored-glass panels—that best synthesized the filmmakers' approach to using color and light to convey the themes of confinement and escape. Take a real element, the passage from one room to the next, and make it symbolic and luminous—a portal between worlds. Reminiscent of Piet Mondrian's abstractions of New York's grids of color, the door exemplified a mixing of colors as harmonious and gleaming. It was a gateway to another world, a place for Tony and Maria to live beyond the segregation that structured the streets. This was "Somewhere" else on film.

If the play of light and shadow built the filmic city as a place of confinement and yearning, the color red added passion, anger, and blood tragedy. Red suffused the sets and the technological enhancements. Jorge Luis Borges, the renowned Argentine writer, loved watching *West Side Story*, even though he was blind by 1961, when the movie debuted. He was drawn to the epic qualities of the story, the awe and tragedy of youthful desire, battle, and bravery. After viewing the movie yet again with a companion, he commented on cities that become literary characters, on "the rivalry between the gangs, on the role of the women, on the use of the colour red." The color red? "His world was wholly verbal: music, colour and form rarely entered it," his companion wrote. And yet Borges saw the story and the city as red. He certainly had been told what the movie looked like, but the music, story, and passion created unusually powerful visual imagery as well. The movie became a way to see the city for the blind Borges, and red was as much a foundation of that city as black pavement and gray buildings.[42]

The use of color is perhaps most notable in the transitions between scenes, one of the critical—and awkward—spots in the move from stage to screen. The editing and special effects team spent more time on the transition from the bridal shop to the dance at the gym, near the beginning of the film, than any other. The stage version had rendered a precedent that was difficult to match. As Maria tries on the new white dress that Anita has repaired, she twirls as the stage set of the shop is pulled off and streamers come down to set the scene for the pivotal dance hall scene where she and Tony meet. The film followed that idea but utilized cinematic techniques to make the transition. Special effects dissolved the image of Maria in a white dress twirling, using a succession of filters that "progressively slipped out of sync with each other, resulting in flaring color fringes. The zoom continues on out of focus, producing a blaze of whirling colors which dissolve to gyrating red abstract forms that gradually evolved into a red mask, showing a distorted group of dancers."[43] The blurry images of dancers set in a blood-red background become more and more distinct and varied in color until the viewer joins the dance at the gym in full swing. This blurred haze connected the scenes and also moved the anticipation of the virginal Maria into the excitement, color, and energy of the dance hall. (The abstract effect was not enough to please Robbins, who, late in editing, entreated the person in charge of special effects "to give early part of gym some treatment to make it less real."[44])

Similarly, the transition between the quintet—different characters anticipating the night's actions in "Tonight"—and the rumble between the Jets and the Sharks pulsated red. "As the gang of boys file past the camera, the scene zooms forward into a red, blurry mass as abstract lines appear and zoom back, turning into a glistening chain link fence superimposed over the setting for the gang fight to follow."[45] The gang members climb those fences and jump down to the underbelly of the highway. "Rarely has color been used more effectively on film, not to provide a tinted background, but as a structural adjunct, imaginatively and handsomely related to the emotional content. You could say that it dramatizes the very bricks," pronounced a reviewer.[46] Arthur Knight, in a trenchant analysis of the film, claimed that it had "a style reminiscent of the Manhattan canvases of Ben Shahn"—perhaps assuaging Robbins's worries that the film's style leaned too far to the realistic. "The settings share his sense of unexpected beauty and color in drab slums and are tinged with the same melancholy suggestion that this beauty is both adventitious and unnoticed."[47] Light and shadow created a city of startling contrasts— aspiration and restriction on every corner—and color tracked people's action in the picture, making clear the human imprint on buildings, highways, and streets.

As much as color and light conveyed thematic elements of urban life, the eye of the camera itself did perhaps even more in fusing real and unreal, streets and dance, city and story. Wise, Robbins, and the director of photography Daniel Fapp blended big-screen techniques— swoops, grand vistas, panoramas—with close-ups and intimate shots, the latter not having been much utilized in movie musicals.[48] Another reviewer called the effect "stimulating," using "both stage and screen techniques; i.e., long holds on individual scenes and bits of action which suddenly switches to dynamic movement."[49] "From the opening helicopter shots of New York's soaring skyline, gradually closing down to the ominous, snapping fingers of a teenage gang lounging against the mesh fence of a mid-city playground, we know that this production has been re-created in terms of the camera," Knight wrote. Here is where camera angle and action on-screen combined to create a vital picture of the city, one animated by people moving.

Knight connected this innovative use of the camera to the importance of dance in the film. The action of people necessitated a more active camera. "Only once, in the gymnasium dance, was I sharply reminded of the theater's one, restricted point of view. Then sud-

denly, into that very shot, leaped two pair of legs within inches of the
lens, and we were back in film once more."[50] This lapse in the overall
fluid portrayal is telling in that the dance in the gym is the only dance
scene not filmed by Robbins. After long delays, skyrocketing costs,
and frustrations over his pugnacious style, the Mirisch brothers fired
Robbins in October 1960, in the midst of rehearsals for the scene.
True to form, after being dismissed on a Friday, Robbins went back to
the soundstage and railed against the dancers, telling them that they
were all expendable. When they showed up for work again on Monday,
they realized it was he who was expendable.

Most wondered how it would be possible to complete the film without him. Robbins was a tyrant, but he was also deeply entrenched
in the story, the movement, the necessary attention to differences
between stage and screen, and the *vision* of the film. Tony Mordente,
playing Action and a veteran of the Broadway and London companies, stepped up as a dance coach to get the cast through the dance
hall scene. Wise took over filming, moving along at a good pace, even
if it was still more delayed and over-budget than the Mirisch brothers
wanted.

Spurned, Robbins turned his back on the film, heading home to
New York. He asked that his name be taken off the film completely.
Finding some cool, he then agreed to wait and see a rough cut before
making the decision. What he saw must have convinced him of its
value overall because he consulted with Wise throughout the editing
of the film. Wise sought out his opinion on the dance scenes in particular. Robbins could not help but respond with copious, detailed
notes and suggestions. "The main problem of the picture is to fix the
Dance Hall sequence," Robbins declared with his characteristic directness.[51]

The dance hall scene pointed to the difference between the eye of
an accomplished film director and that of an accomplished choreographer. Wise had started with a wide-angle view of the dance—seen
from the outside. When the camera ventures into the scene, it is most
often to capture movement and story outside of the dance, such as the
entrance of Maria and then of Tony. It is the one scene in the movie

that is overflowing with people—not just the primary members of the Jets and Sharks, but their women and gang members in training, and the outnumbered and ineffective adults. This is the community in full—and thus offers a dramatic backdrop upon which to show the rift between the two gangs.

Dramatizing the rift is the intent of the dance. The social worker starts with a clearly naïve suggestion for a "get-together dance," instructing the young people to form two circles—men on the outside, women on the inside—moving in opposite directions; when the music stops, men and women are to dance with the partner opposite. Not acceding to this masquerade of tolerance, Riff and Bernardo make it into a challenge and pull their own women to dance with them when the circles stop. Then the battle begins. The dance proceeds as a competition, from larger groups to smaller with increasingly virtuosic moves. But it is really a marking—a claiming—of space that the dance signifies, both in the gang plotline and in the film's portrayal of New York. This is clear in the movement of lines of dancers that charge toward one another; the Sharks initially dominate the space, which is then intruded upon and dominated by the Jets. A half-circle that forms around one couple soon breaks into two—the Sharks surrounding Bernardo and Anita, the Jets encircling Riff and Graziella.

The rift was clear but not dramatic. Wise kept the staging oppositional and flat. The camera went from wide-angle views to chest-high views, and the few moments of suspense—when leaps and movement charged directly at the camera—were settled, and drained of any challenge, by quick cuts back to the fuller picture. Robbins felt the scene undercut the "tense *action* of plot and story" by diminishing the rivalry of the gangs into "general dance enthusiasm." He scolded Wise—the far more experienced film director—that each shot mattered: "Before the Sharks start their own mambo you do not see them (in any shot including both groups) leave the Jets and move to their own conference. The Sharks (in a shot including the Jets) should be seen to withdraw and then take over the dance hall: then the Jets (in a shot including the Sharks) should be seen gathering and taking it back and dispersing the Sharks: then the Sharks reassemble and take it back, and the Jets re-counter."[52]

Robbins knew that the point of the scene was not dance but a battle over possession of space. From the competition between the leading couples of the gangs, "one doesn't get the impression that this is a highly pitched and desperate gang fight for supremacy. . . . This is terribly important to remedy" because the lovers need to meet at the "fiercest moment of the gangs crescendoing competitive dance."[53] In the end, the dancing of the lead couples of each gang is stretched, not heightened, by the filming, which cuts from one to the other with no compulsion. The scene is vibrant because of its colorful fullness—its swishing skirts, gymnastic movement, and crowd revelry—but its staging and filming sanitizes the city, staging a closed competition about dance rather than a necessary and inevitable battle over turf, pride, and belonging.

Robbins's filming of "America" presents a stark contrast. Similar in that it is a face-off between two groups—women and men in the case of "America" in the film—it possesses, from the beginning, more intimacy, involvement, and urgency. Some of this is due to lyrics; we're following a witty repartee (with discriminatory notes). There's also a set that differentiates the space, a rooftop with obtruding air vents and the web of urban infrastructure in the background. This arrangement opens up a V-shaped place of action, going from narrow in the back to wider in the front, already giving depth to the movement that the boxlike set and staging of the dance at the gym did not.

Beyond the physical setup, the staging and filming of the scene draw viewers into the story, into the city, and into the barely contained needs and yearnings of the Sharks. The song starts with a close-up of Anita, and the camera follows her into movement. At one point, the camera trails the backs of Anita and her friend, in effect engaging us in the dance with them. This active camera work contrasted to the static, reactionary camera in the dance at the gym. Robbins does not leave the visual frame of the scene open. Instead, he moves dancers into and out of the frame, most prominently in one shot that features lower legs crossing in front of the frame, through which we see the larger movement of dance. The competition between the groups is staged not only as oppositional but as combative and responsive. The men move upstage clicking their heels; the women follow, mimicking them, and are pushed back when the men turn around. While the lyrics and singing enhance the effect, it is not a battle told to us but one in which we are directly engaged.

The battle over space that dancing symbolizes in the film has a friskier edge in this scene, as it is primarily a battle of the sexes. The union—the passionate sharing of space—is what is desired, only enhanced in this rendition by the teasing taunts. The ending of the scene exhibits this broad claiming of space as the couples come together. After passing off dance moves from women to men at an ever swifter pace, for the first time in the scene the camera pulls back and up, quite high. This exposes the full stage, revealing the squareness Robbins shrank and arced by moving the dancers. The overview provides a climax to the coupling as well, with individual men and women pairing off for the first time in the dance. It ends with the men hoisting the women on their shoulders in a triumph of shared exuberance, if not agreement. They have found a kind of possession. It is a rooftop, but it is theirs: a proclamation of belonging in the city.

In this scene focusing solely on Puerto Ricans—seen here in more detail than in any other blockbuster movie to date—the empathy prompted by the intimate, active camera work raised the stakes of the drama. The screen version of "America" exhibited the influence of criticism the musical had received for its portrayal of Puerto Rico, first in the lyrics of the song. Gone from the lyrics were "tropical diseases" and the "ugly island" of Puerto Rico; now Anita and the women defend the United States, exclaiming that "skyscrapers bloom in America" and extolling "Lots of new housing with more space." Women celebrate the freedom they attain in New York. Men respond with direct accounts of discrimination: "One look at us and they charge twice"; "Lots of doors slamming in our face"; "Free to wait tables and shine shoes." "Life is all right in America," the women insist, a claim the men promptly qualify: "If you're all white in America." Movement embellishes these differing interpretations. Women tease the men, swinging their skirts to show their legs. They dance together, in camaraderie, indicating their strength. Men, on the other hand, demonstrate the bigotry they encounter with mock slaps, slamming doors, kicks in the butt, and gunshots. As in the dance at the gym, Spanish elements enter in the dance, with the men kicking their heels with arms up and shouts of "Olé" at the finale.

The changes in the film version of "America" reflected a more racialized vision of the problems Puerto Ricans faced, even more noticeable given the almost complete absence of African Americans in this picture of New York.[54] The musical had prompted some charges of racism for its perpetuation of stereotypes of spitfire women and dangerous, knife-wielding men. The creators of the film may have absorbed some of that criticism and taken into account the intensifying civil rights movement between 1957, when the musical debuted, and 1961, when the film came out.[55] The problems of discrimination became far more overt in the new lyrics of "America," which changed from primarily a critique of Puerto Rico to primarily a critique of the United States.

The medium of film abetted this more racialized rendering of discrimination and the characters of the Sharks as well. One of the most marked changes in the narrative between the musical and the film in this regard was in the ending. In the musical and the film Jets and Sharks surround Tony's dead body and carry it offstage. In the film, however, the scene then widens to show Chino being led away by the police for the murder of Tony: criminalization of the story's actions only impacts a Puerto Rican.[56] The visual elements of film heightened the defining of the ethnicity of Puerto Ricans in racial terms as well. Darkening actors' skins (most notably that of George Chakiris, who played Bernardo) fit into the visual renderings and research of contemporary city streets. Rita Moreno complained that all of the Puerto Ricans were one "homogenous" brown.[57] (Even though one of the Shark women, Joanne Miya (later Nobuko Miyamoto), was Japanese-American.[58]) Cosmetic changes occurred in stage versions as well, but the close-ups in the film made the darker hair and skin more obvious. And the consistency of the darkness heightened the contrast between white and dark skin.

This difference posited outsider status, even though Puerto Ricans had been American citizens since 1917. This was hardly a well-known fact, however. The internal film industry assessment imposed by the Production Code, for instance, held a category in its notations on the "portrayal of 'races' and Nationals" and declared the Puerto Rican characters in the film as either not citizens or of "unclear" status. Perhaps most tellingly, the assessment's analysis designated the film's "significant story element" as "racial," bypassing the category "political."[59] Both the musical and the film prompted confrontation with the fact that "Puerto Rico is *in* America," as the song acknowledged, but not widely recognized as such. The film relayed the dilemma this gave rise to even more forcefully through its more racialized portrait of Puerto Ricans.

This on-screen portrait was more racial but also had some depth that the stage version lacked. The inclusion of men in its version of "America," for instance, provided a more nuanced picture of Bernardo, in particular, who was more one-dimensional—all threat—in the stage version. Bernardo in the film is loving and playful in "America"—a humorous, caring boyfriend as well as a knife-wielding gang leader. The characters of the Jets, on the other hand, are built more squarely upon membership in a gang, with little that distinguishes one from another. "The Jet Song" and "Gee, Officer Krupke" display their bonds and dilemmas, affording little influence to the women they scoff at, from the girlfriends to Anybodys. The roots of Bernardo's and Anita's anger are shown more thoroughly and more seriously, not in the jest of "Gee, Officer Krupke," which skewers the systems of social work, psychology, and juvenile courts. The discrimination the Sharks face is overt and, as rendered in their encounters with Sargeant Schrank, spiteful. The Sharks compel sympathy because they rise above discrimination to love and, particularly in the character of Anita, to show a full range of emotions from love, playfulness, and loyalty to anger and betrayal.[60] One reviewer noted this imbalance in portrayals of the gangs and predicted that only the actors playing Sharks (Rita Moreno and George Chakiris) would receive Academy Award nominations—which they did; both won.[61]

As in the musical, music and movement diminished the sense of threat the Puerto Ricans aroused, but the city spaces they occupied in the film relayed their broader marginalization even as it enhanced their racialization. The stage version of "America" takes place inside; the film version is on the rooftop, "one of the few places where a kid can be alone," as a Youth Board worker told the screenwriter Ernest Lehman. Streets, alleys, rooftops, "empty space between bldgs, where a tenement has been razed"—these are the leftover spaces of the city for pushed-aside people.[62] Robbins further intensified identification with the Sharks by the way he choreographed the camera, taking viewers into their danced hopes, struggles, and vitality. Combining "camera and choreography," he made movement—the space necessary for it and the ethnic and racial identities portrayed by it—central to the life of the city.[63]

Seeing the city and its inhabitants anew, though, depended on a disorienting but alluring frame for all that followed. "What I wanted to do was to show a New York that people hadn't seen, a different look of the city, almost an abstract one," Wise recounted.[64] Everyone involved in the production recognized that the prologue was the key to the film overall. The debates on realism and abstraction, color and light, choreography and camera angle, resolved in straight-down shots of the canyons in a view of the city that few had ever seen before. The deliberate, slow-motion sauntering over well-known locations—the United Nations, the blocks and blocks of tenement houses, the circulating spokes of Stuyvesant Town, the new highway interchanges. Many swooned at the sight. These are "the most remarkable shots ever taken of New York City from the air," one film critic wrote. "As supernaturally clear as a surrealist painting, the city practically knocks your eye out."[65] The film laid out the seamless relationship between real and abstract even before the aerial shots. A seemingly random collection of vertical lines appears on the screen saturated with changing colors—yellow, red, purple, blue, orange, green—as the now familiar music plays. Then the lines dissolved into a harbor-view of the skyline of lower Manhattan. The abstraction of lines had been made from a frame of the aerial scene: from real to abstract back to real.[66]

The prologue had to set the stylistic and thematic frame while also introducing the setting, the rivalry, and what was at stake in forbidden love—and it did so with almost no words for ten minutes. This was longer than the five minutes onstage because Robbins recognized that it took more time in film to "accept our particular frame of reference . . . to seduce an audience, to adjust them to the atmosphere, to train their eyes on what we want them to see, and to gain the proper emotional reaction."[67] After months of debate, the film opened with the entire prologue shot on location in New York. Panning the city, the filmmakers decided upon two shooting locations: a schoolyard on 110th Street between 2nd and 3rd Avenues, in the heart of Spanish Harlem, and the demolition site for the Lincoln Square Urban Renewal Project, specifically the area of 68th Street and Amsterdam Avenue, just northwest of what would soon rise as the Lincoln Center for the Performing Arts.[68]

Each site had its challenges. On 110th Street, the crew had to contend with curious neighbors leaning out windows from buildings across the street and filling up the sidewalks to watch the filming. Even though police lined the film set, the production company hired six Puerto Rican gang leaders to help keep the set calm. ("We had a gang of real JDs to guard a couple of reel JDs," as dancer Bert Michaels put it.[69]) They proved useful. They warned the crew to stop blaring the "Jet Song," which contained the line "every Puerto Rican is a dirty chicken" and were more successful getting an older woman on the block to hang blue laundry on her lines. ("Stick it up your asses," she first responded to Robbins.[70])

The west-side location posed challenges other than curious neighbors. The production company had to convince the demolition company to delay its work so that some buildings would remain lining the street. Broken windows had to be replaced and some of the stoops cleaned up so that they looked inhabited. "It was deserted, no sign of inhabitants, except for the studio crew and equipment. There were barricades at both ends of the street, and this thundering sound of a wrecking ball, several blocks away, knocking down building after building," dancer Robert Banas remembered.[71] The mostly empty thirteen-block area, though, offered unusual opportunities to film.

FIGURE 5.14 Filming on 68th Street, with a crowd lining the street and standing on the rubble, ca. 1960. Robbins is at the bullhorn by the camera. Photofest.

Carving a pit in the ground, Robbins and the cameramen laid down to shoot upward more easily. The area conveyed the lingering devastation and bombed-out feel of demolition and massive upheaval that urban renewal had wrought in the city. The filmmakers joined these two sites in their view of New York. The Jets jumped up on the east side and landed on the west—real and unreal—and merged the aspirations of new construction with the implacability of entrenched segregation and poverty.

From the surprising initial aerial shots that opened the prologue the camera honed in on people, and small gestures built to bigger movement. As the Jets make their way out of the basketball court, the camera holds on the upper half of their bodies as they turn together, synchronized, to face backward and then forward again. As the camera pulls out to show their full bodies, Riff reaches one arm up. Two dancers move into the sailing step, one leg and both arms opening

FIGURE 5.15 Rubble strewn lot, ca. 1960, looking south at the Amsterdam Houses, a public housing project finished in 1948. Jerome Robbins Dance Division, New York Public Library for the Performing Arts, Astor, Lennox and Tilden Foundations.

forward and then to the side, surveying and broadening their range. A few make assertions into the street with a swift glissade. Walking in the pack, someone breaks into a stylized motion, then nonchalantly returns to the pack, formal gesture absorbed into informal. They run crouched over the word "Jets" spray-painted on the street. And, then, the iconic move: the reach of one arm upward with a leg splayed sideways, the body pulled in different directions, in arc at the hip and ultimately off-balance. The technical aspect of this movement is telling: to keep oneself from falling into the bend of the body requires stretching upward.

The Sharks intrude first in the form of Bernardo—in a startlingly red shirt. The Jets taunt him and he moves across them and then slams his fist against a painted-red brick wall with a glare back to the Jets. (Rumors spread that that one slam of the fist inspired numerous film offers for Chakiris.[72]) Bernardo is joined by one Shark and then another, and they begin their buildup in collective movement first

FIGURE 5.16 Vacant tenements on the north side of 68th Street, awaiting demolition, ca. 1960. Jerome Robbins Dance Division, New York Public Library for the Performing Arts, Astor, Lennox and Tilden Foundations.

with fingers snapping and a crouched run that eats up space across the word "Jets" in the street and on to a broad space in front of a flat backdrop of row houses: bounded space, as Robbins needed, allowing movement but also suggesting a kind of entrapment. After the iconic stretched arm and leg movement, transferred from Jets to Sharks (from the settled to the newcomer), the phrase breaks open at the end with the first vision of the sky—"the place of escape and room," according to Robbins—piercing blue.[73]

The encounters between the Jets and Sharks escalate, with Jets overtaking sidewalks (pushing women to the side, unnoticed as background, as Leven suggested). Leftovers from Bass's interpretation appear: the Jets stand behind a truck with a loud "Keep Off" sign, seemingly directed at the Sharks; a yellow warehouse in the background proclaims "se habla español." A confrontation on the basketball court leads to the first dance-action as fight and escalates the skirmishes, which are now enhanced by "whips," quick blurred shots

FIGURE 5.17 Looking northwest from the southeast corner of 66th Street and Amsterdam Avenue, 17 September 1960, Collection of the Museum of the City of New York.

that connect incidents, such as chases through alleys, Jets climbing
up a mound of demolition rubble only to have junk hailed upon them
by Sharks on the other side of the heap. The final sequence starts with
bright paint—Baby John finishing writing "Sharks Stink" on a wall
in yellow-orange and white as Bernardo appears atop the wall. The
chase of Baby John by the Sharks passes another drawing of a Shark
on the wall and then through a bare lot with a wall of colored doors—
another Bass addition that appears again in the credits at the end
of the film and reinforces the theme of barriers—to the basketball
court, where the dance devolves into a brawl. Police intrude and the
authority of movement transfers to words.

   The prologue encapsulated the visual style of the film as well as a
resonant view of New York. The fragility of places in the city that Robbins quipped about in finding locations for the film spoke to the defining disappearing-and-appearing quality of the built environment

FIGURE 5.18   Looking east to the Hudson River from the southwest corner of 70th Street and Amsterdam Avenue, 17 September 1960, Collection of the Museum of the City of New York.

of the midcentury city and the marginalization of people in those visions. The tension between abstraction and reality also mirrored ongoing debates in urban planning. Panoramic shots visualized the perspective of the master builder Robert Moses, who saw the city in a kind of abstraction, a network of highways, bridges, and tunnels. The panoramic map Moses built for the 1964 World's Fair, in which he could move around buildings like toy blocks, modeled his view of the city. Moses's methods—razing, implantation, prioritizing infrastructure over people—prompted criticism and backlash, but his birds-eye view of New York City conveyed the city as a mechanical operation with moving parts, as in the opening shots of the film. ("What a city for seagulls, if not for people!" as one writer put it.[74]) The aerial vision that introduced the action of the story caught the new scale of a metropolitan region, which drew planners to concentrate less on a central urban core than on a growing and linked zone defined by the circulation of cars.[75]

The zoom in to the street can be seen as the arrival of Jane Jacobs and others into the debate over the forceful changes in the urban landscape. Jacobs celebrated the chaotic collection of quirky people whose diverse uses of the urban environment created a "sidewalk ballet," in her landmark book *The Death and Life of Great American Cities*, which debuted the same year as the film. *West Side Story* is both a statement in support of Jacobs's views and a comment on them. Much of the musical and movie echo Jacobs's claims about the centrality of the street to urban life. Gangs, the era's prominent example of the threat to safety, propelled much of Jacobs's argument against the imposition of superblock structures and housing projects. And yet the film's prologue in particular asserts the importance of minute-by-minute living in the city—aware, reactive, assertive—that encompasses the aspiration of gangs and feel of urban life on the ground. The film not only brings alive these differing views of cities but humanizes them. It adds sound and movement to aerial visions and fear and discrimination to the geniality of the streets; the mobility of the camera allowed for illumination of what was rarely noticed, and dancing heightened the vitality at stake.

In the shift from stage to screen, *West Side Story* became a visual representation and narration of New York that reverberated because of these debates. The creators researched, argued, and experimented, utilizing filmic techniques in special effects but also paying obsessive attention to the visual elements of style—color, light, camera angle, and perspective—to reveal the changing metropolis in its specificity, its aspirations and sacrifices. Movement carried much of this meaning and the dances seemed "as indigenous to the pavements as the seeping hopes and hates," as one reviewer reflected.[76] Those movements had a place that gave them their meaning—the streets of the city. What dance does in *West Side Story* is attach people to their place, hopes and hates to pavement. It is not only that the city provided inspiration for the movement but that the production itself—with dance at its core—created a humanized portrayal of a city, as fluid, vital, and, ultimately, fragile. If the camera did not exactly dance, as Robbins wanted, the visual images were startlingly new. They showed a city teeming with passion, drama, vitality, and tragedy. Through "commingling the real and seemingly real," the film created a believable if fictional world, where gangs danced and lovers sang.[77] The power of this visual representation is that it set the city moving. Not just in seeing anew its architecture and infrastructure, from atop, but in conveying the intractability of urban problems as matched by the dynamism and fullness of people and place.

* 6 *

"New York Rhapsody"

1962–70

On October 18, 1961, just four years after the musical's debut, *West Side Story* the film opened at the Rivoli Theater at Broadway and 49th Street in New York. The Mirisch brothers chose to release the film in road-show style, a convention much like theatrical debuts, where the production opened in one city at a time. As television became more common and convenient, road-show openings sought to entice viewers back to a theater, with stereophonic sound and large-screen formats. (*West Side Story* was one of the first films shot in Super Panavision 70.) There were advanced sales of reserved seats, an intermission, and escalating expectations. Five months prior to the opening of the film, sales had already reached $56,000.[1] Anticipation was high, to say the least. "What can you call it? A dance drama, a tragedy with music, a jazzed-up *Romeo and Juliet*, a shocker of racial conflicts, a gang war thriller, a phenomenon of the theater, a sociological study of juvenile delinquents, a slice of Americana? It is all these things—perhaps even, to our shame, that last."[2]

Most reviewers knocked themselves out to find ways to praise the film, some calling it more successful than the play, others seeing in it a revival of movie musicals. Many picked up on the technical and artistic achievements in walking the fine line between reality and dramatic reinvention. "The frame of photographic realism is quickly and strongly overlaid with a splash of emotional expression that is above and beyond reality. It is the explosive projection of a vigorous creative conceit, conveying an artist's idea of what stirs in the beings of these kids," the *New York Times* reviewer wrote, which must have gone some way toward assuaging Robbins's anxieties about the film.[3] The influential critic Pauline Kael's scathing review, however, may have unsettled him again. Calling it "highly overrated," she blasted the technical wizardry, clunky clichéd language, pretentious moralism, pounding music, and, even, the "huge and sudden" movement, "so portentously 'alive' they're always near the explosion point."[4]

Few endorsed Kael's opinion, however. The film received eleven Academy Award nominations, tying it with its primary competitor, *Judgment at Nuremberg*, a fictionalized treatment of the accounting for Nazi war crimes. *West Side Story* won the competition with ten awards—Supporting Actor (George Chakiris), Supporting Actress (Rita Moreno), Musical Score, Sound Recording, Art Direction/Color, Cinematography/Color, Costume Design, Editing, Director, and Motion Picture—losing to *Judgment at Nuremberg* only in screenwriting. In addition to sharing the Oscar for Best Director with Wise, Robbins received an honorary award for his choreographic achievements on film.

As the film was picking up Oscars, it was traveling around the world. Three months after its opening in Tokyo in early 1962, the theater was still beyond 100 percent capacity at the film's showings, with four hundred people standing or sitting on steps. The same phenomenon was occurring in other places around the world. In Stockholm, where the distributor United Artists for the first time instituted mail order to buy tickets, the theater had to stop taking orders because the "staff was inundated and unable to handle the volume." All of this added up to unforeseen profits. "The figures are such that I have difficulty believing them," the usually unflappable Arnold Picker, executive vice-president of United Artists, announced. A year after its debut, the film was playing in twenty-one countries and had grossed 21 million dollars (approximately 163 million dollars today). It went on to play for five years continuously in Japan and France, winning the award for best foreign film in those countries as well as in Finland

and Mexico. At the movie theater in Paris, the manager claimed that one man had seen the film sixty-two times—and that was two years before it finally stopped running there.[5] At another cinema in Amstead, Netherlands, a man who had seen the movie sixty-nine times led a protest to keep it running nearby rather than transfer to a downtown theater.[6]

Beyond profits, the production's impact was still unfolding. The film and its achievements solidified the story as a "slice of Americana," not just New York. But just what that slice said about America caused increasing unease. Herb Caen, a trenchant cultural critic, synthesized the conundrum of its Americanism. Clair Engle, a US senator from California, praised the film after its compilation of Oscars, saying, "I am sure you share my pride that the top award went to a picture that was American in type, character and spirit. The locale was America, the music was America, and the young people who gave it charm, style and distinction were Americans." Caen demurred: "Let's see now. Racial hatred, poverty, sadistic and/or moronic cops, teenage rumbles, three murders."[7]

These were the contradictions as the film and musical spread across the world. It was American artistry at its best—vital, energetic, resonant. It exposed the hypocrisy of American ideals and tragic consequences of discrimination. It embodied a kind of self-criticism that was rare among nations and an essential feature of a healthy democracy. It was a "glorification of a bunch of psychotic jerks."[8] It could pave the way for American good in the world, going ahead of the Peace Corps—newly deployed in the fall of 1961—to "see what would happen."[9] It served anti-American propaganda at a moment of sharp global tension. These opposing perceptions weaved through the crisscrossing of the musical and film across the world in the early 1960s. The musical and film became increasingly intertwined, one an echo of the other. The amount of attention and concern both aroused was a sign of the story's power and worth, a way to understand the United States, differing political ideologies, and attachment to one another and to place.

The London production of the musical ran into 1961, prompting concerns from the agent there about the competition the film would

FIGURE 6.1 The continuous screening of the film in France, in its fourth year. Robert Wise on left, 1966. Robert Wise Collection, Cinematic Arts Library, University of Southern California.

soon create.[10] More troubling was the inevitable decline in quality and rise in squabbles among the cast in a theatrical production on a long run. Ken LeRoy, who played Bernardo on Broadway, then London, but was passed over for a role in the film, held on to his bitterness long after that. He quit abruptly after more than three years in the production, blaming Robbins for his on-again, off-again authoritarian control when Robbins panned the London version two years after it opened.[11] Robbins felt that the "whole performance was a curiosity as I felt I was seeing a revival ten years in the future," appalled by how weak and shoddy it had become.[12] In particular, the substitution of British actors for Americans was causing problems. Robbins insisted that the role of Riff needed to be played by an American. But this would violate the terms of the agreement with British Equity that had allowed the all-American cast at the beginning of the run only if British actors replaced them as they left. Robbins suggested a compromise: let British actors play the Puerto Rican parts. An "English actor-dancer-singer throws the show out of joint in the American roles," he argued, which then jeopardized it overall.[13] However diminished Puerto Rican authenticity already was in the play, more could be sacrificed to ensure the necessary "Americanness" of the Jets' roles.

The first international tour of the musical perpetuated this attention to its American quality. For the creators, putting the show on worldwide display required keeping it in English, played by an American cast, and bringing along at least some musicians who would be able to play the complex score (filling in the rest of the orchestra locally). Back-and-forth appeals to the State Department for financial support got nowhere, even as American embassies were flooded with requests from local impresarios and companies. The creators had to find producers willing to take on all the complexities—and all the costs—and figure out a way to at least come out even and perhaps make a profit.

London was a good model but also an exception, given its longstanding theatrical tradition, previous productions of Broadway shows, and English language. In contemplating the leap across the

Channel, one possibility was to have the London company tour the European continent. The list of possible cities was long: Paris, Brussels, Amsterdam, Berlin, Copenhagen, Stockholm, Helsinki, Prague, Vienna, Munich, Geneva, Rome, Milan, Naples, Florence, Madrid, Hamburg, Salzburg, Belgrade.[14] As the London company became ragged, though, this option held less appeal. (Eventually the London company toured only Scandinavia in 1962.)

Hal Prince was fed up with the creators and their relentless demands and had already given up the idea of producing the musical elsewhere abroad. The creators soon found a savior in the enterprising Israeli impresario Giora Godik, who was willing to take on the difficult role of figuring out how to tour the complicated production. In the 1950s, Godik began bringing foreign entertainers to Israel, most famously Marlene Dietrich. But it was in the importation of musicals that Godik would achieve his greatest fame. Godik was soon crowned the "King of Musicals" in Israel, *West Side Story* his first big achievement.

In 1959, Godik traveled to New York at the invitation of theater managers hoping to entice him to carry a production to Israel. On the first night, he saw *My Fair Lady*; on the second, *West Side Story*. After that second night, he cleared his schedule of all other shows and proceeded to see *West Side Story* every night of his stay. He wanted to bring the show to Israel because it was a musical—that rare genre so tied to America—but also because of the prejudice and conflict it dealt with, which he thought were comparable to those in Israel. ("Sixty-nine countries are represented in Israel and the problem is close," Alfred Ottenheimer recalled Godik telling him.[15]) Godik worked with producer Pete Kameron to convince the creators to place their precious show in his hands. First Israel, then Paris and Turin, perhaps more. In January 1961, just a few weeks after the closing of the Broadway production, a cast of players from the national and Broadway productions flew to Tel Aviv.

Among them was Ottenheimer, long-running player of Doc on Broadway and the domestic tour, and one-month felon for refusing to answer questions regarding his affiliations with the Communist

FIGURE 6.2 View of Tel Aviv (Bay) from Jaffa, 1960s, with a skyscraper under construction, a harbinger of changes to come. Photograph by Leni Sonnenfeld, Sonnenfeld Collection, Oster Visual Documentation Center at Beit Hatfutsot—The Museum of the Jewish
People.

Party. Ottenheimer's first travel outside of the United States was to
Israel. As a Jew with German heritage, the trip seemed auspicious in
a variety of ways: an endorsement of professional talent, an overcoming of political suspicion (he received his passport without question),
and a personal journey to find a way of belonging in the riven world.

The cast members settled into Tel Aviv for a month of rehearsals
and performances. Given their long stay, they lived with Israelis to
defray the cost of lodging. (Unlike today's tours, where the producing companies arrange and pay for lodging and meals, actors had to
find and pay for these daily expenses.) Ottenheimer ended up with a
German refugee who was married to an American from the Bronx.
Unpretentious and basic, their "middle-class flat . . . might very well
be in the Bronx."[16] What struck Ottenheimer about Tel Aviv was its

dust, partly due to ongoing apartment construction "everywhere" and partly because "suddenly, in the midst of paved streets and side-walks, one will unaccountably come upon unpaved streets and some places that aren't even streets, but dusty (when it's dry) lanes that meander like a country road."[17] In the intense traffic and ongoing construction, Ottenheimer saw Tel Aviv "trying too hard to be a big city," like Paris or New York.[18]

West Side Story entered into Tel Aviv's transition to an urban metropolis, playing for four weeks in front of thirty-two thousand people. While the story spoke to the tensions of urbanization, the spatial representation of those problems played out differently. The show's Hebrew title, *Sipur Haparvavim*, translated as "The Story of the Suburbs." Ottenheimer suggested that there was "some misunderstanding here as to exactly what the West Side of New York is," but the title placed the story where it resonated in Tel Aviv.[19] Newer, teeming suburbs surrounded the older downtown core of the city, and conflicts erupted there.

Reviews of the performances in Tel Aviv confirmed the aptness of this allusion to local geography. The show was a "suburbial tragedy" set in the suburbs of New York, which are the "poor quarters of the big city."[20] Israeli papers also often noted the change in the story's origins, from a religious conflict between Jews and Catholics to a racial one. One mentioned the Jewish backgrounds of most of the show's creators, calling both Robbins and Bernstein Zionists.[21] All of these connections made the story familiar: "Although New York and Tel Aviv are thousands of miles away from each, the subject is known and actual to us."[22]

Israeli critics, however, did not make explicit connections between the ethnic conflicts in the play and local conflicts with the Palestinians or the newer stream of immigrants from Morocco or the sixty-nine countries Godik referenced. The conflict they saw was not around them in Israel but the one that had so affected Jews in Europe—the haunted homeland that defined the making of the nation. In that framework, the Sharks (and, by association, the newer immigrants) were less threatening than the Jets. "The Jets frighten

FIGURE 6.3 Cutout images of dancers in front of an abstracted, vertical cityscape. Program cover, Habimah Theater, Tel Aviv, 1960. Albert M. Ottenheimer Collection, 132, b.44 f.3, Special Collections & University Archives, University of Oregon Libraries, Eugene, Oregon.

me more than the Puerto Ricans because they were for a few moments a reflection of the youth that went blind after villainous leaders in a different country brought disaster on us and the entire world," one reviewer confessed.[23] Threat depended on context and history, and the Jets reminded some Israelis of Nazi youth.

Ultimately, however, the play evoked Broadway—the idea more than the actual street. Hollywood had long parlayed the dreams of the United States on-screen. Now big-city entertainment and art had come from New York to Tel Aviv via a play. Dancing, singing, acting—a live and lived story—created a spectacle of aspiration and hope amid tragedy on the dusty streets of Tel Aviv.

From there, the cast moved on to a kibbutz in Ein Gev on the shores of Galilee, to Haifa, and to Jerusalem. Performing conditions were often difficult, with crowded backstage spaces that forced part of the scenery out the stage door in Ein Gev, for instance. But the reception throughout Israel was "without precedent," with the audience "demanding far more curtain-calls than we ever took anywhere in the US, while the people stood and crowded down the aisles toward the stage." Jerusalem hosted the largest single one-day audience in the production's history; "over 3000 at each of two showings, played back-to-back on the same day, 6:30 and 9 pm."[24] The crowds in Ein Gev prompted United Nations personnel to notify nearby Syrians of the show so that they would not become alarmed at all the cars near the border. The success of the show in Haifa even entered local political discussions regarding a proposed 17 percent increase in the tax rate. As opponents argued that the tax was too burdensome, the mayor noted that the number of people paying high-ticket prices for *West Side Story*—some fourteen thousand in a week—represented a third of Haifa's taxpayers, "so a few piasters more in taxes won't hurt them."[25]

From the cheering audiences to the similarities between Tel Aviv and New York, Ottenheimer noted the bond that *West Side Story* forged—seeing ethnic conflict in ways that Israeli critics were not admitting. A moment in the kibbutz stood out. At the slightest provocation, singing broke out, an accordion appeared, and everyone began dancing the hora. "I noted, dancing side-by-side, one of our Puerto Rican boys and a dark skinned Moroccan Jew—each representing a 'color' problem in their respective countries."[26]

After performing in front of approximately fifty-six thousand in Israel, the cast traveled by land and boat to Paris in March 1961. Here *West Side Story* encountered the suspicions that musicals—indeed, American culture in general—did not reach the level of art. The opening night shattered those suspicions. "The ovation that WSS received tonight is the kind of thing you read about in fiction, or that only happens to the heroines of movies of back-stage life," wrote Ottenheimer. "This audience, dressed to the nines in evening clothes, made up of (I'm told) of everybody who is anybody in the theater and the press in France, reared up and roared out of a hurricane of applause at the finish of tonight's premiere."[27] In the audience, playwright Arthur Laurents described the scene similarly, writing to the "WSS Brass" that it was perhaps the "most exciting performance of the show ever." The curtain calls went on and on. Reeling, Laurents exclaimed, "I almost believe [Ingrid] Bergman who thinks it is the best show she has ever seen in her life."[28] The show provoked so many curtain calls that three men taking turns were needed to crank the curtain up and down, a task that had previously never required more than two.

Reviews confirmed the audience's cheers. With astonishment, surprise, even shock—one was "punched in the chest"—critic after critic hailed the show.[29] The cast garnered much of the attention; critics applauded their talent in acting, singing, and dancing and recognized that Europeans could not meet those standards. "Everybody can do everything, dancing, singing, laughing, talking, jumping, climbing fences, and fighting," the critic of *Le Figaro* exclaimed.[30]

The work was a masterpiece of "total theater, the one advocated but not carried out by Wagner," more than one critic declared.[31] This was an accolade that put the American genre within the embrace of European heritage and aims. Other critics figured out ways to keep the masterpiece at a distance: "It is not the first time that the Americans demonstrate that it is possible to go from the barbaric to the decadent state without going through the civilized one."[32] Or: "Its biggest quality is a 'levelling at the top.' Its universal success proves that it is not necessary to make any concessions to vulgarity or to intellectualism to win all the audiences."[33] Nearly every review rehearsed the question of to which category the spectacle belonged—musical comedy? operetta? opera? commedia dell'arte? Some assigned it to new categories—"choreographic drama" or "musical tragedy" or, resigned, a "mysterious genre." Most ended by discarding the exercise altogether in the face of something both new and of high quality. Some even conceded that recognizing the achievement of *West Side Story* did not require "throwing away forty years of work" Americans had created in musical theater.[34] This way of middling the achievement both undermined it and matched it to the ambivalence anything American generally caused. Even so, the adulation made publicity easy. An advertisement in the metro called it "Le Plus Grand Spectacle du Monde." "Modest," Ottenheimer averred.[35]

As in Israel, local conditions in Paris created a situation that was ripe for comparison with the themes of the story. Parisian gangs, called *blousons noires*, were an indelible part of the urban landscape. The term literally translated as "black shirts" but was more generally understood as "greasers," a mimicking of the style of James Dean and Marlon Brandon in *Rebel without a Cause* and *The Wild One*. These were young men flirting with danger and crime, wearing T-shirts, leather jackets, and rolled-up jeans, hair slicked back. These groups pervaded the outer ring of the city, amid immigrants and working-class residents, "les habitants des villes enfumées." As in Tel Aviv, the west side of Manhattan aligned most clearly with the poorer neighborhoods that began circling growing cities, particularly those with a historic inner core. As with the Teddy boys in London, the *blousons noires* utilized fashion to signal their rebelliousness. It was often a generalized, media-fed defiance that sometimes connected to violence and sometimes did not. Ottenheimer saw a scuffle break out in the middle of the Place de la Republique over scooters and recognized the combatants as *blousons noires* ("though not so clad"). What struck him most, though, was the similarity of the fight to that in *West Side Story*. "I noted that when the boys squared off at first, the one who was on the offensive invited the other to come closer with the same gesture that Bernardo uses in the rumble: crooked elbows, palms turned up, and a come-on gesture with the cupped fingers."[36] And when the prefect of police in Paris went to and enjoyed the show but complained that the "police always arrive very late," he was met with a quick reply by a Parisian: "And that shocks you?"[37]

Comparisons to the show went beyond street scuffles and police ineffectiveness. As in New York, when fights burst out on city streets in response to local pressures, they often reflected national and global conflicts. Algerian independence movements had, since 1954, been waging a war against French colonialism, and the rage spilled out on to the streets of Paris at the time *West Side Story* appeared there. Ottenheimer recorded the increasing threats of violence during April 1961. Security at the theater tightened, with police stationed around the front of it. The revolt collapsed but the anxiety remained. Ottenheimer also noted the racialization of the discomfort by comparing the treatment he received in his hotel versus that of "two Negroes . . . one of them in magnificent African dress—colorful toga and all that." "The manager tipped me a wink which made it clear that though to him I'm a foreigner, I'm not as foreign as all that."[38] This growing tension pervaded the theater as well. At the gunshot in the final scene, Ottenheimer heard the first scream in the audience since the company had performed in the United States.[39]

After four weeks in Paris, the company performed in Turin and Florence to smaller audiences and less enthusiastic reviews. The authenticity of Shakespeare's Verona seemed to be more at stake in Italy than in England, with one critic claiming that "there are no possible points of comparison" between *Romeo and Juliet* and *West Side Story*. Italian critics could discern "charm" but not in the "warm way" that French critics had.[40] Such traveling, though, confirmed the spread of *West Side Story*—and not only among theater critics. On a train in Italy, Ottenheimer spoke to Americans who had seen the show in Detroit and Chicago—and then met Israelis who had seen the show in Tel Aviv.[41]

After an additional three weeks in Paris, the cast headed to Germany, where it received the most mixed response of the tour. German critics declared the show kitsch, the music and story a clichéd confection. Only the dancing stood out as distinctive. The American genre of musicals barely tempted a German critic's heart. Perhaps the most disparaging review compared it to "how the unity of workers is demonstrated in some bad, built-up geared productions in the East."[42] Despite the critical drubbing, audiences applauded. In Munich, the show received a record number of curtain calls—seventeen—and audiences in Hamburg, the last German city visited, came out in enthusiastic hordes.

For Ottenheimer, touring the German cities reverberated personally. As in other places, he saw changes in the landscape that reminded him of home. Looking out the window on the train beyond the red roofs, there were "long stretches when we might have been speeding along the New York Thruway or on the New Jersey Turnpike."[43] Even more, though, the trip made him feel the ghosts of Jews. "Not till the first drugstore scene got underway, however, did I think of the Jewish overtones in action and speech of Doc as I play him."[44] A visit to his ancestral town of Göppingen was particularly haunting. All of his relatives there were gone, either from age or the gas chambers. He looked at the men his age on the street, thinking that they must have been a part of the Nazi Party and a part of the war. "They look to me," he thought, "like so many of their US counterparts, the American Legion boys. It's not a comforting idea."[45]

From Stuttgart, the cast traveled to Amsterdam and Rotterdam. American musical theater had rarely been seen in the Netherlands, although *My Fair Lady* had completed a successful tour in Dutch. A critic, though, worried that the country was not ready for *West Side Story*, seeing the "streets under construction" near the theater in Amsterdam as symbolic of the unpreparedness for the show. Roaring ovations proved otherwise. As in Paris, the portrayal of gangs, in particular, hit a nerve. Like the *blousons noires* there, the Teddy boys in London, and *die Halbstarken* (literally, "half strong") in Munich, Amsterdam's *nozems*—young men imitating the American style of James Dean and Marlon Brando, with greased quaffs of hair

FIGURE 6.4 Street advertisements for the film lining a construction site in Amsterdam, February 1962. AHF/Ben van Meerendonk Collections, International Institute of Social History (Amsterdam).

and leather jackets, listening to American rock 'n' roll and speeding around the city on mopeds—gave audiences a version of the Jets and Sharks on the streets outside the theater. The *nozem* in Amsterdam, in fact, separated into two primary gangs, the Dijkers and Pleiners, which paralleled the show even more clearly. A critic praised the show for its serious look at the "nozem problem," echoing references to the "Puerto Rican problem" in the New York press. "There is neither preaching to the parents nor to the youth. That said, there is a frequent mocking of Americanism, social labor, and law cases with psychological reports . . . and of love. It seems that the U.S. is capable of facing nozem-hood in a healthy way."[46]

The rebuilding of Amsterdam and Rotterdam after World War II was also akin to the remaking of New York by urban renewal. In the Netherlands, though, the change was more abrupt, from old-style

European city to new-style American one, particularly in Rotterdam. There the cars filling the streets were mostly American models such as Chevys and Fords, and the heart of the city was now a shopping center. Building continued apace, with cranes "marching over the landscape in all directions." Ottenheimer called it "the most modern new city in the world . . . with the possible exception of Brasilia."[47]

Despite the continued resonance and the adulation the company received, the show was beginning to fray. The producers no longer offered much money or organizational support. Cast members had to find their own places to live, and by this point many were traveling by car and scooter and camping. Choreographer Michael Bennett put up a tent on any space near the theater.[48] Tempers flared, people left, and the show thinned.

Berlin and Hamburg were the final stops. The cast performed to relatively small audiences in Berlin at the Titania Palast in early August 1961. While some complained that the publicity was inadequate, others began to realize that the city was preoccupied with other events—such as the high rate of defections across the border from east to west. Ottenheimer traveled to East Berlin and was held up at the Fredrichstrasse train station as police entered and took a passenger off the train. The company left Berlin for Hamburg on the morning of August 14, wondering if their train would be allowed to leave. In Hamburg, they received the news that a wall was being constructed between East and West Berlin.[49] Ottenheimer gave his 1,297th and last performance as Doc. The first international tour of *West Side Story* ended "with a whimper instead of a bang."[50]

Just weeks after the musical ended on a whimper, however, the film launched its international bang. As with the musical, there were challenges to showing the film abroad, language chief among them. While many films in English were dubbed for non-English-speaking places—and had singing scenes dropped because of dubbing difficulties—director Robert Wise decided early on that dubbing would not work. And eliminating the singing was clearly not an option with *West Side Story*. The lyrics were essential, as well as the sound, clarity, and quality of the voices. Surtitles had run above the stage in some of the musical performances and proved effective enough, so Wise pushed for subtitles for the film. He also mandated that the film run its full length, with no cuts, and be presented under its original title, rather than being reinterpreted in the language of the country in which it was playing. All of this led to a branding of the name, the story, the look, and the sound.[51] If the musical was inherently malleable because of the time-bound nature of performance, the film gained its power through repetition and reach. (The possibilities of repetition might have even led to an incantation for Borges and others who saw the film repeatedly.)

The film's consistency in celluloid, however, did not prevent local interpretation. When it ran in northern India, a synopsis came out in a literary magazine published in Gujarati. Not only did the title of the article—"A Plea for Hope"—suggest a particular reading of the story; the summary used a class and caste framework, presenting the film as a story of "Conflict, Revenge, Love and Hate":

> In the prosperous and beautiful city of New York is a neighborhood known as the West Side. In a New York bathed in light, this is a neighborhood filled with dark and filthy alleys as in a moonscape. As the saying goes, there is a garbage dump in every town and so, accordingly, the residents of this neighborhood were simple, backward, uncultured, uneducated and alienated from society, far removed from a life of good fortune. Their lives and personal relationships were rife with conflict, vengeance and violence. Arguments and fights broke out frequently. Battles with knives and soda bottles were commonplace and without the timely intervention of the police, there would have been bodies lying in pools of blood. A life of Culture, Civility and Progress was but a mirage.

Love stood out in the ongoing, perpetual battle between civilization and savagery in this interpretation, more extreme poles of difference that the world of caste evoked. When Tony and Maria meet, they recognize one another—and love: "It feels as if we were renewing a love from a previous life," Maria says, alluding to reincarnation. Creating cultural affinities also bumped up against the creeping consumerism of the film, though. Product placement structured the war council where, "as was the custom, everyone was given a Coke." In the end, the Gujarati summary synthesized the conflict of the film with local beliefs. A timeless cradle of life heightens Maria's rage at the end: "In your wild fighting, intoxicated by violence, you forgot your humanity. In pursuit of power, you have cheapened life. If I want, I could exact revenge. But I cannot indulge in this behavior. I have bathed in the sea of love and am enriched. Those of you who have ruined my life, your lives will never be at peace again."[52]

In a short time, the film outpaced the stage version and became the most common way people knew the production. But film and musical also became intertwined. A later German production of the musical replaced some of the script of the musical with that of the film, for example.[53] The two distinct spectacles fused together. As the Israeli producer Giora Godik described reaction to the musical: "The audience is convinced that they are in a cinema."[54] The film, though, had consistency, reach, access; it could travel at far less expense and led to a global recognition of the story. Similar to stage musicals, musical films had shown only lackluster appeal abroad. *West Side Story* changed that, proving popular not only in Europe but in South America and Asia. By January 1965, the gross income of the film abroad nearly matched that from US showings.[55] Industry analysts attributed its success to the wordless language and spectacle of dance and a story of "universal appeal (i.e. not something strictly American like *Music Man*)."[56] Hollywood learned the lesson well. *My Fair Lady* and *The Sound of Music*—rather than *Damn Yankees* and *The Music Man*—continued the musical film's successes after *West Side Story*.

Increasingly, too, the film served as an introduction to the musical. This was the case in Japan, where the story on stage and screen would be played almost continuously for over a decade. The film debuted in Tokyo in December 1961 and stayed in movie theaters there for five years. The play appeared in November 1964 as the first performance of an American musical with an American cast and performed in En-

glish. (A Japanese language production of *My Fair Lady* played just
before *West Side Story*.) The all-female theater troupe Takarazuka
first produced the musical in 1968; large all-Japanese casts took it
over in the 1970s and 1980s. Even at the end of the twentieth century,
West Side Story was still popular. The leading music magazine polled
readers and people in the music business to name the greatest musical works of the twentieth century. *West Side Story* ranked third,
after Igor Stravinsky's *Rite of Spring* and Gustav Mahler's Ninth Symphony.[57]

The musical's first performance in Japan came on the occasion of
the first anniversary of the Nissei Theater in Tokyo, a 1,334-seat performing arts theater housed in the building of the Nissei life insur-
ance company. Opened in October 1963 in the center of the city, the
new theater hosted opera, plays, musicals, and concerts, by both its
own production company and those from overseas. The prospect of an
American musical played by an American cast prompted a great deal
of preparation, as much to combat concern over an English-language
production in a little-known genre as in celebration of the anniversary. The press began covering the show weeks before it opened, sending reporters to rehearsals and printing large photographs of dancers
and interviews with the primary actors. The articles floated issues of
cultural dissimilarities in performance. The actor playing Tony wondered about the difference in applause patterns he had heard about—
that Americans applaud after every song and Japanese only after the
curtain first opens and during the finale. How might this "mess up
our flow," he asked.[58] This concern prompted a reply from a Japanese actress who had appeared in *Flower Drum Song* on Broadway.
"I ask everyone, from the bottom of my heart, to send them timely
applause," she pleaded to her fellow Japanese.[59]

The Nissei published a large brochure with essays that described
the plot in detail and explained musical theater and its distinctive
integration of song, dance, and drama. Two other articles situated
Broadway in New York City, drawing together the dynamism of the
city with the energy and spectacle of the genre. "Broadway musicals
satisfy the demands of New York with its hard tempo and upbeat

rhythm, its mixture of eroticism and sadism, and a hint of playful humor. This is a city that wants 67 seconds in a minute," the author noted.[60] Another ambled the west side of Manhattan describing how the production accurately displayed a condensed version of the place.[61]

As in Paris, Japanese critics saw *West Side Story* as an example of "total theater," the aim of Wagner and comparable to Japanese forms of theater such as Noh, Bugaku, and Kabuki in the entangling of life and art. This wholeness came from the high quality of dance, music, and drama but also from tackling difficult social problems. It was art grounded in reality, neither an escape from it nor a fantasy about it. "This musical was unafraid of exposing the unsolvable dirt and problems that exist behind America's prosperity," one reviewer wrote.[62] It is a matter of working toward an ideal rather than proclaiming the country has reached that ideal, another clarified.[63]

The press stories, the Nissei's promotional brochure, and the long-running success of the film prepared a strong foundation for the stage version. But issues of respect were still key. Japanese audiences questioned the authenticity and quality of the cast, a traveling troupe that had not performed on Broadway. The producer, Paul Szilard, negotiated these issues, aware that the questions about the cast, for instance, were part of the larger diplomacy of respect that the Japanese sought from Americans. Szilard pressured Robbins to write an ingratiating note for the Nissei Theater brochure, thanking the Japanese for the opportunity to perform. Even more, he succeeded in getting Robbins to come to Japan to oversee the final rehearsals, inviting the press to watch a three-hour rehearsal. Robbins's appearance confirmed the legitimacy of the production in Japanese eyes, both the American cast and the Japanese theater. The "Nissei Theatre is up to par in every way with the many theatres in New York. I'm very excited to see how Japanese fans will react to this piece," Robbins confirmed.[64]

The obsequiousness paid off. Yet again, reviewers raved. Earphones provided simultaneous translation for those who needed it, but for most the dance carried the story and the success. Many insisted on the difference from the film, one arguing that the story was "originally meant for a stage performance and especially the fighting scenes have a kind of power that cannot be felt from the film. It's kind of like seeing fresh fish jumping around at the market, and for us Japanese that love sashimi I'm sure that the rawness of the performance is something exquisite."[65] Others defended the cast, recognizing that they were the traveling troupe but "they were chosen directly by Robbins himself after all."[66]

Critics also honed in on particular parts of the story that reverberated. In Osaka, the police used the film to "as a weapon against juvenile delinquency." They posted a poem, entitled "West Side of Japan," alongside an advertisement for the film (as translated for *Variety*):

> Fairies in red tight-pants and blue
>   pirate-striped jackets!
> They swagger on the street of
>   morality with non-gravity!
> They streak on the short cut to the
>   sexual reaction!
> Now, let me tell you whose energies
>   are spent in wrong way,
> The right way to the right mind.
> Go straight into the new light with
>   big courage.[67]

Rita Moreno claimed that the Japanese understood the story even better than Americans. Since they are "unaware of racial or religious differences," according to Moreno, the Japanese see the "beauty without the squalor," the purity of love and hope between two young people.[68] But there was at least some recognition of constraints in Japanese society that resonated for others. A Japanese reviewer of the Nissei production thought the story was about "people who can't be individuals because their society won't allow it."[69]

Individualism served as one thread of the Americanism that the production displayed. In Japan, the love of Tony and Maria crossed the barriers put up by families rather than gangs, harking back to the musical's origins in *Romeo and Juliet*. In France, political tensions associated with the breaking up of the French empire played out on the streets of Paris in seeming parallel with the rumbles onstage. Reviewers in a variety of countries pointed to juvenile delinquency as a common theme of the era. "The young gangsters of *West Side Story*, with their blue jeans, elaborate hair styles, cowboy boots, and switchblades, are not peculiar to New York. They can be seen lounging outside a dance hall and a movie house in the solitary main street of the English country town, or drifting after nightfall along city streets in France, Italy, Belgium, and Germany," a writer in London claimed.[70]

Juvenile delinquency abroad increasingly took on an "American Look," as an expert in the subject wrote.[71] Mass media contributed to the circulation around the world of James Dean, Marlon Brando, and the Jets and the Sharks. But the popularity of these images rose alongside political actions and a new global conversation about juvenile delinquency as well. In the United States, John F. Kennedy's administration beefed up the attention to the issue started by Dwight Eisenhower, who began with studies and conferences in the mid-1950s. In May 1961, Kennedy initiated a commission on youth crime; in September, Congress passed the Juvenile Delinquency and Youth Offenses Control Act, which gave additional resources to state and local communities to combat crime among youth. When later asked why such attention and money was given to the issue, the Kennedy administration official in charge of the effort gave one answer: "*West Side Story*."[72] The American initiative then went global. UNESCO sponsored a conference on the topic in Paris in June 1962. A report followed two years later, tagging juvenile delinquency "a problem for a modern world."[73]

Given the apparent universality of concern over juvenile delinquency, the supporters of *West Side Story* in the US theatrical world again lobbied the State Department to support the show abroad. A testy discussion about it consumed the meetings of the drama advisory panel of the Bureau of Educational and Cultural Affairs in September 1963. In addition to insisting that delinquency was a connector between countries, the drama panelists reiterated that showing a story that held critical viewpoints of the United States was a sign of the strength of our democracy, not of weakness. It was a positive propaganda move: "The poets lead the way," Edward Kook, the head of a theatrical lighting company, summarized.[74]

The panelists threw down an ultimatum: accept the judgment of the experts or the panel would be "emasculated" and "fall apart eventually." Why not use *West Side Story* as a test case, to see whether or not there could be positive political benefits from such a story, rather than censor it on plot alone? The move would not only clarify the impact of such a show but also might lead to a "common ground of understanding with those who veto our decisions." The State Department official in the meetings balked—and parried. If the panel chose to put forth *West Side Story* as its sole recommendation, it would be the end of the theater program. The panelists caved. They ranked *West Side Story* as their first choice but added *Carmen Jones*, *Annie Get Your Gun*, *Kiss Me, Kate*, and *The Pajama Game* as the next best alternatives.[75] Opinion recorded, but ignored. The State Department did not sponsor *West Side Story*. American democracy did indeed have its limits.

The film, though, crossed boundaries more easily than the staged musical, through networks well established and oiled by profit. The State Department still tried to blunt the impact. Soon after the release of the film, assistant secretary of state Philip Coombs contacted Robert Wise to express a common concern—that the story lent "itself to exploitation by the Communists." Could lines be added at the beginning that would be "a tribute or dedication to the people of all racial and nationality backgrounds in the United States who, working together, have made great strides toward overcoming the conflicts depicted, and who are still working hard on the unfinished business of our democratic society"? Coombs went on to enumerate over two pages the main points that needed to be addressed.[76] Wise sent a considered reply, gently revealing the hypocrisy in the request. If there were any foreword to the film, he wrote, neither acceding to nor denying the request, it "must be done in a most subtle way so as not to be singled out as any kind of propaganda device."[77]

The question of the propaganda potential of the film and the mu-sical was really concerned solely with the story's reception should it travel to the Soviet Union. In fact, the transference of the story to the US-Soviet rivalry was the basis of a parody in *Mad* magazine in April 1963. The satirists moved the story to the east side, replacing the youth gangs with "two rival gangs at the U.N." and rewriting "When You're a Jet," for instance, as "When You're a Red." Others still saw this parallel as an opportunity rather than a barrier to the traveling of the production. Yet another Soviet dance company (150 Ural dancers) at-tended the show in Paris and declared that it depicted a problem they knew well at home. This bolstered Ottenheimer's and others' belief that juvenile delinquency served as grounds for commonality rather than disparagement of the United States. The ability "to make art of our problems and our daily life," Ottenheimer argued, outweighed the acknowledgment of the plight of Puerto Ricans and the ongoing problems of racism.[78] Following the efforts of Hal Prince a couple of years earlier, the European tour producers Godik and Kameron pressed American officials to allow a tour to the Soviet Union. *West Side Story* would raise the reputation of the United States in the eyes of the Soviet people, advocates believed, not serve Soviet propaganda. The State Department remained adamant: no tour.

Still, the show traveled. Initial interest in the stage production in the late 1950s, and the publication of the script in Russian in a Soviet theater journal, did not lead to any productions. But the album leaked in. Soviets who were able to travel to London, Paris, and New York made a beeline to the show. The cosmonaut Gherman Titov, who was the second person (and second Russian) to orbit the Earth in August 1961, went to see the film in May 1962 in Washington with forty other Russians.[79] The film, in fact, arrived on Russian soil before a stage production took place. The official US entry in the 1962 Moscow Film Festival was *The Great Escape*, the heroic tale of American prisoners' escape from a Nazi camp. The films shown out of competition—*Some Like It Hot, Ben Hur*, and *West Side Story*—had more appeal. Rus-sians stood in line for four hours to see *West Side Story*, and it was considered one of the most popular films of the festival.[80] The US delegation, though, attempted to slant the viewing—just as the State

Department official had wanted. Director Stanley Kramer opened the film by saying that the audience should understand that the depiction of gangs in New York "represents only one section of the city, not the whole city." It was a slice of US life that was not representative.[81] American exhibitors even requested that the lyrics to "America" not be translated into Russian. *Izvestia*, the Soviet government newspaper, promptly printed a full translation.[82]

The one prominent review, in the news organ of the youth wing of the Communist Party, *Komsomol'skaya Pravda*, found much to praise. The invention and artistry of filmic technique was impressive and, instead of criticizing the movie "for the things that are not in it," "we shall shake the hands of its creators for what they have done."[83] Meaning, however, still derived from a different ideology. The struggle for "ownership" of the street was an inevitable result of the American lifestyle.[84] The central conflict between the Jets and the Sharks came from living in a "bourgeois world: they would be better off being friends . . . helping each other in this strange city, in this concrete asphalt jungle, yet they reveal knives instead."[85] A more thorough critique of the film a few years later pointed out that only the people were alive in a landscape that had no tree, grass, dogs, cats, or birds: "The air is full of the heavy, hot fumes of cars and of asphalt. Air which tickles the throat."[86] Even if the creators did not search for "an exact answer" to this dilemma, the *Komsomol'skaya Pravda* review concluded, they displayed a "sincere love" for the people "living in countless west sides of America."[87] Or, as another reviewer put it, "Yes, the stamp 'Made in America' is here on everything. But in this case it is not the stamp of commerce or political calculation, but a stamp of true art."[88]

In the USSR, as in Japan, the film prompted a stage production. The National Academic Opera Company in Erevan performed the musical in October, just three months after the Moscow Film Festival.[89] Over a year later, in December 1964, *West Side Story* opened in Tallinn, in the Soviet Republic of Estonia, while the safer *My Fair Lady* played in Leningrad and Moscow.[90] But *West Side Story* was coming to Moscow, reports on the other side of the iron curtain declared. Robbins, Bernstein, Laurents, and Sondheim rallied the lawyers again, who shot off a threatening letter to the State Department. This time the lawyers targeted the International Business Practices Division, rather than the Department of Cultural Affairs. The specific situation "may afford your department with an opportunity to advance the cause" of protecting foreign property rights for all American authors, the lawyer reasoned.[91]

Even the appeal to capitalism did not inspire foreign diplomats to intervene on behalf of *West Side Story*'s creators. The Moscow Operetta Theater scheduled *West Side Story* with only a day's notice in July 1965.[92] An added spoken prologue framed the action: "Comrades, we would like to tell you about good boys brought up in hatred and shackled by hatred"—a twist on the State Department request for the film's premiere.[93] The production faithfully translated the name of the Sharks into Russian (*Akuli*) and the Jets became "radioactive" (*Reactivni*), another symbol of the nuclear moment, if not a kind of airplane. Slang, too, was put forth literally, so had little meaning, and the racial theme was muddled. But the shooting of Tony prompted a collective gasp.[94]

The reviews were mixed. One lamented the lack of "humor and happiness" in the play, a sign that "Gee, Officer Krupke" might not have been rendered in the same way.[95] In fact, it is difficult to know exactly what music or dance was used. Records were available, but scores were harder to come by. Similarly, with dance, the film might have served as inspiration for movement, but there was little of the training in jazz dance that was so necessary to Robbins's choreography. Even so, a few weeks after the premiere, a Soviet intellectual declared that "gone are the days of artistic passivity and of mediocre ordinary mannerism intended for an unexacting public." Operettas were out. New, more experimental theater—with social commentary that blurred with propaganda—was in.[96]

The barriers of Bernstein's music and Robbins's choreography, infractions of intellectual property, cultural confusion, and political tensions—none of this stopped the production from rolling through the Soviet Union. From November 1968 to August 1971, the Leningrad Lenin Komsomal Theater put on *West Side Story* in cities from Leningrad to Chelyabinsk, east of the Ural mountains. Here the "immorality of American social culture" crushed individualism and the potential and empathy of "simple human understanding."[97] It is likely that alterations enhanced this interpretation: a review of a 1974 production described the ending as a celebration of the police.[98]

It is not surprising that the Soviets revised *West Side Story* to serve their own ideological purposes; what may be more surprising is the number of places where there was no need for changes for the production to resonate. Its theme of the quest for belonging aligned with many different political contexts. Increasingly, in the 1960s, it was in places defined by racial discrimination that the production spoke most directly. Diana Ross led the Supremes in an emotional rendering of "There Is a Place for Us" in front of Britain's royal family in London in November 1968. After that violent year—with the assassinations of Martin Luther King Jr. in April and Bobby Kennedy in June—she spoke as the song faded: "There's a place for us. A place for all of us. Black and white, Jew and Gentile, Catholic and Protestant. So was the world of Martin Luther King and his ideal. If we keep this in mind, then we can carry on his work." While referencing King, though, a local incident may have prompted the declaration. The day before the concert, a controversial British politician urged the government to repatriate its immigrants of color to what he conceived as their homelands.[99] The song was an eloquent plea for a world in which all belonged, wherever they lived.

Theater companies in Rhodesia and South Africa—countries severely divided by racial segregation—wanted to use the production to convey this message as well. But to sanction a production in South Africa would have meant breaking a worldwide cultural boycott that attempted to keep the country from enjoying the artistic and intellectual labors of others who abhorred its apartheid policies. Arthur Laurents and Hal Prince felt that the "nature of the material and its possible influence on people" had to be taken into consideration— and perhaps the guarantee of a thousand pounds in royalties as well. Robbins, however, consistently denied permission to companies in both Rhodesia and South Africa. He was not swayed by accounts from theater companies there that they performed to integrated audiences—fully integrated, not just with special seating for whites and blacks. Nor did he think the message mattered. "I don't think we will move them about anything they are already *very* aware of. They know the problem and have been [unable?] to change it. WSS would only 'entertain' such people."[100] Robbins followed his own instinct on the issue but also sought out advice from Miriam Makeba, the activist and singer from South Africa, who convinced him that any interaction with South African or Rhodesian theatrical companies legitimized the segregated racial order by placing ticket prices "beyond the buying power of the Black African."[101] Despite personal appeals from a South African actor, Prince gave up. "Until such time as discriminatory practices change with respect to theatre audiences in Capetown, there isn't a prayer they'll give their consent to performing WSS in South Africa," he wrote.[102]

South Africa, though, was defiant in the face of international scorn. The country's copyright act of 1965 contained a piracy clause that asserted that authors' refusal to give permission to put on their plays was unreasonable and constituted a kind of illegal theft. In the mid-1960s, the Johannesburg Operatic and Dramatic Society sought permission to perform *West Side Story, Fiddler on the Roof,* and *Man of La Mancha.* They were denied rights for all three. The Society then turned to the Supreme Court Copyright Tribunal of South Africa. The copyright holders engaged one of South Africa's top lawyers to argue that the piracy clause contravened the Berne Convention, which set up the first commonly accepted global intellectual property rights in the late nineteenth century and to which South Africa was a signatory. (Neither the United States nor the Soviet Union, however, were signatories. The US joined other treaties, such as the Universal Copyright Convention of 1952, which better accommodated its internal copyright laws. The US Senate eventually ratified a more complete international treaty, the Berne Convention Implementation Act of 1988.) In February 1969, the South African court ruled that the Johannesburg Society constituted a highly professional company that could produce such plays and pay the necessary royalties.[103] The same year, though, the country banned the viewing of *West Side Story* the film by nonwhites, a good indication of the distinct audiences the different mediums reached.[104]

The licensing of performances, both at home and abroad, was strengthened after World War II. Following the path established by recorded music at the beginning of the twentieth century, copyright and licensing provided a legal and moral armature for the United States to spread its cultural capital around the world. While Coca-Cola and Levis were perhaps more obvious products of consumption, selling Americana as much as a soft drink or a pair of pants, movies, records, and, increasingly, stage performances became a bigger part of this wave of circulation of cultural goods. Copyright and licensing contributed to the control that US creators kept over their works, and powerful and successful artists such as Robbins and Bernstein pushed their lawyers to ensure that the law—and its provisions for credit and royalties—be enforced. While countries such as South Africa and the Soviet Union eluded this growing legal and financial armature, most bowed to it. Small high schools in rural Finland sought permission to perform *West Side Story* alongside well-known producers gunning to profit from the next revival. By the end of the twentieth century, a fully authorized and licensed production of *West Side Story* in China cinched the circle of control in intellectual property rights of musicals from Broadway.[105]

But at least some of *West Side Story* existed beyond the ideological, legal, and commercial structures of its worldwide distribution. A 1995 production in South Africa recognized that the tradition of the Broadway musical was built from a particular place at a particular time. The show demanded "'attitude,' that kind of self-focussed confidence that borders on arrogance and loves to make a display of its own power. . . . You see it in the step of the dancers, in the snap of the fingers and the angle of the heads. If it is not there, you miss it. It is also something that many years of cultural boycott have blotted out of our stage dancing tradition." The wonder of the production in South Africa, then, was that a squad of dancers had begun to possess that attitude. They belonged to the stage, to the show, "with the sheer exuberance of their bodies." This was, the reviewer claimed, a "New York Rhapsody."[106]

* 7 *

"Somewhere"

As *West Side Story* traveled around the world on stage and screen in the early 1960s, a friend of Albert Ottenheimer's declared that it would likely next appear on Mars and Venus. "What an epic!" he announced.[1] It was an epic of artistry, of ideals, and of longing. But, despite intergalactic predictions, it was not an epic of the future, on earth or any other planet. In many ways, *West Side Story* ended an era rather than forecasting a new one. In the crisis-drenched 1960s in New York, and in cities around the United States and the world, the rumble between Jets and Sharks seemed almost romantic. A robbery at the Rivoli Theater in February 1962 made the point. As the film played, two men tied up three employees and stole over seven thousand dollars.[2] Battles with knives were quickly overwhelmed by guns, torched buildings, and tear gas fired into crowds by police. The production had warned of the animosity and violence lurking in the city, but it did not foresee—and could not contain—the rage, fight, and demand that burst forth. The musical's vision of "Somewhere" slid from a hoped-for future into nostalgia for a never-been past.

The dream ballet of "Somewhere" was omitted in the film because its otherworldliness could not fit the hyperrealism of the medium, but its absence portended the steps away from *West Side Story*'s vision of hope. The embedded allusions to atomic warfare and the Cold War flickered in the distance as the daily, grinding, mazelike fighting in Vietnam became near and consuming. The touch of sentimentality and outdatedness that clung to *West Side Story* became a durable part of its appeal. The imagined world of the story may have seemed less attainable but more desired, the bickering of the gangs more adolescent and more manageable. It registered the end of an era.

Political events changed the perception of the production, but aspects of the production itself also contributed to a growing sense that this vision of belonging was unattainable. The initial salvo was Nuyoricans' anger, when the musical opened, over its portrayal of Puerto Ricans, especially in the lyrics of "America." That outrage increased with the racialization of Puerto Ricans in the film. The six young men a social worker brought to the Broadway production in 1958, who chaffed against the musical's condemnation of their parents, were likely not the only ones who found it unrealistic that a gang member's sister would stand by the murderer of her brother. By the mid-1960s, with violence on the upswing, that idea became blatantly absurd. The stakes in crossing ethnic or racial boundaries became increasingly stark. If death had been a surprise in the rumble between the Jets and the Sharks—where knives came out only after an interrupted fistfight—it was now to be expected, as racial and ethnic rage were more often accompanied by firebombs and machine guns. Perhaps even more telling, young people began to put gang warfare in another framework: one of conspiracy. "The gang thing was more or less imposed on us, anyway . . . by the white power structure. The majority. They wanted to divide us," one adolescent summed up.[3] Us and them became more rigidly redefined as black and white. And there was only pitched battle, little yearning love.

Part of the increasingly jaded view of the production resulted from leaks about the internal creative battles of the production itself, particularly in the making of the film. Early publicity about Robbins's absence from the film set did not reveal the drama of artistic and financial battles. Ultimately the codirector credits—and the Oscars—softened the clashes between the film's creators and producers that had occurred on the soundstage. But within a few months of the film's debut, Marni Nixon, the singing voice of Maria, began demanding screen credit and more royalties for her vocals. Betty Wand, who dubbed some of Anita's singing (in "A Boy Like That"), soon followed. (Jim Bryant, who sang Tony's songs, did not join the battle, as his contribution to the film had long been known, if also not acknowledged by a screen credit.)[4] Also, none of the creators of the musical besides Robbins thought highly of the film, viewing it as Broadway gone Hollywood with melodrama and overproduction tipping the delicate balance of realism and fantasy toward unbelievability. Laurents, in particular, inveighed against swishy boys dancing on the street, which he thought made it impossible to take the gang drama seriously. Robbins stood staunchly by both versions (even if there were always criticisms to make).

Robbins continued his involvement in (and dominance of) the production by being the most concerned with licensing decisions—more often saying no while the other creators said yes (never in a casino, for example)—and returning again to similar themes in different forms. His rendering of a ballet based on many of the movements of *West Side Story* followed soon after the opening of the musical. *NY Export: Opus Jazz* (1958) earned raves as a more stylized version of the movement of the show, less narrative and more balletic but still dynamic. And another ballet on the same themes, *Events* (1961), debuted at the time of the film. It was a dire view of the world. It included one section on racism, another on religious fanaticism, and, perhaps the most disturbing, a rendering of a pedophilic relationship between two men. The dance critic John Martin in the *New York Times* dismissed it as "another session with the Jets and Sharks, this time gone completely paranoid, both gangs. They slouch and twitch and roll in morbid self-pity, until at last the atom bomb gets them."[5] A friend of Robbins remembered *Events* as the most anti-American dance Robbins ever created.[6] And yet his continuing success on Broadway, on film, and in ballet led critics to crown him the most American of choreographers. From "tutus to T-shirts," Robbins was heralded for bringing "modern man into ballet."[7]

Bernstein was similarly touted for the vitality that he was bringing to classical music. He quickly capitalized on *West Side Story*'s success by developing an orchestral suite of it in 1961, played by symphonies around the world. Bernstein became conductor of the New York

Philharmonic in the midst of *West Side Story*'s first Broadway run, in 1958, and conducting and touring became the focus of his work for the next decade. Occasional compositions—*Kaddish Symphony* (1963), dedicated to John F. Kennedy, and *Chichester Psalms* (1965)—spiked an otherwise whirlwind decade of promoting classical music to young people on television and, with the Philharmonic, recording and touring to South America, Europe, and the Soviet Union. But *West Side Story* haunted Bernstein, prodding him to replicate its success in more classical form. He resigned from the Philharmonic in 1969, determined to devote himself to composition.

Laurents, on the other hand, dedicated himself to Broadway. He, Robbins, and Sondheim quickly moved on to another massively successful show, *Gypsy* (1959), this time one that skewered show business itself. Laurents continued working with Sondheim in the 1960s on *Anyone Can Whistle* (1964) and *Do I Hear a Waltz?* (1965), but achieved his other most significant successes writing the movie *The Turning Point* (1977) and then directing the musical *La Cage aux Folles* (1983). If *West Side Story* stuck to Robbins most of all, it was *Gypsy* that clung to Laurents. He directed revivals of it 1974 and again in 2008.

Sondheim's career after *West Side Story* defined the generational difference between him and Robbins, Bernstein, and Laurents. He was determined to write not just lyrics but music and to conceive a Broadway show himself from its origins. But the collaborations with Robbins and Laurents pulled him into their projects. He grudgingly agreed to write just the lyrics again for *Gypsy*; he relied on Robbins to fix the staging of *A Funny Thing Happened on the Way to the Forum* (1962); he worked with Laurents on *Anyone Can Whistle* and *Do I Hear a Waltz?* Robbins and Bernstein even talked him into a misguided attempt to reimagine a Bertolt Brecht play as a musical in the late 1960s. (Robbins eventually walked out on the collaboration and the musical never came into being.) But it was working with another *West Side Story* partner that finally launched Sondheim toward creating the works that pushed the genre to change. Through the 1970s, Hal Prince directed *Company* (1970), *Follies* (1971), *A Little*

Night Music (1973), *Pacific Overtures* (1976), *Sweeney Todd* (1979), and *Merrily We Roll Along* (1981)—conceived, composed, and written by Sondheim—a collection of musicals that banished sentimentality from the musical form. Sondheim had learned from the masters, working first with Rodgers and Hammerstein, then Laurents, Bernstein, and Robbins, before setting out on his own path. *West Side Story* later embarrassed him with its melodic swoons and treacle lyrics. He was ever grateful for the auspicious entrée to the musical theater world, but it laid the foundation against which he would rebel.

Ultimately neither Sondheim, Laurents, nor Bernstein was bound to the story in the ways that Robbins was. The story cleaved to him, even as he further investigated his personal demons in *Fiddler on the Roof* (1964).[8] *Fiddler* sought to heal the wounds between father and son, between religion and self, even bridging divides between Jews and Gentiles by insisting on the fragility of tradition. *West Side Story*, though, had led Robbins to the "futility of intolerance" in general.[9] It was a step removed, investigating Puerto Ricans and gang life, but it took him closer to the personal wounds that still loomed surrounding religion, family, sexuality, and politics. Robbins dedicated years of his life to *West Side Story* and its motivating ideas, intermittent yet constant, from ballets about group in/exclusion to the original Broadway show and film and then its first Broadway revival, which he directed in 1980. He would go back to it again near the end of his life, building *Jerome Robbins' Broadway* (1989) around it and adapting the dance into *West Side Story Suite* (1995) for the New York City Ballet.

Beyond the creators, the show had the most impact on those who played the role of Anita. George Chakiris won an acting Oscar for his Bernardo, but his career in film flailed, as did most of the others'; he survived but was not launched to fame. Natalie Wood's legacy was secure before the film and remained so after. The role of Anita, however, confirmed the talents of Chita Rivera, particularly on the stage, and finally jolted Rita Moreno into fame across movie, television, and stage. The later Broadway revivals recognized the dominance of this role, casting the well-known African American dancer and actress

Debbie Allen in 1980 and the new sensation Karen Olivo in 2009. This role—more than any other—has launched stars. Anita is magnetic in her verve, honesty, and transformation. But the character also spoke to one of the most enduring legacies of the production: its racialized ethnic stereotyping. Rita Moreno turned down movie offers for over a year after winning the Oscar, objecting that all the possibilities were some version of a sex-driven Latina spitfire. She began to involve herself in politics instead and attended Martin Luther King's March on Washington in August 1963.[10] Just a few weeks later, an African American actress in Chicago accused the director of a production of *West Side Story* at the Encore Theater of discrimination. She wanted to try out for the role of Maria; he insisted that she was better suited for Anita, "who is brassy and a better role for a Negro."[11] Almost two decades later, in the 1980 Broadway revival, Debbie Allen as Anita still provoked concern from at least one Puerto Rican who claimed, "Puerto Ricans are not black." Even more, the protester insisted, the role of Anita was the theatrical opportunity of a lifetime for Puerto Rican actresses, and they should have first priority for the role—a pragmatic embrace of a still ambivalent image.[12]

The musical did become a way for many to prove their talent, particularly on the growing summer stock and regional theater circuit. The aging, fragile star Dorothy Dandridge grasped the role of Anita as a way to hold on to fame, and the operatic singer Anna Maria Alberghetti finally became Maria after failed auditions for both Broadway and Hollywood productions. A young Christopher Walken was Riff; Richard Chamberlain and Pat Boone applied their sweetness to Tony; and aspiring choreographer Michael Bennett tried to outdo the master Robbins.[13] Despite the difficulty of the music and dance, the production became a surefire hit in regional theaters, summer stock, and, increasingly, high schools. Its enduring audience became young people, eventually appealing more to teenagers than adults. They took the story as their own. Teenagers in Chicago identified an alley near Milwaukee Avenue and Irving Park Road as a "perfect setting for a West Side Story type movie," and started filming themselves in blue jeans and turtleneck sweaters, "snapping their fingers."[14] Teenagers recreated the story in their own settings, shaping it to their own places.

Much as the producers had first imagined, the production continued to be used to reach teenagers about the ravages of discrimination and gang life. Paul Newman chose the film to exemplify the wrongs of banning films for obscenity in a New York legislative hearing in 1962. Parents, not the state, he argued, should decide whether children could see such films as *West Side Story*. He had taken two of his children, and "the effect of the total experience is that people should get along well together. They came away with the senselessness of gang warfare. . . . I wouldn't think of divesting them of that experience."[15] Programs fighting poverty and delinquency began to use films to start discussions about the problems facing young people. *Raisin in the Sun, On the Waterfront, East of Eden*, and *West Side Story* provided points of comparison to their lives, even if overdramatized.[16]

Tellingly, *West Side Story* was paired with older films in these programs for youth. By the early 1960s, contemporary artistic visions of troubled youth had become even more unvarnished. Novels such as *The Cool World* (1959) by Warren Miller—and the filmic version that came out in 1963—stood on the shoulders of *West Side Story* but moved beyond it. *The Cool World* was a bleak portrait of an African American gang based in Harlem, some of whose members appeared in the film. The story centers on one primary aim: being able to buy a gun so as to gain respect. "Aint nothing like a piece. I hold a piece in my hand once made me feel like I own the whole motheren world," a gang member asserts. Claiming a block has little to do with it. The city barely exists outside a "projeck," and the characters see the buildings around them as existing only for demolition, construction, and then repeat. At fourteen, the main character Duke sells weed to get the money to buy a gun, aims to become president of the gang when the current president becomes hooked on heroin, and beds the gang's prostitute without having to pay for the pleasure. The book notes assignations with gay men in Central Park as another avenue of revenue. Unrequited love exists only in the form of a gun out of reach.[17]

West Side Story punctured Broadway's rosy visions of life. It did not go as far as *The Cool World* but may have helped bleaker portraits into being by giving mainstream attention and sympathy to an ongoing problem. Attention given, fictional accounts such as *The Cool World* and nonfiction accounts such as *Up from Puerto Rico* (1958) by Elena Padilla and *Down These Mean Streets* (1967) by Piri Thomas filled out the particulars. But among Broadway musicals, *West Side Story* remained a rare tragedy. Then, in 1968, the boundaries got pushed again: *Hair* arrived. Also a story of youth, this musical gave hippie culture its moment onstage. Drugs, rock 'n' roll, biracial sex, homosexuality, and, of course, long hair, were meant to provoke society at large. On Broadway, explicit lyrics about cunnilingus, fellatio, and the differing sexual delights of "white boys" and "black boys" revved up the first full nudity seen onstage. "*Hair* will be the *West Side Story* of the sixties," a *New York Times* critic declared. It was also an indication of how much had changed in a decade. Try to imagine Maria's girlfriends singing, "Black boys are nutritious" instead of "I Feel Pretty," the critic gibed.[18] Resisting authority, flouting convention, and sex were center stage.

The comparison was acute when the revival of *West Side Story* at Lincoln Center occurred at the same time *Hair* was playing on Broadway in the summer of 1968. Everyone seemed to take for granted *West Side Story*'s outdatedness. Riots had replaced rumbles, polarized and violent civil rights battles made the ethnic squabbles seem quaint, the common use of crude language made "Krup you" almost sweet, the Rolling Stones pushed Bernstein's music to the safe, ignored realm of classical music, and the quirky, sexual roll of Twyla Tharp's choreography in *Hair* only emphasized Robbins's balletic foundation. "There is also the slightly disappointing realization," a critic went on, "that *West Side Story* is constructed of the common clay of many a Broadway musical: handsome boy, pretty girl, male and female chorus, exotic background, show-stopping comedy number, etc."[19] The latest sensation on Broadway confirmed the classic nature of an older one.

Becoming a classic, however, did not end the production's appeal; in fact, it extended it. As the 1960s marched on, *West Side Story* beckoned with its burnished classicism. It no longer served as drama of the daily headlines, but it achieved a kind of universalism for the contemporary age. Instead of being tied to a particular historical moment, the story stood in for enduring characteristics of New York and the United States. This seemed to be particularly true for dancers. Rudolph Nureyev saw the musical in Paris while touring with the Kirov in April 1961. The production overwhelmed him and, "as they came out into the street, in a burst of euphoria he launched into an impersonation of the Jets, cha-cha-chaing along the Champs-Élyseés."[20] Two months later, he defected. Just a few years later, a young student at the Royal Danish Ballet saw *West Side Story* and said, "That's where I'm going."[21] Peter Martins went on to join the New York City Ballet and has been its head since the death of George Balanchine. Dancers may have been attracted to a dance-led story and Robbins's inventive choreography, but the self-criticism of the story also had its appeal. On a mission sponsored by the United States Information Agency to promote US films in 1964, the actor Kirk Douglas was swayed by this assessment from university students and teachers abroad. Most countries did not allow the kind of self-criticism that *West Side Story* portrayed. The United States came across as a place trying to better itself by reviewing its faults, not slavishly promoting its ideals.[22]

This was not a perspective shared by many Puerto Ricans, however. What had begun as a random assignment of difference in an updated *Romeo and Juliet* became the primary channel for defining Puerto Ricans and what it meant to belong. The story portrayed their marginalization, but it also served to perpetuate stereotypes. And the production's worldwide spread and success made it particularly hard to see Puerto Ricans beyond the characters of Bernardo, Anita, and the Sharks. Any even uneasy embrace of the story began to loosen as the endurance of it solidified. There were attempts to make it their own. The Teatro Musicale de Puerto Rico in San Juan requested permission to put on *West Side Story* in English and Spanish in 1964. Robbins said no. In fact, he turned down most requests to put on the show by any groups from Puerto Rico or with Puerto Rican connections, leaving behind no reasoning for his denials. Robbins—or the other creators—never claimed to know well the experiences of Puerto Ricans. They were stand-ins (with a useful colorful heritage in music and dance) for those who did not belong. Recognition of this problematic use, lack of knowledge, and stereotypic generalization may have burrowed into the sensitive Robbins. He may have been wary of knowing even more about how Puerto Rican themselves would adapt and interpret the story.

Even without permission to put on *West Side Story* in theatrical venues, Puerto Ricans began to assert their own stories of adaptation to the mainland in the 1960s. Some of this had to do with the changing nature of migration. The economic forces of Operation Bootstrap expanded the back-and-forth travel of Puerto Ricans, as the federal government pushed to move the island from an agricultural to an industrial economy. Those in the mainland began to go back to the island as jobs opened up in this campaign to bolster US corporations' place there. "The homesick Puerto Rican lass of 1957's *West Side Story* no doubt has moved back to San Juan. What's more, her derisive friend who likes the isle of Manhattan may by now have followed her," one reporter claimed.[23] Those on the mainland also began to assert their rights as part of the broadening of the civil rights movement. The Puerto Rican gang the Young Lords remained powerful, but so did organizations working against it, such as the Real Great Society, formed in the Lower East Side in 1964 to combat poverty and promote education. Its theatrical troupe, Theatre of Courage, put on a local version of *West Side Story*. When the group expanded to East Harlem in 1967, it received funding to renovate two buildings on Madison Avenue near East 110th Street, a couple blocks from the school playground that served as one of the main sets for the filming of *West Side Story*.[24]

By the 1970s there were even more cultural organizations dedicated to the experiences of Puerto Ricans. Building from the mambo of the 1950s, salsa synthesized music and dance traditions from Puerto Rico, Cuba, and Latin America more generally in the 1970s. A literary movement swelled on the Lower East Side under the umbrella of the Nuyorican Poets Café, begun in 1973. One of the founders, playwright

Miguel Pinero, found fame soon thereafter with his play *Short Eyes*, a brutal tale of life in prison, which debuted on Broadway in 1974. The play won awards, traveled to Europe, and was produced as a book. But a musical about the zoot suit fracas that ensnared Chicanos in Los Angeles in the 1940s, which picked up on some of the themes of *West Side Story*, fared less well. *Zoot Suit* opened and closed without much excitement in 1979.

In the midst of this flourishing of the arts of Latino/as, *West Side Story* still dominated their representation among musicals, however. A revival of the production, directed by Robbins with consultation by Laurents, toured nationally in 1979 and landed on Broadway in 1980 with Debbie Allen as Anita, Puerto Rican actress Josie de Guzman as Maria, and Alvin Ailey dancer Héctor Jaime Mercado as Bernardo, the first two Latino/as in those latter roles on Broadway. Robbins made no attempt to change the show, as he believed it remained relevant.[25] Most critics disagreed. They confirmed its continuing appeal but argued that its only perspective on the troubles of urban life now was that there could be no easy solutions. "The final moment, when Jets and Sharks together lift Tony's lifeless body from the ground, is an impressive ritual of social healing. If only this healing were so easily come by (in this context even three deaths is 'easily') on the real streets of the real West Sides of our cities," a writer in the *Village Voice* summarized.[26]

As *West Side Story* continued to rove the world in the 1980s and 1990s as a classic of Broadway, if not a contemporary picture of New York, the musical that received the most attention as another Puerto Rican story was Paul Simon's *The Capeman*. Simon explored the story of Salvador Agron, a sixteen-year-old convicted of murder in a gang battle in the Hell's Kitchen neighborhood of Manhattan in August 1959. Agron was born in Puerto Rico and was likely developmentally delayed. In the midst of a difficult home life, he became part of the gang life of New York, first associating with the Mau-Maus of Brooklyn and then the Vampires in Manhattan. On a steamy August night, Agron went out with a few others from the gang expecting an encounter with members from a rival gang, the Norseman. The few Vampires found teenagers in a playground and Agron, wearing a black, red-lined cape, attacked and stabbed two of them. (It was later determined that the teenagers were not gang members.) At the time, the incident confirmed the realism of *West Side Story*, soon to begin its national tour.

By 1998, however, when *The Capeman* debuted on Broadway, this was no longer seen as an accurate view of Puerto Rican life in New York, in 1959 or 1998. The show suffered from Simon's determined control of the material and the changing attitudes toward which stories get told and by whom. In this newly politicized framework, *West Side Story* came under more vigorous attack. The scholar Alberto Sandoval-Sánchez excoriated the production's inauthenticity and persistence. *West Side Story* smothered Puerto Ricans, he claimed, presenting the first conversation point others raised to show they knew the story of the island and its inhabitants. The poet Judith Ortiz Cofer recalled being serenaded with the song "Maria" as she rode on a bus from London to Oxford; "Maria has followed me to London, reminding me of a prime fact of my life: you can leave the Island, master the English language, and travel as far as you can, but if you are a Latina, especially one like me who so obviously belongs to Rita Moreno's gene pool, the Island travels with you."[27]

The popularity of the production obscured the actual experiences of Puerto Ricans. Sandoval-Sánchez then turned the lens around. The story is a more accurate view of the "east side history of hatred/ racism," he charged. The primary end of the story is a more seamless assimilation of Puerto Ricans *to* white America, the criminalization of Puerto Ricans the necessary part of confirming the innocence of white Americans.[28] "*West Side Story* is . . . nothing short of a Puerto Rican *Birth of a Nation* (1915)," Frances Negrón-Muntaner continued, comparing the film to an earlier symbol of whitewashing America's long history of discrimination with vicious caricatures of African Americans played by white men in blackface.[29] A high school in Amherst, Massachusetts, canceled its production in response to student protests in 1999. In its valorized stereotyping, widespread distribution, and easy embrace, *West Side Story* marked the acceptance and endorsement of prejudice—not its unraveling. These condemnations resonated with many Puerto Ricans inside and outside the academy. The accounts named the unease that had been rumbling for decades. If the show had been a guide to America in the 1950s and 1960s, a story of liberalism's possibilities, by the 1990s it had become a guide to its failures, particularly in its handling of ethnic and racial issues.[30]

As Puerto Ricans eschewed the show, though, white gay men embraced it. "A Place for Us" became an anthem for gay rights; many saw the yearning for belonging it expressed as a hidden message from the gay creators about themselves.[31] This did not prompt revivals of *West Side Story*, however, as other Broadway shows soon told the story of gay men more overtly. Sondheim suggested the possibility in *Company* (1970), his breakaway hit that centered on the dysfunction of marriage and the appeal of bachelor life. *A Chorus Line* (1976), conceived, directed, and choreographed by Michael Bennett, who took Jerome Robbins as his model, incorporated the tragic consequences of closeted life for a gay dancer. And then Laurents directed the first explicit story about a gay couple on Broadway in *La Cage aux Folles* (1983). Broadway went on to uncover other struggles to belong hinted at in *West Side Story*.

There was not a major revival of the show on Broadway from 1980 to 2007, an indication of its discomfiting issues of representation, naïve politics, and the turn to spectacle in the genre with high-grossing productions like *Cats* (1980), *The Phantom of the Opera* (1986), and *Les Misérables* (1987). Despite that, the musical continued to be licensed around the world and toured cities in the United States and the United Kingdom in the 1990s. Its ongoing, less flashy or controversial, fame was as a story of wayward, longing youth. What remained resonant was not so much the story of Puerto Ricans or of New York in upheaval as its portrayal of juvenile delinquency. Michael Jackson saw this and featured competing, dancing gangs in the video for "Beat It" (1982) and the setting of a New York subway station in his video for "Bad" (1987).[32] There was a limit to how young the story would skew, however. Disney proposed an animated version between cats, to which Laurents replied, "One paw, one heart?"[33] The creators said no to that and often refused permission to stage the show with middle school students.

The creators, led by Robbins, kept a tight rein on how the show would be used, perhaps realizing how quickly it could become fodder for parody.[34] As it soon did. John Leguizamo's spoof in *House of Buggin'* (1995) opened the floodgates. The 1950s Sharks with colored jeans and shirts and pompadours prance in a concrete playground to face the Crips, who are seeking to sell drugs and are loaded with guns and howitzers. By the early 2000s, the production was most visible in commercials and parodies, from three widely celebrated commercials for the Gap in 2000 (with the Khakis as the Jets and Jeans as the Sharks) to a caricature by Robert DeNiro in *Analyze That* (2002) to spoofs on *Scrubs* (2002), *Family Guy* (1999), and *The Simpsons* (2011). More recently, both *Ugly Betty* (2007) and *Glee* (2011) have incorporated *West Side Story* into plots that put its nostalgic view of youth alongside more contemporary realities. *West Side Story* is common enough to be known, well worn enough to poke fun at; its righteous naivety serves as a reliable straight man. It is ripe for reinvention.

The fiftieth anniversary of the musical, in 2007, prompted reviews of its impact and relevance—and also talks of a Broadway revival. Undertaken by Laurents, at the age of ninety-one, *West Side Story* opened again on Broadway in March 2009. Laurents sought to update it with two major changes: incorporating Spanish into the lyrics and dialogue and focusing more strongly on the story of love between Tony and Maria. "I Feel Pretty" became "Siento Hermosa," a "Boy Like That," "Un Hombre Así."[35] These changes, particularly the move to Spanish, caused consternation among the largely non-Spanish-speaking audiences that attend Broadway shows. Subtitles were tried and quickly dismissed. Finally, more English returned.

This fiddling required the talent and skills of Lin-Manuel Miranda, a young artist who had leapt to Broadway fame just a year earlier with *In the Heights* (2008), a heart-warming tale of love and longing among Latino/as on the far upper west side of Manhattan, in the neighborhood of Washington Heights. Laurents engaged Miranda to adapt the lyrics and dialogue from English to Spanish. This move not only utilized Miranda's language and creative talents: it bound a more contemporary tale of New York to an earlier one. (*West Side Story* even stole Karen Olivo to play Anita from her starring role as Vanessa in *In the Heights*.) Miranda had a Puerto Rican father, had played Bernardo in a sixth-grade production, and directed his high school version, with the Sharks played by no Latino/as but "various shades of brown, and Asian."[36] He also had the typical ambivalent response to *West Side Story*, understanding it as both a blessing and a curse for Puerto Ricans.[37] *In the Heights* was his riposte: of the neighborhood, in the neighborhood, and celebrating the neighborhood, it was a tale of belonging not denied but found. Opening with upbeat, rhythmic hits of a clave—reminiscent of but different from fingers snapping—Miranda's musical sets out to create a vision of home on a New York City street corner. A bodega, a hair salon, a cab company, a beloved *abuela* overseeing it all. The only overt nod to *West Side Story* comes when Usnavi, Miranda's character, is asked if he can dance: "Like a drunk Chita Rivera" is the reply, lighting on the most famous Puerto Rican in the original production. The mixture of Latino/a identities in the city is the foundation of the neighborhood. "My mom is Dominican-Cuban / My dad is from Chile and P.R. / which means / I'm Chile- . . . Dominica-Rican! / But I always say I'm from Queens!" one explains. Characters variously aspire to finish a degree at Stanford, return to the Dominican Republic, or move downtown, but, ultimately, the theme is an embrace and claiming of the city. Usnavi realizes that "this corner is my destiny." The show ends with the entire cast singing, "I'm home."

In the Heights received thirteen Tony nominations and won four, including Best Musical. Its joyousness was infectious, and it fit into the longer tradition of musical theater's happy stories. Apart from a slap at gentrification and lingering color lines, there were few mentions of social ills to trouble the love stories. The musical conveyed its contemporary view of New York less through its cheerful story than in its focus on youth. It built on the success of *Rent* (1996), which had utilized *West Side Story*'s formula: take the story line of a classic—Puccini's *La Boheme*—and drop it in contemporary New York. In *Rent*, young men and women search for love in a city ravaged by AIDS, drugs, and the growing economic inequality of early-1990s New York—all accompanied by a rock score and frank lyrics à la *Hair*. *In the Heights*, then, took the focus on youth, grounded in a New York City neighborhood, and added hip-hop. It gave a stage to arts of the streets, infusing the vitality of these expressive styles into an older and more conventional form.

As in *West Side Story*, the music and dance of *In the Heights* tied the stage to the streets outside the theater. The trail from the older show traveled as much through those streets as through the conventions of the Broadway musical itself. If the story and politics of *West Side Story* became nostalgic, its dancing did not. It remains visceral, explosive, and immediate. Partly this is the magic of dance: it only exists in the moment—except now when captured on-screen. Much to Robbins's dismay, the Jets and the Sharks danced on 68th Street on the west side and 110th in Spanish Harlem, and those images traveled around the globe.

Did that inspire others to do the same?

Dancing in the streets became common in the 1960s, as part of civil rights struggles and hippie be-ins, R & B and rock 'n' roll. What had been confined to stages and dance halls spilled out into parks, sidewalks, and streets. With the growing ubiquity of media that could capture motion, dance became a new way to see and express identity and belonging. The steady plodding of the marchers of Selma was an indication of their conviction, the wavy lassitude of the crowds at Woodstock a sign of their mellowness. And then there was the poppin' of James Brown, snapping his body in sharp rhythm and dropping to the ground in a beat. It was Brown and the rhythms of R & B, funk, and soul that moved into the neighborhoods of the South Bronx and Harlem, following African Americans and Puerto Ricans pushed out of the gleaming glass towers of midtown or living near the marble shrine of Lincoln Center. B'boyin'—or breakdancing—along with scratching records, rappin' lines, and spray-painting walls and trains

FIGURE 7.1 Claiming space through dance on the upper west side, 1983. The open and blocked windows are reminiscent of the abandoned buildings used for backdrop of the prologue in the film (figure 5.16). Photograph © Martha Cooper.

took over the streets. Dancers formed into gangs, who staged battles. A piece of cardboard for spinning heads on the concrete corner and the rumble was on.[38]

West Side Story lurks behind the rise of b'boying and hip-hop, not as a definitive cause but as a cipher. "Breaking is a way of using your body to inscribe your identity on streets and trains, in parks and high school gyms. It is a physical version of two favorite modes of street rhetoric, the taunt and the boast," as the dance writer Sally Banes first described it. "It is a way of claiming territory and status, for yourself and for your group, your crew."[39] Breakdancing pulled together movement from West Africa, capoeira from Brazil, social dancing from Harlem's dance halls, and, perhaps, inspiration from Jerry Robbins. "What's at stake is a guy's honor and his position in the street. Which is all you have," Fab 5 Freddy, one of the defining members of hip-hop in the late 1970s, explained.[40] Breakdancing speaks to the need to find yourself in others, with others, and in defiant display to others. "When You're a Jet" updated to meet the burned-out carcasses of

FIGURE 7.2 Looking south from the west side of Manhattan, with Lincoln Center in the foreground and the Empire State Building piercing the fog, August 1964. Photograph by Bob Serating.

buildings lining the streets of the South Bronx, in the face of outright discrimination, neglect, and abandonment. That is its place.

West Side Story is not a vision of New York today. The west side is now one of the most expensive areas to live, with Lincoln Center as a temple to the high arts at its heart. Rising real estate values have pushed grime, grit, the homeless, and new migrants and immigrants to the outer boroughs. Drugs have changed the purpose of gangs. Minorities are the majority in the city. Puerto Ricans still account for one in three Spanish-speaking New Yorkers, but the total number in the city has declined since the early 1980s. The home of some of hip-hop's creators, an unassuming apartment building in the South Bronx at the edge of the Cross Bronx Expressway, is recognized as worthy of historic preservation. And *West Side Story*'s vision of an idyllic "Somewhere"—a green oasis outside the city—has been reversed in a renewed embrace of the ideals of urban life as sustainable, diverse, and communal. The quest of young people searching for their place has moved far beyond the musical and the film, and even beyond New York. The city is no longer the one Jerome Robbins lived in and remade, the story is no longer a resonant view of Puerto Ricans or rebelling adolescents.

It is still a story that defines us, though, by showing what we are not but also what we remain. Dividing the world into opposing camps. Looking through chain-link fences to visions beyond. Yearning to belong. Dancing to identify, explode, and connect. Searching for our place.

ACKNOWLEDGMENTS

Putting on a show takes a lot of people. So does writing a book. If a show is an intensive collaboration that bursts into a collective, exuberant moment, a book is more often a meandering journey bolstered and held together through the years by a wide variety of people who may not even know the roles they played. It is a pleasure to be able to acknowledge those roles now.

The idea for this book occurred as I was writing another one. That other one is still unfinished, but the research for it, on the rise of Lincoln Center, has been the foundation of most of my thinking, teaching, and writing about the intersection of arts and urbanization over the last few years. I am forever grateful to the Rockefeller Archive Center for sponsoring me as a Scholar-in-Residence, which allowed for a deep dive into the archival material on Lincoln Center. My work and conversations there over the years have continued to inspire research, workshops, events, curricula, and more research. Robert Battaly, Camilla Harris, Erwin Levold, Jack Meyers, Tom Rosenbaum, James Allen Smith, Darwin Stapleton, and Roseann Variano have been instrumental in supporting and expanding my ideas about the arts, cultural policy, foundations, and New York City.

Other institutions played supporting roles as well. The New School began as a riposte in the long-standing debate about higher education, and traces of that rebelliousness remain in the support it gives to faculty crossing disciplines and engaging a wider public. There are few places where my interests in the arts, urbanization, and history could play out in dialogue with so many others. I spent a sabbatical year immersed in the archival materials of the Performing Arts Library of the New York Public Library, with trips to the University of Oregon, the Wisconsin Historical Society, the Margaret Harrick Library of the Academy of Motion Picture Arts and Sciences, and the Cinematic Arts Library of the University of Southern California. Jonathan and Sarah Veitch made the research trip to Los Angeles a personal pleasure as well as a professional one. I am also grateful for the support of the Harry Ransom Center at the University of Texas at Austin for research in the papers of Ernest Lehman, and for the research help of Daria Lotareva, Elizabeth Constant Jordan, Mark Ocegueda, and Bianca Rowlett in archives that I could not visit in person. As any historian knows, archivists and librarians are the backstage heroes of any book.

Maggie Adams at MGM embraced my obsession with *West Side Story* and not only shared visual material for the making of the film but also connected me to dancers from the film with their own stories to tell. I am grateful to Robert Banas and to Bert Michaels, especially, for their fresh anecdotes, youthful enthusiasm, and wise insights into how show business works. Freddie Gershon of Music Theatre International discussed with me how musicals travel to places far from Broadway. Karin Ida Maria Ander, Yulia Cherkasova, Aissatou Diallo, Divina Hasselman, Al-Noor Hirji, Pieter-Paul Pothoven, Meghan Robison, Akari Shono, Mariya Smrinov, Aya Tasaki, and Lina Maria Villegas Guiterrez provided invaluable assistance in translating materials from around the world so that I could follow where *West Side Story* traveled.

Puerto Rico was a resonant place to delve into the various meanings this story has had for Puerto Ricans, and Brian Herrera, Deborah Paredez, Alberto Sandoval-Sánchez, and Elizabeth Wells were the ideal discussants for that at a roundtable of the American Studies Association conference. The Dance Studies seminar at Columbia University, which Lynn Garafola originated and organized, provided another welcome context for ideas in formation. I was lucky to be paired with Alisa Solomon, whose book on *Fiddler on the Roof* provided such an inspirational model. Aaron Shkuda and Jeffrey Trask helped connect the filming of *West Side Story* to concerns of urban historians, and Aaron created a larger conversation about the arts in US cities after World War II at a conference panel and then as a special section for the *Journal of Urban History* in which I joined him as coeditor. I have also benefited from conversations with Tony Anemone, Thelma Armstrong, Laura Auricchio, Lauren Erin Brown, Joanna Dee Das, Oz Frankel, Terri Gordon-Zolov, Joseph Heathcott, Rachel Heiman, Elizabeth Kendall, Jessica Lautin, Madge McKeithen, Gustav Peebles, Victoria Phillips, Claire Potter, Tim Quigley, Max Rivera, David Scobey, Lisa Servon, Liz Sevcenko, Jeff Smith, Robert Snyder, Radhika Subramaniam, Sigrid Svendal, Ellen Tolmie, and Almaz Zelleke. Shannon Mattern and Aleksandra Wagner were as supportive in friendship as in writing.

The first response of Alan Thomas at the University of Chicago Press to two chapters buoyed me through writing the rest of them. I am grateful to Randolph Petilos, Joel Score, the anonymous readers, and all the others at the press who have helped turn my research and writing into a show of its own. Thomas Lisanti of the New York Public Library and Christopher Pennington of the Jerome Robbins Rights Trust were instrumental in the amassing of critical visual material in the book. I am especially grateful to Rosaria Sinisi, overseer of the Oliver Smith estate, who generously opened up files on Smith that taught me more about him, the production, and the ongoing lives of musicals.

There are starring roles in this production as well. Casey Nelson Blake has a more insightful understanding of *West Side Story* than I do, and has generously shared those ideas and encouraged my own perspective. Lew Erenberg has been pushing me out on the proverbial academic stage since I began graduate school and continues to prod and sharpen my thinking still. Alison Isenberg has been an unfailingly generous compatriot as we have been writing our books over many years. Our manuscript retreat made the final stage not only enjoyable but a meaningful reminder of what more can be dug out of topics from ongoing conversations. And two graduate student assistants have been more than students and more than assistants:

Lina Maria Villegas Guiterrez and Katerina Vaseva have been crucial partners in this production.

When the stage goes dark, there are the people who make my place in the world: my mother and the still vibrant memory of my father, my brother and sister and their families, the Kane and Gough families, Donna and Malik Geraci, Mark Larrimore, Kasia Malinowska, Jena Osman and Amze Emmons, Karen Plafker and Brian Horrace, Leslie Schwerin. Brian, Brisa, and Earl have lived with *West Side Story* more than any person or cat should have to. Yet they continue to point out any snapping fingers that might be an echo of others — and risk hearing more from me about what this might reveal. This book is dedicated to Brisa, whose childhood has been defined by this story that obsesses her mother. If the youth of *West Side Story* heed the advice of no adult in an attempt to define their own world, I can only hope that my own child follows their lead.

NOTES

PROLOGUE

1. *New York Times* (27 September 1957); *New York Post* (19 October 1961). Both in box 67, folder 6 (hereafter abbreviated, e.g., b.67 f.6), JRPP/NYPL.

CHAPTER 1

1. Original materials are in b.81 f.1, JRP/NYPL.

2. Robbins's note appears in the margins of a letter from Amberson Enterprises Inc., Bernstein's management company, to Floria Lasky, Robbins's lawyer, 8 March 1995, b.80 f.15, JRP/NYPL. The letter contains an overview of the creation of *West Side Story* for a new pressing of the record. The overview was eventually scrapped. For more on disagreements between Bernstein and Laurents, see Laurents's April 1949 letters to Bernstein, reprinted in Simeone, ed., *Leonard Bernstein Letters*, 252–55.

3. There is little explanation of the working title "Gang Bang" on an early outline (b.81 f.1, JRP/NYPL). Whether a mocking suggestion or one that was truly considered is hard to know. While the phrase now refers to harrowing sexual violence, the men may have meant simply to emphasize gangs and the sexual drive that motivates the young lovers. "Gang Bang" never reappeared as a title even in the working drafts.

4. Rough drafts of scripts in b.81 f.1, JRP/NYPL; Louis Calta, "'Romeo' to Receive Musical Styling," *New York Times* (27 January 1949), 19.

5. *West Side Story* has received its share of attention, both popular and scholarly, but little of it has focused on the centrality of New York City to the story and its production, on the interweaving of the musical and the film, or on its international and ongoing resonance. For overviews of the making of the musical, which largely center on Bernstein, see Garebian, *Making of West Side Story*; Wells, *West Side Story*; Simeone, *Leonard Bernstein*; Smith, *There's a Place for Us*; and Oja, *Bernstein Meets Broadway*. Berson, *Something's Coming*, looks at both the musical and the film. The most trenchant commentary has come from those looking at the film's portrayal of Puerto Ricans. See Sandoval-Sánchez, *Jose, Can You See?* and "*West Side Story*"; Negrón-Muntaner, *Boricua Pop*; Paredez, "Queer for Uncle Sam"; Herrera, *Latin Numbers*; Acevedo-Muñoz, *West Side Story as Cinema*.

6. See the Bernstein biographies by Burton, Secrest, Seldes, and Shawn; Bernstein's own *Findings*; and Simeone, ed., *Leonard Bernstein Letters*. On Robbins, see Jowitt, *Jerome Robbins*; Greg Lawrence, *Dance with Demons*; and Vaill, *Somewhere*. In the last decade of

211

his life, Laurents went on a memoir torrent: see *Original Story By*, *Mainly on Directing*, and *The Rest of the Story*. On Sondheim, see Zadan, *Sondheim & Co.*, and Sondheim's own *Finishing the Hat* and *Look, I Made a Hat*.

7. Jowitt, *Jerome Robbins*, 49. In the corresponding footnote (524), Jowitt explains that this comes not from Robbins himself but from Brian Meehan. It has the hint of exaggeration with a basis in truth.

8. Vaill, *Somewhere*, 18–19.

9. Robbins, ["My city lies between two rivers . . ."], n.d. [1940s?], b.25 f.6, JRPP/NYPL.

10. Robbins, ["A Story of Four Young People . . ."], n.d. [1940s?], b.25 f.6, JRPP/NYPL.

11. Robbins, [". . . like a little town . . ."], n.d. [1940s?], b.25 f.6, JRPP/NYPL.

12. Oja, *Bernstein Meets Broadway*, offers an in-depth exploration of the making of *Fancy Free* and *On the Town*.

13. [Robbins], "Fancy Free," typed draft with headings "Music and mood" and "Action" for Bernstein, June 1943, b.40 f.6; Bernstein to Robbins ["I've been a stinker not to have written sooner . . ."], Tuesday [Summer 1943], b.39 f.17; JRPP/NYPL.

14. Smith to Robbins, 16 March 1944, b.39 f.18, JRPP/NYPL. Works of Oliver Smith copyright Rosaria Sinisi.

15. Scenario for the record, b.39 f.16, JRPP/NYPL.

16. [Robbins], "Fancy Free."

17. Ibid.

18. [Sketches on stationery of Hotel Whitcomb, San Francisco], n.d. [1943?], b.40 f.6, JRPP/NYPL.

19. Bernstein to Robbins, ["I've been a stinker not to have written sooner . . ."], Tuesday [Summer 1943], b.39 f.17, JRPP/NYPL.

20. [Robbins], "Fancy Free."

21. Bernstein to Robbins, ["Your description of the state of the Ballet Theatre sounds gruesome"], n.d. [Summer 1943], b.39 f.17, JRPP/NYPL.

22. Robbins to Donald Saddler, n.d. [1943], b.39 f.19, JRPP/NYPL.

23. Vaill, *Somewhere*, 157.

24. Laurents, "Rough Outline: 'Romeo,'" n.d. [1949], b.81 f.1, JRP/NYPL.

25. Laurents, "Musical Origins," *Playbill* (30 September 1957).

26. Laurents to Bernstein, 19 July [1955], reprinted in Simeone, ed., *Leonard Bernstein Letters*, 342–43. Laurents also sent a copy of the letter to Robbins.

27. Decades after the fact, Laurents claimed he could only have written "movie Chicanos" and insisted on the transfer to the "New York and Harlem I knew firsthand, and Puerto Ricans and Negroes and immigrants who had become Americans"; Laurents, *Original Story By*, 337–38. This seems mildly disingenuous, partly because Laurents's criticisms of the film have focused so exactly on its inauthentic and "anti–Puerto Rican" portrayals of the gang members. New York held appeal for all the creators, as much so or even more for Bernstein and Robbins, so Los Angeles as a setting probably never had much plausibility.

28. Laurents, "Romeo," n.d. [1955], b.81 f.1, JRP/NYPL.

29. Zipp, *Manhattan Projects* (chaps. 4–5), gives the most thorough review of the construction of Lincoln Center in the midst of debates over urban renewal.

30. There was no FBI file on Laurents, although he had to provide a detailed explanation and affidavit in the process of a passport renewal in 1952; AL/LOC, b.128 f.7.

31. For the particularly vulnerable position of Jews in entertainment and gay and lesbians, see Litvak, *Un-Americans* (chap. 6 specifically looks at Broadway), and Johnson, *Lavender Scare*. For an account published in 1973 but still brimming with the effects of the era, see Kanfer, *Journal of the Plague Years*.

32. Hearings of the House Committee on Un-American Activities, 83d Congress, H1428-H-B, 5 May 1953, 1315–25. For Robbins's interactions with the FBI and HUAC, see Vaill, *Somewhere*; Lawrence, *Dance with Demons*; Jowitt, *Jerome Robbins*; the FBI files on Robbins; and Laurents's several memoirs.

33. In letters in May 1999 to Greg Lawrence, a biographer of Robbins, Laurents made clear that he believed Robbins informed because he was "evil," not that he was evil because he informed. The action only confirmed what Laurents saw as a base characteristic of Robbins, also manifest in Robbins's refusal to let go of the "conceived by" credit he insisted upon for *West Side Story* (see p. 106); AL/LOC b.104 f.7.

CHAPTER 2

1. Laurents, "Romeo," n.d. [1955], b.81 f.1, JRP/NYPL.

2. Robbins to Laurents and Bernstein, 18 October 1955, b.85 f.11, JRP/NYPL. The letter includes handwritten comments by Bernstein in the margins. Most often, Bernstein agrees with Robbins's criticisms.

3. Ibid.

4. Ibid.

5. Arthur Laurents, "Musical Origins," 26 September 1957; AL/LOC b.92 f.1. Originally published in the *Playbill* that accompanied the debut of the musical.

6. See the story "This Is New York" in *Look* (18 February 1958), which dramatizes the changes in photographs and statistics. For urban renewal's impact on New York City, see Zipp, *Manhattan Projects*; Berman, *All That Is Solid Melts into Air*; and Schwartz, *New York Approach*.

7. Arthur Laurents, "The Growth of an Idea," *New York Herald Tribune* (4 August 1957), sect. 4, 1.

8. Whalen and Vazquez-Hernandez, *Puerto Rican Diaspora*, 2. See also Haslip-Viera, Falcon, and Rodriguez, eds., *Boricuas in Gotham*; Thomas, *Puerto Rican Citizen*.

9. Lao-Montes and Davila, eds., *Mambo Montage*, 154.

10. Annotated Script Changes, b.81 f.4, JRP/NYPL.

11. Bernstein, quoted in Secrest, *Leonard Bernstein*, 212.

12. Script Excerpts, 1957, b.81 f.3, JRP/NYPL.

13. Scripts, 1957, b.81 f.7, JRP/NYPL.

14. Eric Avila describes the ways in which in those who had little control over the placement of urban infrastructure in the modernist era, such as highways, inhabited the spaces with their own community and cultural traditions. One of the best examples of this is the formation of Chicano Park in San Diego, a place of murals underneath the highway, in the early 1970s; see Avila, *Folklore of the Freeway*, esp. chaps. 4–5.

15. Annotated Script Excerpts, 1957, b.81 f.2, JRP/NYPL.

16. Robbins, ["My city lies between two rivers . . ."], n.d. [1940s?], b.25 f.6, JRPP/NYPL.

17. Character description notes, 1957: "Riff," b.85 f.4; "Riff," b.85 f.9; "Tony," b.85 f.4; JRP/NYPL.

18. Character description notes, 1957, untitled pages and one titled "Bernardo," b.85 f.4, JRP/NYPL.

19. Patsy [no last name] to Robbins, n.d. [Spring 1957], b.82 f.4, JRP/NYPL. I have been unable to identify the full name of this letter writer, although she appears to be a playwright or dramaturg.

20. General Notes, 1957, b.85 f.9, JRP/NYPL.

21. Patsy [no last name] to Robbins, 19 April [1957], b.85 f.3, JRP/NYPL.

22. See, for example, Annotated Script, n.d. [1956?], b.81 f.2, Act I, Scene I, JRP/NYPL.

23. Annotated Script, n.d. [early 1957?], b.81 f.5, Act I, Scene I, JRP/NYPL.

24. Annotated Script, n.d. [1957?], b.81 f.5 and Script, n.d. [1957?], f.7, JRP/NYPL.

25. Script [Jan. 1956], b.17 f.4, SS/WHS.

26. Lyrics manuscripts, b.18 f.1, SS/WHS.

27. Script excerpts, n.d. [1957?], b.81 f.3, JRP/NYPL.

28. Elizabeth Wells gives the most thorough account of the influences in Bernstein's music in *West Side Story*, chaps. 3–4.

29. Flora Roberts, Sondheim's lawyer, claims that Sondheim said this to her; Zadan, *Sondheim & Co.*, 14. On Robbins's visit to Harlem, see Robbins to Tanaquil LeClerq, 20 February 1957, LeClerq Papers, NYCB; on Bernstein, Wells, *West Side Story*, 129.

30. Score, "I Feel Pretty," b.50 f.14, JRP/NYPL.

31. Scenario sent to prospective investor from producer Cheryl Crawford's office, 11 January 1957, b.75 f.1, JRP/NYPL.

32. Score, "America," b.50 f.5, JRP/NYPL.

33. Laurents, "Romeo" [1955], b.81 f.1, JRP/NYPL.

34. Score, "Mix!," b.50 f.19, JRP/NYPL.

35. Annotated script, n.d. [early 1957?], b.81 f.2: 1-4-12, JRP/NYPL.

36. Ibid.

37. Robbins crossed out "brown bellies" in one draft; b.82 f.1, JRP/NYPL.

38. Annotated script changes, 1957, b.81 f.4, JRP/NYPL.

39. Character description notes, ["Bernardo"], n.d., b.85 f.4, JRP/NYPL.

40. Sandoval-Sanchez, *José, Can You See?* (chap. 2), gives the most thorough condemnation of the production from the perspective of Puerto Ricans, deeming it a racist portrayal that has only been a burden to Puerto Ricans. See also Negrón-Muntaner, "Feeling Pretty"; Brian Herrara, *Latin Numbers*; and Paredez, "Queer for Uncle Sam."

41. Wells, *West Side Story*, 126.

42. Ernest Lehman, typed screenplay dated 6-17-60, published by MGM to accompany the 50th anniversary special edition DVD of the film, 67.

43. Annotated script, n.d. [1956?], b.82 f.2, JRP/NYPL.

44. Laurents, *West Side Story*, act 2, sc.1.

45. Script, b.81 f.7, JRP/NYPL.

46. Lyrics manuscripts, b.18 f.1, SS/UWS.

47. [Robbins], "Second Act Ballet Scenario," n.d. [1957?], b.85 f.5, JRP/NYPL.

48. Ibid.

49. Laurents, *Mainly on Directing*, 146. Robbins told "Tony Mordente that the Jets' abuse of Anita reminded him of an episode at Camp Kittatinny, when bigger boys had held him down and teased him by dangling a worm in his face"; Vaill, *Somewhere*, 282.

50. Deborah Paredez fleshes out this reversal with a convincing rereading of the character of Anita in "Queer for Uncle Sam."

CHAPTER 3

1. Cheryl Crawford to Jerome Robbins, 15 June 1956, b.75, f.1, JRP/NYPL.

2. Crawford to Robbins, 15 June 1956, b.75 f.1, JRP/NYPL.

3. Crawford to Arthur Laurents, 20 July 1956; Crawford to Roger Stevens, 10 July 1956, b.83 f.4, CC/NYPL.

4. Crawford to Robbins, 3 January 1957, b.75 f.2, JRP/NYPL; Crawford to Laurents, 11 April 1957, and his response to her, n.d. [April 1957?], b.43 f.2, RS/LOC. On the "invented slang," see Bernstein et al., "Landmark Symposium," 17.

5. Laurents to Crawford, n.d. [April 1957?], b.43 f.2, RS/LOC. See also Laurents, *Original Story By*, 328; Bernstein et al., "Landmark Symposium," 17.

6. The *New Yorker* published an evocative rendering of gang life in Brooklyn the week *West Side Story* debuted; Walter Bernstein, "The Cherubs Are Rumbling," *New Yorker* (21 September 1957), 129–59. The best historical overview of gangs in New York in this period is Schneider, *Vampires, Dragons, and Egyptian Kings*. The journalist Harrison Salisbury wrote an influential series of articles on juvenile delinquency in March 1958 that became the book *The Shook-Up Generation*. See also Gilbert, *Cycle of Outrage*; Snyder, "Useless and Terrible Death"; Flamm, *Law and Order*.

7. Crawford to Laurents, 11 April 1957, b.43 f.2, RS/LOC.

8. Crawford to Robbins, 3 January 1957, b.75 f.2, JRP/NYPL. See also the letter from Edwin Lester of the Los Angeles Civic Light Opera Association to Crawford, 26 December 1956, b.83 f.4, CC/NYPL.

9. Crawford to Frank Ricketson, 23 January 1957, b.83 f.4, CC/NYPL.

10. Crawford to Elia Kazan, 26 March 1957, b.83 f.4, CC/NYPL; Lawrence, *Dance with Demons*, 248. Kazan was known for such films as *On the Waterfront* (1954) but also for his friendly testimony to the House Un-American Activities Committee, touched on in chapter 4.

11. Crawford, *One Naked Individual*, 214.

12. Ibid.

13. Robbins's marginal notes on letter from Amberson Enterprises Inc. to Floria Lasky, 8 March 1995, b.80 f.15, JRP/NYPL. See also the accounts in Sondheim, *Finishing the Hat*, 29–30; Laurents, *Original Story By*, 325–27; Crawford, *One Naked Individual*, 214.

14. Lawrence, *Dance with Demons*, 249; Shull, *Angels*, 117–20.

15. Arthur Gell, "Director Signed for Wouk's Play," *New York Times* (8 July 1957), 20.

16. Vaill, *Somewhere*, 261, 267.

17. Robbins to Tanaquil LeClerq, 25 February 1957, New York City Ballet Archives; Robbins, quoted in John Keating, "Far, Far from Verona: Jerome Robbins Does Research on Leather Jacket Set for Romeo-and-Juliet-Suggested *West Side Story*," *Cue* (13 July 1957), 12, b.69 f.11, JRPP/NYPL. See also the description of dances in Bernstein, "Cherubs Are Rumbling."

18. David Boroff, "Preparing the *West Side Story*," *Dance Magazine* 31, no. 8 (August 1957): 14–19; quote 15.

19. Robbins to LeClerq, 25 February 1957, New York City Ballet Archives.

20. Robbins, quoted in Boroff, "Preparing the *West Side Story*," 15.

21. Casting and Contact Lists, b.85 f.12, JRP/NYPL. Emphasis in original.

22. Robbins, quoted in Garebian, *Making of West Side Story*, 110.

23. Charles D. Rice, "Juliet Lights Up Broadway," *Los Angeles Times* (1 December 1957), 1.

24. Zadan, *Sondheim & Co.*, 18.

25. Lawrence, *Carol Lawrence*, 38–39.

26. Lawrence, *Dance with Demons*, 249. Prince came to expect this anxiety from Robbins, even though he thought Robbins was better prepared for rehearsals than many other directors. Robbins, he recalled, found it difficult to face the eager, expectant cast members. Prince, *Contradictions*, 33.

27. For in-depth treatment of Bernstein's score, see Wells, *West Side Story*, chap. 3; Smith, *There's a Place for Us*, chap. 5.

28. Boroff, "Preparing the *West Side Story*," 19.

29. Lawrence, *Dance with Demons*, 253; *West Side Stories*.

30. Muriel Fischer, "Charming Misfit: Lee Becker Strikes a Happy Balance between Stage Role and Realism," *New York World-Telegram* (15 February 1958), b.69 f.14, JRPP/NYPL.

31. Vaill, *Somewhere*, 286.

32. Script excerpts, b.81 f.3, JRP/NYPL.

33. Chauncey, *Gay New York*, gives a detailed view of gay life in the city that ends in the 1940s: see especially the epilogue. D'Emilio, *Sexual Politics*, picks up the story in the 1950s and chronicles the impact of anticommunism, the growing urban subculture, and the new organization of a political movement for civil rights in chap. 3. D. A. Miller in *Place for Us* theorizes the role Broadway musicals played as an externalized genre of the secretive, isolated, and closeted life of many gay men. In his memoirs, Laurents describes a vivid gay life, cruising on the Upper East Side in Robbins's neighborhood, going to cocktail parties and dinner parties; see *Original Story By*, esp. 403.

34. Robbins's Annotated Script, n.d., b.82 f.1, JRP/NYPL.

35. "Tony and Maria" annotated script, n.d. [Spring 1956?], b.82 f.5, JRP/NYPL.

36. Robert Wise, "W.W.S.—Notes," n.d. [1960?], b.37 f.12, RW/USC.

37. Lyrics manuscripts, b.18 f.1, SS/WHS; Sondheim, *Finishing the Hat*, 42–43.

38. Manuscripts of lyrics can be found in SS/WHS. One version of these songs—with commentary by Sondheim—has also been published in Sondheim, *Finishing the Hat*, 31–53.

39. Ibid., 33.

40. Prince, *Contradictions*, 34.

41. Ibid., 35.

42. Vaill, *Somewhere*, 286–87.

43. Dorothy Kilgallen, "What's in a Name? Side Finds Out," *Washington Post* (24 July 1957), B8; Arthur Laurents, "The Growth of an Idea," *New York Herald Tribune* (4 August 1957), sect. 4, 1. For photographic spreads, see Friedman-Abeles, "Broadway's New Season Begins to Stir," *New York Times* (28 July 1957), 65. For discussion of Robbins's research, see Keating, "Far, Far From Verona."

44. Washington reviews include Richard L. Coe, "'West Side' Has That Beat," *Washington Post* (20 August 1957), B12, and Maxine Chesire, "Composer Bernstein Tells Capitalities: West Side Story Is 'Poetry,'" *Washington Post* (20 August 1957), B3. For a story based on the AP wire, see "New Musical Show Scores in Premiere," *Los Angeles Times* (20 August 1957), 23.

45. *Evening Star* (Washington DC) (20 August 1957), b.69 f.11, JRPP/NYPL.

46. Jay Carmody, *Sunday Star* (Washington, DC) (25 August 1957), b.69 f.11, JRPP/NYPL.

47. "Musical's Authors Get Key to Capital," *New York Times* (31 August 1957), 18.

48. Zadan, *Sondheim & Co.*, 25.

49. *Life* (16 September 1957), 103–6; Bernstein, "Cherubs Are Rumbling"; Hirschfeld drawing, *New York Times* (22 September 1957), 133; article on casting, Murray Schumach, "Talent Dragnet," *New York Times* (22 September 1957), 135. See also the spread by photographer Fred Fehl, *New York Times* (8 September 1957), SM31, as well as Robert Bvett's review, which concentrated on Bernstein, "Bernstein's *Romeo & Juliet*," *New Republic* (9 September 1957), 21.

50. Brooks Atkinson, "Theatre: Jungles of the City," *New York Times* (27 September 1957), 14; Walter Kerr, "West Side Story," *New York Herald Tribune* (27 September 1957), 10.

51. Leo Lerman, "The Playbill Diarist" (column in *Playbill*), week of 14 October 1957, Playbills Collection, NYPL. For views of both a critic and a few audience members, all of

whom praise the show, see "What Audience Thought of Play," *New York Journal American* (27 September 1957), 18.

52. Brooks Atkinson, "West Side Story," *New York Times* (6 October 1957), 133. "Jungles of the City" had been the subtitle of Atkinson's first review, *New York Times* (27 September 1957), 14.

53. John Chapman, n.p. [*Daily News?*], n.d. [27 September 1957?], b.69 f.11, JRPP/NYPL.

54. Oliver Smith to Robbins, 5 April 1956; personal collection, Rosaria Sinisi. Works of Oliver Smith copyright Rosaria Sinisi.

55. *New York World-Telegram*, n.d. [27 September 1957?], b.326, Scrapbook, HP/NYPL.

56. Marya Mannes, "Theater: A Question of Timing," *The Reporter* (14 November 1957), 38.

57. Marya Mannes, "Black and White in New York," *The Listener* (9 January 1958), 59.

58. *New York World-Telegram*, n.d. [27 September 1957?], b.326, Scrapbook, HP/NYPL.

59. Howard A. Rusk, "The Facts Don't Rhyme," *New York Times* (29 September 1957), 83.

60. "Protestas de Críticos Porque 'West Side Story' Denigra a los Boricuas," *El Diario* (New York) (2 October 1957). Translated by Lina Maria Villegas Gutierrez.

61. "Chita Rivera desempeña una parte destacada en 'West Side Story,'" *La Prensa* (10 September 1957), and an editorial by Eliseo Combas Guerra in *El Mundo* (10 October 1957) berate Isern; Isern's response can be found in "Señala él había censurado error en 'West Side Story,'" *El Mundo* (12 October 1957). Translated by Lina Maria Villegas Gutierrez.

62. "Muñoz elogia West Side Story," *El Mundo* (15 October 1957), 12. Translated by Lina Maria Villegas Gutierrez.

63. Henry Raymont, "Señalan el exito West Side Story," *El Mundo* (9 September 1957). See also a return to the question in *El Mundo* a few years later by Arturo Parrilla, "'West Side Story' sigue triunfando en Broadway" (27 August 1960), 10. Translated by Lina Maria Villegas Gutierrez.

64. *El Mundo* (28 September 1957); Virginia Maldonado, "'West Side Story' no denigra a los Puertorriqueños," *El Imparcial* (26 October 1957), S-4. Translated by Lina Maria Villegas Gutierrez.

65. "Actitud equivocada," *El Diario* (2 October 1957), 13. Translated by Lina Maria Villegas Gutierrez.

66. Maldanado, "West Side Story no denigra."

67. Snyder, "Useless and Terrible Death," gives a compelling synopsis of this transformation by looking at the death of Michael Farmer in Washington Heights in late July 1957. See also Schneider, *Vampires, Dragons, and Egyptian Kings*; Flamm, *Law and Order*.

68. Sondheim, *Finishing the Hat*, 52.

69. Henry Hewes, "The Cool Generation," *Saturday Review* (5 October 1957), 22.

70. Harold Clurman, "Theatre," *Nation* (12 October 1957), 250–51. Brooks Atkinson, in his second review in the *New York Times* (6 October 1957), 133, also derides the Krupke number as making a laugh out of a serious problem; Arthur Todd, writing in *Dance Observer* (November 1957), 136, calls the song "tasteless" but does not condemn the show overall because of it.

71. Robbins, on *Look Up and Live*, 1958, produced by Jack Kuney, Jerome Robbins Collection/NYPL.

72. Crawford to Laurents, 11 April 1957, b.43 f.2, RS/LOC. Emphasis in original.

73. The idea of having gang members and teenagers see the show came up almost immediately in the reviews of it; see letters to the editor: "Found in the Drama Mailbag," *New York Times* (13 October 1957), 123, as well as letter from a 17-year-old who recommended that every teenager see it, *New York Times* (3 November 1957), 139. For a review of the

practice that mentions the recorded session by Young, see "Story Acts as J.D. Deterrent," by John McClain in *New York Journal American* (2 November 1958), n.p.

74. "*West Side Story* discussion [sound recording]," n.d. [1958], Harold Prince audiovisual recordings, Rodgers and Hammerstein Archives of Recorded Sound, NYPL.

CHAPTER 4

1. Walter Kerr, "West Side Story," *New York Herald Tribune* (27 September 1957), 10.

2. Walter Kerr, "Sharks and Jets Battle in Dance," *New York Herald Tribune* (6 October 1957): sect.4, 1.

3. *Daily News* (27 September 1957), b.69 f.12, JRPP/NYPL.

4. Robbins, quoted in Boroff, "Preparing *West Side Story*," 17.

5. See *Life* (9 September 1957 and 16 September 1957).

6. A. Bloom, "Letters to the Editor: West Side Moral," *Washington Post* (6 September 1957), A10.

7. Henry Hewes, "The Cool Generation," *Saturday Review* (5 October 1957), 22.

8. Peter Stearns, in *American Cool*, and Joel Dinerstein, in both "Lester Young and the Birth of Cool" and the Smithsonian exhibit and catalog *American Cool*, detail the long history of this style and approach. *The Cool World*, a 1959 novel by Warren Miller (made into a film released in 1963), fused this style with gang life in Harlem. The numerous jazz renditions of *West Side Story*, by musicians from Andre Previn to Oscar Peterson, Stan Kenton, and Dave Brubeck, also connect "Cool" to the lingo's original setting.

9. Grover Dale, who played Snowball in the original cast of the musical, described the dance in Lewis Segal, "Keeping 'West Side Story' Cool," *Los Angeles Times* (8 June 1997), 49.

10. Walter Terry, "The 'West Side' Dance Story," *New York Herald Tribune* (20 October 1957), sect. 4, 7.

11. Marya Mannes, "Theater: A Question of Timing," *The Reporter* (14 November 1957), 38.

12. "Shows on Broadway: West Side Story," *Variety* (2 October 1957), 72.

13. Atkinson, "Jungles of the City," 14. For another view of the power of the dance, see Richard P. Cooke, "The Theatre: Tough and Tender," *Wall Street Journal* (30 September 1957), 8.

14. "The Bad Loser," *Time* (10 October 1960), 28. For more on relations between Khrushchev and Macmillan, see Geelhoed and Edmonds, *Eisenhower, Macmillan and Allied Unity*. For more on Khrushchev's visit to the United States, see Fursenko and Naftali, *Khrushchev's Cold War*; Taubman, *Khrushchev*. For a more personal investigation of the shoe banging and what it might have entailed, see Nina Khrushchev, "Case of Khrushchev's Shoe."

15. Noonan, *Strange Career of Porgy and Bess*, 196; chap. 4 discusses the international tour more generally. For the role of jazz, dance, visual arts, and literature in cultural diplomacy in the 1950s and 1960s, see Von Eschen, *Satchmo Blows Up the World*; Prevots, *Dance for Export*; Croft, *Dancers as Diplomats*; Barnhisel, *Cold War Modernists*.

16. For a fuller treatment of this visit, see Hallinan, "1958 Tour."

17. *New York Post* (8 May 1958), b.69 f.14, JRPP/NYPL.

18. "2D Day in City Busy for Soviet Visitors," *New York Times* (9 July 1958), 29.

19. Harold Prince to Robbins, 2 July 1958, b.75 f.2, JRP/NYPL.

20. Edith Evans Asbury, "'West Side Story' Plays Host to Frolicsome Bolshoi Dancers,"

New York Times (30 April 1959), 36. See also *New York Mirror* (29 April 1959) and *World Telegram*, n.d. [29 or 30 April 1959?], b.69 f.15, JRPP/NYPL; Stuart Little, "Half of Bolshoi Dancers Attend 'West Side Story,'" *New York Herald Tribune* (30 April 1959), 17.

21. Harold Prince to Hugh Beaumont, managing director of H. M. Tennet Ltd. (whose nickname was Binkie), 25 May 1959 and 9 June 1959, b.194 f.29, HP/NYPL.

22. For a detailed look at one such visit, see Croft, "Ballet Nations."

23. Prince to "fellas," 5 June 1959, b.75 f.2, JRP/NYPL.

24. Khrushchev, quoted in "Last Words," *Time* (31 October 1960), 20.

25. Prince to Art Buchwald, in the Paris office of the *New York Herald Tribune*, 16 March 1960, b.198 f.4, HP/NYPL. This version of what happened did not make it into the papers.

26. "Russians to See U.S. Plays," *New York Times* (1 September 1959), 21.

27. Prince to Gennady Osipov, Chairman Statue Committee for Cultural Relations with Foreign Countries (Moscow), 2 September 1959, b.198 f.4, HP/NYPL.

28. Prince to Buchwald, 16 March 1960, b.198 f.4, HP/NYPL.

29. Prince to Ambassador Lacy, 30 December 1959, b.198 f.4, HP/NYPL. William Lacy, the former US ambassador to Korea, had negotiated the 1958 cultural exchange agreement with the Soviets.

30. Frank G. Siscoe, Director East-West Contacts Staff, to Prince, 29 February 1960, b.198 f.4, HP/NYPL.

31. The script was published with the title "The History of the Western Outskirts" in *Sovremennaya Dramaturgija* (Soviet Dramaturgia), vol.14 (Moskow: Iskusstvo Pub., 1959), 275–342 (translation by A. Afonina and L. Moroshkina); RSAL. Translation by Mariya Smirnov, with research help in Moscow by Daria Lotareva.

32. Prince to Ambassador Lacy, 30 December 1959, b.198 f.4, HP/NYPL.

33. Drama Advisory Panel Meeting, International Cultural Exchange Service, 21 February 1958, b.102 f.6, BEC/UA.

34. Drama Advisory Panel Meeting, International Cultural Exchange Service, 22 May 1959, b.102 f.6, BEC/UA.

35. Drama Advisory Panel Meeting, International Cultural Exchange Service, 22 May 1959, b.102 f.6, BEC/UA. For an analysis of the sunny, heterosexual love story of most musicals, see Wolf, *Changed for Good*.

36. Prince to Micheline Rozan, MCA Paris, 23 September 1958, b.196 f.3, HP/NYPL.

37. [No author, n.p.] (6 November 1958), b.69 f.14, JRPP/NYPL; "'West Side Story' Off to London," *New York Herald Tribune* (6 November 1958), 23.

38. Griffith to Robbins, 14 July 1958, b.75 f.2, JRP/NYPL.

39. See, for example, the letters from Griffith and Prince to Robbins, n.d. [1958?], and from Harold Freeman, Laurents's agent, to Griffith and Prince, 31 October 1958, b.76 f.9, JRP/NYPL.

40. Walter Terry, "Robbins Musical London-Bound," *New York Herald Tribune* (16 November 1958), sect. 4, 5.

41. Travel Diary of Albert Ottenheimer, 7/13/61, b.42 f.13, AO/UO.

42. "Soup with Robbins," *New Yorker* (4 April 1959), 33.

43. "Musical Turns to Tragedy," *London Times* (13 December 1958), 3.

44. "'West Side Story' Wows West End: Top Musical Sensation since 'Okla,'" *Variety* (17 December 1958), 71; "By the Throat," *Newsweek* (29 December 1958), 28.

45. Paul Phelan, "'West Side's' Second Story: A Smash Hit in London," n.p. n.d. [1959?], b.69, f.20, JRPP/NYPL.

46. Harold Myers, "London Critics' 17-to-1 Vote," *Variety* (8 July 1959), 89.

47. Paul Phelan, "'West Side's' Second Story: A Smash Hit in London," n.p., n.d. [1959?]; Don Cook, "'West Side Story' a Hit in London," n.p., n.d. [1959?], b.69 f.20, JRPP/NYPL.

48. "A Generation in Revolt," *Guardian* (11 September 1962), 3. See also the comments of the American journalist W. J. Igoe writing from London, "The Generation Trapped between Levels of Society," *Chicago Daily Tribune* (30 December 1962), D6, and *A Waste of Public Money*, a contemporaneous novel on the theme of juvenile delinquency by British writer Robin Chapman. For a cultural history of zoot suits, see Peiss, *Zoot Suit*.

49. "Soup with Robbins," *New Yorker* (4 April 1959), 33.

50. Don Cook, "West Side Story a Hit in London," n.p., n.d. [1959], b.69 f.20, JRPP/ NYPL. See also clipping [n.p., n.d.] that claims "its themes of racial intolerance has a contemporary parallel in London," b.69 f.14, JRPP/NYPL.

51. Script draft, January 1956, b.17 f.4, SS/WHS.

52. Albert Ottenheimer's letter to Florence Bean James, another founder of the Seattle Playhouse who also was put on trial before the Canwell Committee, gives a personal and detailed account of his testimony in 1955 in New York. He mentions intentionally evading the period of his working for the labor school and the union in his testimony; Ottenheimer to Florence [Bean James], 21 August 1955, b.2 f.3, AO/UO.

53. Ottenheimer to Norman Felton, CBS TV Network, 26 December 1958, b.5 f.7, AO/UO.

54. Copy of Ottenheimer's testimony on Communist Activities in the New York Area, b.2 f.4, AO/UO. For a personal account of the testimony, see his letter to Florence Bean James; Ottenheimer to Florence [Bean James], 21 August 1955, b.2 f.3, AO/UO. Ottenheimer was contacted in 1970 by a doctoral student looking at the influence of HUAC on American theater and responded extensively to a questionnaire about his activities. His response is a good summary of the intertwining of his career, communism, and anticommunism; see Oppenheimer to Robert Vaughn, 15 March 1970, b.3 f.1, AO/UO. His papers also include poignant letters between himself and his brother that document the personal cost of these activities.

55. Albert Ottenheimer, "Life in the Gutter," *New Yorker* (15 August 1959), 82–86.

56. Ottenheimer to Kenneth Littauer (his agent), 9 September 1959, b.22 f.4, AO/UO.

57. Ottenheimer, draft of "The Not-So-Lonesome Road," b.22 f.5, AO/UO.

58. [No author, no title], *New Yorker* (7 December 1957), 44.

59. "Marjory Adams, "Ability to Do Back Flip Landed Kert in Theater," *Boston Globe* (1 April 1960), 37.

60. *San Francisco Examiner* (11 October 1959), b.326 Scrapbook, HP/NYPL.

61. Claudia Cassidy, "On the Aisle: Chicago Theater in 'The Visit,' 'Look Homeward, Angel,' and 'West Side Story,'" *Chicago Tribune* (13 December 1959), F9; Claudia Cassidy, "On the Aisle: At Least the Town Is a Bit Worked Up about 'West Side Story,'" *Chicago Tribune* (17 December 1959), C11; "Stage Notes," *Chicago Tribune* (5 January 1960), B3.

62. Brooks Atkinson, "Theatre: Musical Is Back," *New York Times* (28 April 1960), 31.

CHAPTER 5

1. Robbins, quoted in "Small Rumble," *New Yorker* (2 April 1960), 35. Recent commentary on the film includes Acevedo-Muñoz, *West Side Story as Cinema*, and a group memoir of dancers in the film, *Our Story*. Berson, *Something's Coming*, and Herrera, *Latin Numbers*, also discuss the musical and the film.

2. Jerome Robbins to Robert Wise, 4 April 1960; Wise to Robbins, 8 April 1960; Robbins to Wise, n.d. [mid-April 1960]; b.78 f.15, JRP/NYPL.

3. W. J. Weatherby, "West Side Diary," *Manchester Guardian Weekly* (1 March 1962), 14.

4. Robbins to Wise, 4 April 1960, b.78 f.15, JRP/NYPL. Emphasis in original.

5. Wise to Robbins, 8 April 1960, b.78 f.15, JRP/NYPL.

6. Robbins, handwritten notes, n.d. [February 1960?], b.86 f.6, JRP/NYPL.

7. Prologue photo collage, b.87 f.10–14, JRP/NYPL. In claiming that Robbins "envisioned the movie as a black-and-white film noir," Vaill may be referring to this collage; *Somewhere*, 322.

8. Robbins's handwritten note, b.87 f.10, JRP/NYPL.

9. Saul Bass, "A Visual Interpretation of the Rough Shooting Continuity—The Prologue," 4 May 1960, b.86 f.6, JRP/NYPL. This is the first mention of aerial shots in connection with the prologue. Wise oversaw the actual aerial shooting in August 1960 but has also taken credit for the idea; see Leemann, *Robert Wise on His Films*, 166. For an overview of the work of Bass, see Jennifer Bass and Kirkham, *Saul Bass*.

10. Bass, "Visual Interpretation."

11. Bass, "Visual Interpretation." Emphasis in original.

12. Bass, "Visual Interpretation"; Partial Storyboard Prologue, "The Time Before," SB/AMPAS.

13. Robbins, "West Side Story Movie—Notes," 12 June 1960, b.86 f.5, JRP/NYPL.

14. "New York Location List," n.d. [February 1960], b.87 f.9, JRP/NYPL.

15. "Tests," n.d. [Robbins's handwritten notes, February 1960], b.86 f.8, JRP/NYPL. Emphasis in original.

16. Wise, quoted in Hollis Alpert, "'West Side Story': A Brilliant Stage Production Starts to Become a Film," *Dance Magazine* (October 1960), 39.

17. Wise to Bob Relyea, "West Side Scheduling," 13 June 1960, b.86 f.3, JRP/NYPL.

18. [Dance . . . Background], n.d. [June or July 1960?], b.86 f.7, JRP/NYPL.

19. Robbins, quoted in Alpert, "West Side Story," 36.

20. Robbins, quoted in *Observer Weekend Review* [*Guardian*, UK] (18 February 1962), 65.

21. Leven received an Oscar for his art direction on the film, but still carried some anger over Bass's role. A passage in a review by Arthur Knight—"It is always difficult to assign credit where it is due in a movie. . . . One can only say that Saul Bass, the visual consultant, and/or Boris Leven, the production designer have made this film as exciting pictorially as it is musically and dramatically"—prompted an angry letter from Leven proclaiming that "Mr. Bass had absolutely nothing, and I repeat, nothing to do with either the conception, or the design, or the color or the ideas for lighting of any of the sets or backgrounds—or with anything that had to do with the visual aspect of the film"; Arthur Knight, "Romeo Revisited," *Saturday Review* (14 October 1961), 40; Leven to Arthur Knight, 13 October 1961, BL/AMPAS. The "visual interpretation" of the prologue that Bass put together, as well as the abstract montage he worked on with Robbins, suggest that Bass did make a crucial contribution to the visual look of the film—even if it was in choosing which approach not to take.

22. Leven to Wise, "West Side Story on Film" [1960], b.1 f.20, BL/USC.

23. *Look* (18 February 1958): "This Is New York," 29–116; "The Changing Face of New York," 65–69; "Behind New York's Façade," 70–71. Wise's files included "The Changing Face of New York," and "Tourist's-Eye View of Manhattan," b.37 f.20, RW/USC.

24. Leven to Wise, "West Side Story on Film" [1960], Leven Collection, b.1 f.20, BL/USC.

25. D'Andrea, in *Our Story*, 182.

26. Moreno, *Rita Moreno*, 32, 37.

27. Ibid., 183.

28. Finstad, *Natasha*, 228.

29. Relyea and Relyea, *Not So Quiet on the Set*, 150.

30. Philip K. Scheuer, "'West Side Story' Takes Over Studio," *Los Angeles Times* (12 December 1960), C13.

31. Relyea and Relyea, *Not So Quiet on the Set*, 155.

32. Robbins to Robert Fizdale, 5 June 1960, quoted in Vaill, *Somewhere*, 323.

33. W. J. Weatherby, "Change of Medium," *Guardian* (10 March 1961), 5.

34. Ibid., quoting Robbins.

35. Robbins, quoted in Alpert, "West Side Story," 36, 39.

36. Robbins to Cheryl Crawford, 12 July 1960; quoted in Vaill, *Somewhere*, 323.

37. Ibid.

38. Ibid.

39. Robbins described the difference between dance onstage and on film using the example of stepping forward and back in Weatherby, "Change of Medium."

40. Banas, in *Our Story*, 95.

41. Evans, in *Our Story*, 92. For confirmations of the hot, intense conditions of filming "Cool," see, also in *Our Story*, the reminiscences of Tony Mordente (13–14) and Robert Banas (95, 115).

42. Manguel, *With Borges*, 23–24 on *West Side Story*, 21 on "wholly verbal world." See also Ronald Christ's interview with Borges, "Art of Fiction No.39."

43. Linwood G. Dunn, ["West Side Story"], description for award nominations for optical and audible effects, ca. 1961, PF/AMPAS.

44. Robbins, "Notes taken at running Sunday, 4/2/61," b.86 f.5, JRP/NYPL.

45. Robbins, "Notes taken at running Sunday, 4/2/61."

46. Paul V. Beckley, "West Side Story," *New York Herald Tribune*, 19.

47. Knight, "Romeo Revisited."

48. Wise, quoted in *Show* (October 1961), PF/AMPAS.

49. "West Side Story," *Variety* (27 September 1961), 6.

50. Knight, "Romeo Revisited."

51. Robbins to Wise, 12 April 1961, b.86 f.9, JRP/NYPL.

52. Robbins, "Notes on West Side Story Film," 12 April 1961, b.86 f.9, JRP/NYPL.

53. Ibid.

54. The only appearance of African Americans in the film is in the gymnasium dance scene, where a few line the walls in the background.

55. The film prompted at least one personal campaign against the "anti–Puerto Rican propaganda" the writer thought it displayed. R. Dominguez to Robert Wise, 31 October 1961, b.37 f.2, RW/USC.

56. Both Sandoval-Sánchez, "*West Side Story*," and Herrera, *Latin Numbers*, give a detailed analysis of this.

57. Moreno, *Rita Moreno*, 187.

58. Miyamoto's story of her transformation from playing a Puerto Rican in the film to embracing her Japanese heritage—and of time in a relocation camp for Japanese Americans during World War II—is a compelling example of the struggle to belong; see *Our Story*, 224–36.

59. Motion Picture Association of America, History of Cinema: Hollywood and the Production Code, reel 32, AMPAS.

60. Paredez, "Queer for Uncle Sam."

61. Sidney Skolsky, "The Mail Bag," *Citizen News* (10 February 1962), CF/AMPAS.

62. Lehman, "Notes WestSide Story," n.d. [November 1959], b.128 f.11, EL/HRC.

63. Robbins, quoted in Alpert, "West Side Story," 36.

64. Leemann, *Robert Wise on His Films*, 166.

65. *New York Post* (19 October 1961), b.67 f.6, JRPP/NYPL. There were dissenters. "Instead of framing a musical with the imaginative power of suggestion, the first ten minutes or so of the film were shot in the streets of New York. It was probably a courageous idea, and some people will doubtless find it acceptable, even piquant. Personally it struck me as pure hokum. Far from looking like shook-up teenage mobsters, to me they just look like a posse of ballet kids, having a ball and camping it up," wrote the dance critic Clive Barnes,

"Clive Barnes on Jerome Robbins and West Side Story," *Dance and Dancers* (March 1962), 14–17; quote 15.

66. Optical effects described by Dunn for Academy nomination, 1961/62; "As the abstract painting had originally been generated from one frame of the aerial scene, a dissolve to this held frame made a smooth transition into the action." PF/AMPAS.

67. Robbins, quoted in Alpert, "West Side Story," 36.

68. For a detailed analysis of the geographical setting of each shot, see http://www.pop spotsnyc.com/west_side_story/.

69. Michaels, in *Our Story*, 49.

70. Relyea and Relyea, *Not So Quiet on the Set*, 149–50. See also a letter from the social worker who gathered the neighborhood boys, thanking the film production for a party for them after the filming: John Gomez to Allen Wood, 22 September 1960, b.37 f.9, RW/USC. Wood was the film's production manager but is perhaps more famous as the inspiration behind the "Vote for Al Wood" posters seen in the prologue.

71. Banas, in *Our Story*, 106.

72. *West Side Memories*.

73. Robbins to Wise, n.d. [mid-April 1960], b.78 f.15, JRP/NYPL.

74. Brendan Gill, "Outsize," *New Yorker* (21 October 1961), 197.

75. Zipp, *Manhattan Projects*, uses the prologue of the film to convey some of these contradictions in urban policy. See especially pp. 157–59.

76. *Hollywood Reporter* (22 September 1961), b.1 f.118, BL/USC.

77. Knight, "Romeo Revisited."

CHAPTER 6

1. "'West Side' Film to Debut Here Dec. 14," *Los Angeles Times* (8 June 1961), C13.

2. Philip K. Scheuer, "'West Side Story' Takes Over Studio," *Los Angeles Times* (12 December 1960), C13.

3. Bosley Crowther, "Musical Advance: The 'West Side Story' Expands on Screen," *New York Times* (22 October 1961), X1.

4. Pauline Kael, "*West Side Story* Is a Highly Overrated Movie," in *I Lost It at the Movies*, 147.

5. Picker, quoted in "'Story' May Set New Musical Pattern in Foreign Sites as It Jingles at B.O.," *Variety* (27 March 1962), 1, 4; quote 4. See also "'West Side Story' Setting Records, Picker reports," *Hollywood Reporter* (27 March 1962), 1, 9; *Motion Picture Daily* (27 March 1962), b.183 f.7, and United Artists Press Release (26 March 1962), b.128 f.22, in EL/HRC. On profits, see Thomas Thompson, "Tuning U.S. Musicals to Overseas Box Office," *Life* (12 March 1965), 55, 58; and records in b.88 f.22, JRP/NYPL. On the Paris fan, see "'West Side Story' 3 Years in One Paris Movie House," *New York Times* (27 January 1965), 27. Multiple reviews of the film are in PF/AMPAS and EL/HRC.

6. "A Real Fan, He," *Chicago Daily Defender* (16 December 1963), 7.

7. Herb Caen, "And Who Will Buy My Violence," *Los Angeles Times* (24 April 1962), A5.

8. Kenneth Harman writing to critic Philip Scheuer, "Paul Gallico Story Sold to Seven Arts," *Los Angeles Times* (30 April 1962), C13.

9. Producer of the first European tour, Pete Kameron, quoted in Buchwald, n.d., n.p. [April 1961], b.89 f.9, JRP/NYPL.

10. Audrey Wood to Hugh Beaumont, 20 March 1961, b.76 f.10, JRP/NYPL.

11. Ken LeRoy to Robbins, 31 March 1961, b.76 f.10, JRP/NYPL.

12. Robbins to Beaumont, 27 December 1960, b.76 f.10, JRP/NYPL.

13. Robbins to Beaumont, 9 January 1961, b.76 f.10, JRP/NYPL.

14. Beaumont to Carl Fisher, 8 April 1959, b.194 f.29, HP/NYPL. See also discussions in b.75 f.2, JRP/NYPL.

15. Interview with Giora Godik by Albert Ottenheimer, 19 July 1961, b.22 f.2, AO/UO.

16. Travel Diary, 1/21/61, b.42 f.9, AO/UO.

17. Travel Diary, 1/29/61, b.42 f.10, AO/UO.

18. Ottenheimer to Florence [Bean James], 18 March 1961, b.8 f.2, AO/UO.

19. Travel Diary, 2/5/61, b.42, f.10, AO/UO.

20. *Haaretz* (15 February 1961); original article and translation from Hebrew b.130 f.5, EL/HRC. My thanks to Oz Frankel for insight into and context for the production in Israel. For additional items from Israel, such as a program and souvenirs, see b.44 f.3–4, AO/UO.

21. *Maariv* (17 February 1961); *Hazofeh* (17 February 1961). Original articles and translations from Hebrew in b.130 f.5 EL/HRC.

22. *Maariv* (17 February 1961); original article and translation from Hebrew b.130 f.5, EL/HRC.

23. *Haaretz* (15 February 1961); for another analogy to Europe, see *Hamishmar* (15 February 1961). Original articles and translations from Hebrew in b.130 f.5 EL/HRC.

24. Ottenheimer to Kenneth Littauer, 23 April 1961, b.8 f.2, AO/UO.

25. Ottenheimer to Florence [Bean James], 18 March 1961, b.8 f.2, AO/UO. See also Travel Diary entries throughout February and March 1961.

26. Ottenheimer to Florence [Bean James], 18 March 1961, b.8 f.2, AO/UO. In another description, Ottenheimer describes the "Morrocan Jew" as a "very dark-skinned Yemenite"; Travel Diary 3/10/61, b.42 f.10, AO/UO.

27. Travel Diary, 3/30/61, b.42 f.11, AO/UO.

28. Laurents to "WSS Brass" [Harold Prince, Robert Griffith, Leonard Bernstein, Jerome Robbins, and Stephen Sondheim], n.d. [April 1961], b.194 f.29, HP/NYPL.

29. Andre Ransan, *L'Aurore* (3 April 1961): "an astonishing cocktail of everything: of drama, comedy, music, singing, dancing and ballet, of theater, musichall, nightclub and even circus." Jean-Jacques Gautier, *Le Figaro* (1 April 1961), was shocked, "punched in the chest." Translated articles in b.130 f.3, EL/HRC. For reviews from the French production, see b.22 f.1 and b.44 f.2–3, AO/UO; b.89 f.9, JRP; and b.130 f.3, EL/HRC.

30. Jean-Jacques Gautier, *Le Figaro* (1 April 1961); b.89 f.9, JRP/NYPL. Translation by Aissatou Diallo.

31. Maurice Tassart, *Le Parisien* (1 April 1961); translated article in b.130 f.3, EL/HRC.

32. Gerard Desille, *Noir et Blanc* (7 April 1961); translated article in b.130 f.3, EL/HRC.

33. Jacques Bourgeois, *Arts* (29 March 1961); translated article in b.130 f.3, EL/HRC.

34. Michel Perez, *Combat* (5 April 1961); translated article in b.130 f.3, EL/HRC. For discussion of what to call the production, see *Combat* (31 March and 3 April 1961); *L'Aurore* (3 April 1961); *Le Parisien Libere* (1 April 1961); *France Soir* (1 April 1961); *Paris Jour* (1–2 April 1961); *Lettres Francaises* (6–12 April 1961); b.89 f.9, JRP/NYPL. Translation by Aissatou Diallo.

35. Travel Diary, 4/16/61, b.42 f.11, AO/UO.

36. Travel Diary, 4/22/61, b.42 f.11, AO/UO.

37. *France Soir* (1 April 1961), b.89 f.9, JRP/NYPL.

38. Travel Diary, 5/21/61, b.42 f.12, AO/UO.

39. Travel Diary, 4/16/61, b.42 f.11, AO/UO.

40. See "Happy Debut at the Teatro Comunale" and other articles in b.44 f.1, AO/UO. Translation by Meghan Robison.

41. Travel Diary, 6/11 and 6/12, b.42 f.12, AO/UO.

42. "Ruhm und Raffinement der West Side Story," *Feuilleton* [n.d. 1961?], b.45 f.1, AO/UO. Translation by Divina Hasselmann.

43. Travel Diary, 6/27/61, b.42 f.12, AO/UO.

44. Travel Diary, 6/16/61, b.42 f.12, AO/UO.

45. Travel Diary, 6/24/61, b.42 f.12, AO/UO.

46. Margreet Koch, "West Side Story: puur theater in gave balans," *Het Vrije Volk* (22 July 1961), 6. Translation by Pieter-Paul Pothoven.

47. Travel Diary, 7/20/61, b.42 f.13, AO/UO.

48. Kelly, *One Singular Sensation*, 28.

49. Travel Diary, 8/12–8/14, b.42 f.13, AO/UO.

50. Travel Diary, 8/18/61 and 8/26/61, b.42 f.13, AO/UO.

51. "'West Side Story' Lyrics Will Be Subtitled for Foreign Bookings," *Variety* (4 August 1961), 1, 14; "'Story' May Set New Musical Pattern in Foreign Sites as It Jingles at B.O.," *Variety* (27 March 1962), 1, 4.

52. *Gujarati Magazine* (June 1962), b.129 f.22, EL/HRC. Translation by Al-Noor Hirji.

53. John Neumeier to Arthur Laurents, 15 January 1979, b.79 f.19, JRP/NYPL.

54. Godik, quoted in "Steiler Zahn," n.p. n.d. [1961], Scrapbook, b.58, AO/UO. Translation by Divina Hasselmann.

55. Film Performance Distribution 1964–65, b.88 f.22, JRP/NYPL.

56. Thomas Thompson, "Tuning U.S. Musicals to Overseas Box Office," *Life* (12 March 1965), 55, 58, quote 58.

57. Craig Urquhart, VP of Public Relations, Amberson Enterprises Inc. to Robbins, referring to the Japanese magazine *Ongaku-no-Tomo*, 21 January 1998, b.77 f.20, JRP/NYPL.

58. N.p. (29 October 1964); multiple original reviews in b.89 f.10, JRP/NYPL. Translation by Aya Tasaki.

59. *Hochi Sport News* (8 November 1964), b.89 f.10, JRP/NYPL. Translation by Aya Tasaki.

60. Omori Minoru, "Broadway Musical and *West Side Story*"; see also Kusakake Hisashirou, "A Place Called Broadway"; *West Side Story* Program, 9 November–27 December 1964, Nissei Theatre. Copy in files of the author. Translation by Aya Tasaki.

61. Toshio Kawatake, "Opinions on Musicals," *West Side Story* Program, Nissei Theatre. Translation by Aya Tasaki.

62. Kazuo Mizuno, "West Side Story, Just as I Saw It," *West Side Story* Program, Nissei Theatre. Translation by Aya Tasaki.

63. Fuyuhiko Okabe, "A Live Musical on Stage Is Wonderful," *West Side Story* Program, Nissei Theatre. Translation by Aya Tasaki.

64. For concern about the troupe, see article in *Hochi* (10 November 1964); Robbins, quoted in *Sport Nippon* (8 November 1964), b.89 f.10, JRP/NYPL. Translation by Aya Tasaki. See also Szilard, *Under My Wings*.

65. *Sankei News* (11 November 1964), b.89 f.10, JRP/NYPL. Translation by Aya Tasaki.

66. *Sankei Sport* (11 November 1964), b.89 f.10, JRP/NYPL. Translation by Aya Tasaki.

67. "Osaka Cops Adopt 'West Side Story' To Hit Own Punks," *Variety* (28 March 1962), 1, 63; quote 63.

68. John L. Scott, "Orientals See a Different Side to 'West Side Story," *Los Angeles Times* (21 October 1962), 8.

69. *Japan Times* (19 November 1964), b.89 f.10, JRP/NYPL. Translation by Aya Tasaki.

70. W. J. Igoe, writing from London, "The Generation Trapped between Levels of Society," *Chicago Daily Tribune* (30 December 1962), D6.

71. William C. Kvaraceus, *Dynamics of Delinquency*, 27. See also Flamm, *Law and Order*; Gilbert, *Cycle of Outrage*; Ellis, ed., *Juvenile Delinquency*.

72. Adam Yarmolinsky, the Kennedy administration official, quoted in Flamm, *Law and Order*, 195.

73. William C. Kvaraceus, "Juvenile Delinquency: A Problem for the Modern World," UNESCO (1964).

74. Office of Cultural Presentations, Ad Hoc Drama Panel, 11 September 1963, MC 468 CU, b.102, f.7, BEC/UA.

75. Office of Cultural Presentations, Ad Hoc Drama Panel, 12 September 1963, b.102, f.7, BEC/UA.

76. Philip Coombs to Wise, 22 November 1961, b.37 f.2, RW/USC.

77. Wise to Coombs, 13 December 1961, b.37 f.2, RW/USC.

78. Travel Diary, 4/17/61, b.42 f.11, AO/UO.

79. "Titov Welcome," *Los Angeles Times* (3 May 1962), 16.

80. "Izvestia Sees Political Angle in Film Accident," *Los Angeles Times* (10 July 1963), 17; Jim Becker, "Kramer Says U.S. Denting Russian Armor," *Chicago Tribune* (23 July 1963), A4.

81. "'West Side Story Gets a Big Ovation at Moscow," *Newsday* (9 July 1963), 3C. See also "'West Side Story' Is Applauded in Soviet Film Festival Showing," *New York Times* (9 July 1963), 28.

82. "Izvestia Sees Political Angle in Film Accident," *Los Angeles Times* (10 July 1963), 17. The song "America" seems to have prompted an interpretive change in lyrics in translation of the film too, referenced in an article on the film: "Everybody is proud and free here/Here, every third is hungry!"; Georgi Makarov, "The Rise and Fall of the Musical," in *The Myth and the Reality: Foreign Cinema Today* (1972), 262; RSAL. Translation by Yulia Cherkasova. Reviews of the musical and film found in the Russian State Art Library with the help of Daria Lotareva.

83. "Soviets Finally Admit They Like 'West Side Story,'" *Chicago Tribune* (15 July 1963), B2.

84. Makarov, "The Rise and Fall of the Musical," 258. Translation by Yulia Cherkasova.

85. Y. Varshavskiy, "Stolen Youth," *Komsomol'skya Pravda* (14 July 1963), 4; RSAL. Translation by Yulia Cherkasova.

86. V. Shitova, "West Side Story," *On the World's Screens* (1966), 48; RSAL. Translation by Anthony Anemone.

87. Varshavskiy, "Stolen Youth."

88. Shitova, "West Side Story," 51.

89. "West Side Story Makes Bow in Soviet Union," *Boston Globe* (8 October 1963), 9; "An Armenian Ballet to Tour Soviet; Inspired by 'West Side Story,'" *Variety* (30 October 1963), 4.

90. "West Side Story Is Staged in Soviet," *New York Times* (31 December 1964), 11.

91. Miles Lourie, Orenstein, Arrow & Lourie, to Harold Levin, International Business Practices Division, State Department, 25 November 1964; b.77 f.25, JRP/NYPL.

92. Theodore Shabad, "In Moscow, 'West Side Story' Becomes Picture of Life in the U.S.," *New York Times* (25 June 1965), 37.

93. Fred Coleman, "'West Side' as Moscow Sees It," *Los Angeles Times* (26 June 1965), 15.

94. Richard C. Longworth, "'West Side Story' Puzzles Muscovites," *Washington Post* (25 June 1965), D13.

95. Y. Ostray, "Successes and Failures of a Certain Premiere," *Moskovskaya Pravda* (11 August 1965); RSAL. Translation by Mariya Smirnov.

96. Stephen S. Rosenfeld, "Russians Make It Da West Side Story" *Washington Post* (4 August 1965), B6; "New Ways of Old Genre," *Sovetskaya Rossiya* (3 August 1965); RSAL. A review in *Evening Moscow* (23 July 1965) mentions Laurents and Bernstein, but not Robbins; RSAL. "Moscow's 'Lady' May Run 10 Yrs.," *Newsday* (19 January 1965), 3C, claims that songs were retained in American musicals in the Soviet Union but set to a score by Russian musicians. Translations by Mariya Smirnov.

97. *Cheliabinskiy Rabochii* (11 July 1970); RSAL. Translation by Mariya Smirnov.

98. *Krasnoe Zanmia* (Tomsk) (16 May 1974); RSAL. Translation by Mariya Smirnov.

99. "Names & Faces in the News," *Boston Globe* (19 November 1968), 2; "People, Places, Problems," *Chicago Defender* (7 December 1968), 13.

100. Prince to Authors, 1 November 1965; Laurents to Prince, 5 November 1965; Prince to Laurents, 8 November 1965; Prince to Bill Ricketts, Chappell & Co., 17 November 1965; b. 198 f.2, HP/NYPL. See also Beaubien, "Cultural Boycott of South Africa."

101. Research by Robbins's office, August 1965; Floria Lasky to Allen Whitehead, Music Theatre International, 17 November 1965; b.78 f.5, JRP/NYPL.

102. David Holliday to Prince, 10 December 1965; Prince to Holliday, 27 December 1965; b. 198 f.2, HP/NYPL.

103. "South Africans Sue to Stage Musicals," *New York Times* (27 February 1968), 37; "Author's Objections Fail to Halt Production of 3 Shows in Africa, *New York Times* (18 February 1969), 34; Jean du Plessis, "U.S. to Fight Music Thefts," *Washington Post* (5 July 1968), A29; "SA 'piracy' clause may be invoked for musicals," *Stage and Television* (7 March 1968), 17.

104. "500 Zulu 'Extras' Not Allowed to See the Film They Made," *Irish Times* (22 November 1969), 11.

105. Music Theatre International to authors, 23 July 1997; Freddie Gershon, Music Theatre International, to Xu Xiaozhong, Central Academy of Drama, 16 July 1997; b.76 f.26, JRP/NYPL. For an overview of U.S. cultural power abroad after World War II, see de Grazia, *Irresistible Empire*, and Belmonte, *Selling the American Way*. For an analysis of dance as intellectual property, see Kraut, "Stealing Steps."

106. "New York Rhapsody: West Side Story Raises Performances to New Heights," *Star* (Johannesburg, South Africa; 4 December 1995); b.77 f.24, JRP/NYPL.

CHAPTER 7

1. Jerry [Simpson?] to Albert Ottenheimer, 23 July 1961, b.8 f.4, AO/UO.

2. "Rivoli Theatre Held Up," *New York Times* (26 February 1962), 55.

3. Bernard Weinraub, "There's a Place for Us?" *New York Times* (27 June 1965), X9.

4. Charles E. Davis Jr., "Hollywood's Ghosts Ask to Be Given Credit," *Los Angeles Times* (25 February 1962), J2; "Suit Charges Star Role Sung by Bit Player," *Los Angeles Times* (9 February 1963), B2. See also Nixon, *I Could Have Sung All Night*, 129–38.

5. John Martin, "Dance: Robbins' Troupe," *New York Times* (18 October 1961), 50.

6. Erin Martin, quoted in Lawrence, *Dance with Demons*, 296.

7. Emily Coleman, "From Tutus to T-Shirts," *New York Times* (8 October 1961), SM20.

8. For a thorough and compelling account of *Fiddler on the Roof* and its interweaving with Robbins's life, see Solomon, *Wonder of Wonders*.

9. Robbins, quoted in Lawrence, *Dance with Demons*, 245.

10. Moreno, *Rita Moreno*, 202.

11. "Encore Theater Accused of Practicing Racism," *Chicago Daily Defender* (18 September 1963), 16.

12. Andrés Roura to Roger Stevens, n.d. [October 1979], b.74 f.9, JRP/NYPL.

13. Hazel Garland, "CLO's 'West Side Story' Is Theatre at Its Best," *Pittsburgh Courier* (21 August 1965), 16. The production that Bennett choreographed included Walken and Alberghetti. For the impact of the show on Bennett, see Kelly, *One Singular Sensation*, 18–21, 36–37.

14. "Skokie Youths Film 'West Side Story,'" *Chicago Tribune* (14 March 1963), N2.

15. Mike McGrady, "Should NY Put Aye on Films," *Newsday* (2 October 1962), 3C.

16. Weinraub, "There's a Place for Us?"

17. Warren Miller, *Cool World*, 219 ("piece"), 100 ("projeck"). See also the 1963 film of the same name produced by Frederick Wiseman with music by Dizzy Gillespie.

18. William Kloman, "'2001' and 'Hair'—Are They the Groove of the Future," *New York Times* (12 May 1968), D15.

19. Dan Sullivan, "Theater: Jets vs. Sharks," *New York Times* (25 June 1968), 32.

20. Kavanagh, *Nureyev*, 119–20; Lawrence, *Dance with Demons*, 396; James M. Halbe, "Russian Ballet Star Who Fled Fascinates West," *Stars & Stripes* (28 August 1961), n.p.

21. Roslyn Sulcas, interview with Peter Martins, "City Ballet's Leader, 30 Years In," *New York Times* (21 April 2013), AR11.

22. Richard L. Coe, "Douglas Found They Like Us," *Washington Post* (11 April 1964), C15.

23. Mike Doerr, "Puerto Rico Pulls Itself Up by Its Operation Bootstrap," *Los Angeles Times* (26 November 1964), B11.

24. See JW Thompson news/NY news brochure (9 August 1968), in the records of the New York Foundation, b.175 f.1, NYPL.

25. *Sun Sentinel* (20 November 1979), b.69 f.16, JRPP/NYPL.

26. Julius Novick, "Clean Streets," *Village Voice* (25 February 1980), 73.

27. Judith Ortiz Cofer, "The Myth of the Latin Woman: I Just Met a Girl Named Maria," in Cofer, *Latin Deli*, 148.

28. Sandoval-Sánchez, "*West Side Story*." Sandoval-Sánchez builds out this interpretation in *Jose, Can You See?*

29. Frances Negrón-Muntaner, *Boricua Pop*, 61. See also Brian Herrara, "Compiling *West Side Story*'s Parahistories."

30. Novick, "Clean Streets."

31. Ronald Forsythe (pseudonym), "Why Can't 'We' Live Happily Ever After, Too?" *New York Times* (23 February 1969), D1; D. A. Miller, *Place for Us*.

32. For a perspective on how Michael Jackson reinvented *West Side Story* in these music videos, see Pugh, *America Dancing*, 288–90.

33. Laurents, *Original Story By*, 351.

34. One of the only parodies that the original creators approved was in a benefit for AIDS in Los Angeles, titled "West Hollywood Story." The licensing company insisted that the AIDS Hospice Foundation "program must include a line in prominent position that the authors of *West Side Story* have made an unusual exception to their general policy of not allowing alternate 'versions' due to their sympathy and support for the Hospice program and AIDS relief"; see Music Theatre International to Craig Smith, Columbia Studios, 9 June 1989, b.79 f.26, JRP/NYPL.

35. Patricia Cohen, "Same City, New Story: Since the Jets and Sharks First Rumbled, New York Has Changed," *New York Times* (15 March 2009), AR1. See Herrera, "Compiling *West Sides Story*'s Parahistories," for an extended analysis of this revised revival.

36. Miranda, quoted in Rebecca Mead, "All about the Hamiltons," *New Yorker* (9 February 2015), 48–57; quote 53. See also Cohen, "Same City, New Story," and a 2011 television interview between Maria Hinojosa and Miranda at http://www.wgbh.org/programs/Maria -Hinojosa-One-on-One-12/episodes/Lin-Manuel-Miranda-15067 (accessed 20 March 2015).

37. Miranda talks of this in his interview with Hinojosa.

38. Mandalit del Barco, "Breakdancing: Present at the Creation," National Public Radio, 14 October 2002 (http://www.npr.org/templates/story/story.php?storyId=1151638). See

also original articles by Sally Banes, reporting in the Village Voice in the early 1980s, reprinted in *Writing Dancing in the Age of Postmodernism*; George, *Hip Hop America*.

39. Sally Banes, "Breaking Is Hard to Do: To the Beat, Y'all," *Village Voice* (10 April 1981), reprinted in *Writing Dancing in the Age of Postmodernism*, 121–25.

40. Fab 5 Freddy, quoted in Banes, "Breaking," in George et al., *Fresh*, 111.

BIBLIOGRAPHY

ARCHIVES

Academy of Motion Picture Arts and Sciences, Margaret Herrick Library, Los Angeles, CA (AMPAS)
Saul Bass Papers (SB)
Linwood Dunn Papers
Boris Leven Materials (BL)
Clipping File, *West Side Story* (CF)
Production Files, *West Side Story* (PF)
Visual Materials, *West Side Story*

Library of Congress, Washington, DC (LOC)
Leonard Bernstein Papers
Arthur Laurents (AL)
Roger Stevens Papers (RS)

Museum of the City of New York, New York, NY
Broadway Production Files, *West Side Story*
Look Photographs

New York City Ballet Archives, New York, NY
Tanaquil LeClerq Papers

New York Public Library, New York, NY (NYPL)
Cheryl Crawford Papers (CC)
Dodger/Eaves-Brooks Costume Plots
Harold Prince Papers (HP)
Jerome Robbins Collection
Jerome Robbins Papers (JRP)
Jerome Robbins Personal Papers (JRPP)
Jerome Robbins Photographs
Peter Gennaro Papers
Judith Scott Papers

Russian State Art Library, Moscow, Russia (RSAL)
Reviews of *West Side Story*, musical and film

University of Arkansas, Special Collections, Fayetteville, AR (UA)
US State Department Bureau of Educational and Cultural Affairs, MC 468 (BEC)

231

232 BIBLIOGRAPHY

University of Oregon Libraries, Special Collections & University Archives, Eugene, OR
(UO)
Albert M. Ottenheimer Papers, Coll. 132 (AO)

University of Southern California, Cinematic Arts Library, Los Angeles, CA (USC)
Clipping Files, Rita Moreno
Ernest Lehman Papers
Boris Leven Papers (BL)
Stanley Scheuer Papers
Robert Wise Papers (RW)

University of Texas, Harry Ransom Center, Austin, TX (HRC)
Ernest Lehman Papers (EL)

Wisconsin Historical Society, Madison, WI (WHS)
Gerald A. Freedman Papers
Walter Mirisch Papers
Jean Rosenthal Papers
Stephen Sondheim Papers (SS)

SECONDARY SOURCES

Acevedo-Muñoz, Ernesto R. *West Side Story as Cinema*. Lawrence: University Press of
Kansas, 2013.
Anderson, Elijah. *The Cosmopolitan Canopy: Race and Civility in Everyday Life*. New
York: Norton, 2011.
Avila, Eric. *The Folklore of the Freeway: Race and Revolt in the Modernist City*. Minneapo-
lis: University of Minnesota Press, 2014.
Ayala, Cesar J., and Rafael Bernabe. *Puerto Rico in the American Century: A History since
1898*. Chapel Hill: University of North Carolina Press, 2007.
Baldwin, James. *No Name in the Street*. New York: Dial Press, 1972.
Banes, Sally. *Writing Dancing in the Age of Postmodernism*. Hanover, NH: University Press
of New England, 1994.
Barnhisel, Greg. *Cold War Modernists: Art, Literature, and American Cultural Diplomacy*.
New York: Columbia University Press, 2015.
Bass, Jennifer, and Pat Kirkham. *Saul Bass: A Life in Film and Design*. London: Laurence
King Publishing, 2011.
Beaubien, Michael C. "The Cultural Boycott of South Africa." *Africa Today* 29.4 (1982):
5–16.
Belmonte, Laura A. *Selling the American Way: U.S. Propaganda and the Cold War*. Phila-
delphia: University of Pennsylvania Press, 2008.
Bender, Thomas. *The Unfinished City: New York and the Metropolitan Idea*. New York: New
York University Press, 2002.
Berman, Marshall. *All That Is Solid Melts into Air: The Experience of Modernity*. New York:
Simon & Schuster, 1982.
Bernstein, Leonard. *Findings*. New York: Simon & Schuster, 1982.
Bernstein, Leonard, Terence McNally, Arthur Laurents, Jerome Robbins, and Stephen
Sondheim. "Landmark Symposium: *West Side Story*" (Dramatists Guide Round
Table Series), *Dramatists Guild Quarterly* 22.3 (Autumn 1985): 11–25.

Berson, Misha. *Something's Coming, Something Good: West Side Story and the American Imagination*. Milwaukee: Applause Books, 2011.

Block, Geoffrey. *Enchanted Evenings*. New York: Oxford University Press, 2009.

Brode, Douglas. *The Films of the Sixties*. Secaucus, NJ: Citadel Press 1980.

Burton, Humphrey. *Leonard Bernstein*. New York: Faber and Faber, 1994.

Busch, Justin E. A. *Self and Society in the Films of Robert Wise*. Jefferson, NC: McFarland & Co., 2010.

Bushard, Anthony. "From *On the Waterfront* to *West Side Story*, or There's Nowhere Like Somewhere." *Studies in Musical Theatre* 3.1 (2009): 61–75.

Caro, Robert. *The Power Broker: Robert Moses and the Fall of New York*. New York: Knopf, 1974.

Caute, David. *The Dancer Defects: The Struggle for Cultural Supremacy during the Cold War*. New York: Oxford University Press, 2003.

Chaplin, Saul. *The Golden Age of Movie Musicals and Me*. Norman: University of Oklahoma Press, 1994.

Chapman, Robin. *A Waste of Public Money*. London: Hodder and Stoughton, 1962.

Chauncey, George. *Gay New York: Gender, Urban Culture, and the Making of the Gay Male World*. New York: Basic Books, 1995.

Christ, Ronald, with Jorge Luis Borges. "The Art of Fiction No. 39." *Paris Review* 40 (Winter–Spring 1967): 116–54.

Cofer, Judith Ortiz. *Latin Deli: Prose and Poetry*. New York: W. W. Norton, 1995.

Colon, Jesus. *A Puerto Rican in New York, and Other Sketches*. New York: International Publishers, 1982.

Crawford, Cheryl. *One Naked Individual: My Fifty Years in the Theatre*. Indianapolis, IN: Bobbs-Merrill, 1977.

Croft, Clare. "Ballet Nations: The New York City Ballet's 1962 US State Department-Sponsored Tour of the Soviet Union." *Theatre Journal* 61 (2009): 421–42.

———. *Dancers as Diplomats: American Choreography in Cultural Exchange*. New York: Oxford University Press, 2015.

Dash, Irene. *Shakespeare and the American Musical*. Bloomington: Indiana University Press, 2010.

de Grazia, Victoria. *Irresistible Empire: America's Advance through 20th Century Europe*. Cambridge, MA: Harvard University Press, 2005.

D'Emilio, John. *Sexual Politics, Sexual Communities: The Making of a Homosexual Minority in the United States, 1940–1970*. Chicago: University of Chicago Press, 1983.

Denby, Edwin. *Dancers, Buildings and People in the Streets*. Liberty Corner, NJ: Horizon Press, 1965.

Dinerstein, Joel. "Lester Young and the Birth of Cool." In Gena Dagel Caponi, ed., *Signifyin(g), Sanctifyin' & Slam Dunking: A Reader in African American Expressive Culture*, 239–76. Amherst, MA: University of Massachusetts Press, 1999.

Dinerstein, Joel, and Frank H. Goodyear III. *American Cool*. New York: Delmonico Books, 2014.

Ellis, Heather, ed. *Juvenile Delinquency and the Limits of Western Influence, 1850–2000*. New York: Palgrave Macmillan, 2014.

Enck-Wanzer, Darrel. *The Young Lords: A Reader*. New York: New York University Press, 2010.

Ezrahi, Christina. *Swans of the Kremlin: Ballet and Power in Soviet Russia*. Pittsburgh, PA: University of Pittsburgh Press, 2012.

Finstad, Suzanne. *Natasha*. New York: Crown Publishing Group, 2001.

Fisher, James T. *On the Irish Waterfront: The Crusader, the Movie, and the Soul of the Port of New York*. Ithaca: Cornell University Press, 2009.

Flamm, Michael. *Law and Order: Street Crime, Civil Unrest, and the Crisis of Liberalism in the 1960s*. New York: Columbia University Press, 2005.

Fursenko, Alexandr, and Timothy Naftali. *Khrushchev's Cold War*. New York: W. W. Norton, 2006.

Garebian, Keith. *The Making of West Side Story*. Oakville, Ontario: Mosaic Press, 1995.

Geelhoed, E. Bruce, and Anthony O. Edwards. *Eisenhower, Macmillan and Allied Unity, 1957–61*. New York: Palgrave MacMillan, 2003.

Genter, Robert. *Late Modernism: Arts, Culture, and Politics in Cold War America*. Philadelphia, PA: University of Pennsylvania Press, 2010.

George, Nelson. *Hip Hop America*. New York: Viking Press, 1998.

George, Nelson, Sally Banes, Susan Flinker, and Patty Romanowski. *Fresh: Hip Hop Don't Stop*. New York: Random House, 1985.

Gilbert, James. *A Cycle of Outrage: America's Reaction to the Juvenile Delinquent in the 1950s*. New York: Oxford University Press, 1986.

Grant, Mark N. *The Rise and Fall of the Broadway Musical*. Boston: Northeastern University Press, 2004.

Grossvogel, David I. *Scenes in the City: Film Visions of Manhattan before 9/11*. New York: Peter Lang International Academic Publishers, 2003.

Hallinan, Victoria. "The 1958 Tour of the Moiseyev Dance Company: A Window into American Perception." *Journal of History and Cultures* 1 (2012): 51–64.

Haslip-Viera, Gabriel, Angelo Falcon, and Felix Matos Rodriguez, eds. *Boricuas in Gotham: Puerto Ricans in the Making of Modern New York City*. Princeton, NJ: Markus Wiener Publishers, 2005.

Herrera, Brian Eugenio. "Compiling *West Side Story*'s Parahistories, 1949–2009." *Theatre Journal* 64.2 (May 2012): 231–47.

———. *Latin Numbers: Playing Latino in Twentieth-Century U.S. Popular Performance*. Ann Arbor: University of Michigan Press, 2015.

Hoffman, Walter. *The Great White Way: Race and the Broadway Musical*. New Brunswick, NJ: Rutgers University Press, 2014.

Homans, Jennifer. *Apollo's Angels: A History of Ballet*. New York: Random House, 2010.

Horowitz, Joseph. *Artists in Exile: How Refugees from Twentieth-Century War and Revolution Transformed the American Performing Arts*. New York: Harper Collins, 2009.

Hubbs, Nadine. *The Queer Composition of America's Sound: Gay Modernists, American Music, and National Identity*. Berkeley: University of California Press, 2004.

Iglesias, Cesar A. *Memoirs of Bernardo Vega*. New York: Monthly Review Press, 1984.

Jacobs, Jane. *The Death and Life of Great American Cities*. New York: Random House, 1961.

Johnson, David. *The Lavender Scare: The Cold War Persecution of Gays and Lesbians in the Federal Government*. Chicago: University of Chicago Press, 2004.

Jowitt, Deborah. *Jerome Robbins: His Life, His Theater, His Dance*. New York: Simon & Schuster, 2004.

Kael, Pauline. *I Lost It at the Movies*. Boston: Little, Brown, 1965.

Kanfer, Stefan. *A Journal of the Plague Years*. New York: Atheneum, 1973.

Kavanagh, Julie. *Nureyev: The Life*. New York: Pantheon, 2007.

Kelly, Kevin. *One Singular Sensation: The Michael Bennett Story*. New York: Doubleday, 1990.

Khrushchev, Nina. "The Case of Khrushchev's Shoe." *New Statesman* (2 October 2000), 33.

Knapp, Raymond. *The American Musical and the Formation of National Identity*. Princeton, NJ: Princeton University Press, 2005.

Kowal, Rebekah. *How to Do Things with Dance: Performing Change in Postwar America*. Middletown, CT: Wesleyan University Press, 2010.

Kraut, Anthea. "'Stealing Steps' and Signature Moves: Embodied Theories of Dance as Intellectual Property." *Theatre Journal* 62.2 (May 2010): 173–89.

Lambert, Gavin. *Natalie Wood*. London: Faber and Faber, 2004.

Lao-Montes, Agustin, and Arlene Davila, eds., *Mambo Montage: The Latinization of New York*. New York: Columbia University Press, 2001.

Laurents, Arthur. *Home of the Brave*. New York: Dramatists Play Service, Inc., 1945.

———. *Mainly on Directing: Gypsy, West Side Story, and Other Musicals*. New York: Knopf, 2009.

———. *Original Story By*. New York: Knopf, 2000.

———. *The Rest of the Story*. New York: Applause, 2012.

Lawrence, Amy. *The Passion of Montgomery Clift*. Berkeley: University of California Press, 2010.

Lawrence, Carol. *Carol Lawrence: The Backstage Story*. New York: McGraw-Hill, 1990.

Lawrence, Greg. *Dance with Demons: The Life of Jerome Robbins*. New York: Berkley Books, 2001.

Leemann, Sergio. *Robert Wise on His Films: From Editing Room to Director's Chair*. Los Angeles: Silman-James Press, 1995.

Levitt, Helen, director. *In the Street*. 1948.

Lewis, Oscar. *La Vida: A Puerto Rican Family in the Culture of Poverty*. New York: Random House, 1965.

Lindner, Christoph. *Imagining New York City: Literature, Urbanism, and the Visual Arts, 1890–1940*. New York: Oxford University Press, 2015.

Litvak, Joseph. *The Un-Americans: Jews, the Blacklist, and Stoolpigeon Culture*. Durham, NC: Duke University Press, 2009.

Look Up and Live. Television program, produced by Jack Kuney. CBS, 1958.

Lynch, Kevin. *The Image of the City*. Cambridge, MA: MIT Press, 1960.

Madsen, Peter, and Richard Plunz, eds. *The Urban Lifeworld: Formation, Perception, Representation*. New York: Routledge, 2002.

Manguel, Alberto. *With Borges*. London: Telegram Books, 2006.

Mayor, Loren Adele. "Broadway at the Crossroads: Urban Planning and Theatrical Production in NYC in the 1950s." PhD diss., Northwestern University, 1999.

McCourt, James. *Queer Street*. New York: W. W. Norton, 2005.

Mirisch, Walter. *I Thought We Were Making Movies, Not History*. Madison: University of Wisconsin Press, 2008.

Miller, D. A. *Place for Us*. Cambridge: Harvard University Press, 1998.

Miller, Warren. *The Cool World*. Boston: Little Brown, 1959.

Monush, Barry. *Music on Film: West Side Story*. New York: Limelight Editions, 2010.

Mordden, Ethan. *Coming Up Roses*. Oxford: Oxford University Press, 1998.

———. *Medium Cool: The Movies of the '60s*. New York: Knopf, 1990.

Moreno, Rita. *Rita Moreno: A Memoir*. New York: Celebra, 2013.

Morris, Gay. *A Game for Dancers: Performing Modernism in the Postwar Years, 1945–60*. Middletown, CT: Wesleyan University Press, 2006.

Most, Andrea. *Making Americans: Jews and the Broadway Musical*. Cambridge, MA: Harvard University Press, 2004.

Negrón-Muntaner, Frances. *Boricua Pop: Puerto Ricans and the Latinization of American Culture*. New York: New York University Press, 2004.

Negrón-Muntaner, Frances. "'Feeling Pretty': *West Side Story* and Puerto Rican Identity Discourses." *Social Text 63* 18.2 (Summer 2000): 83–106.

Nixon, Marni, with Stephen Cole. *I Could Have Sung All Night: My Story*. New York: Billboard Books, 2006.

Noonan, Ellen. *The Strange Career of Porgy and Bess: Race, Culture, and America's Most Famous Opera*. Chapel Hill: University of North Carolina Press, 2012.

Oja, Carol J. *Bernstein Meets Broadway: Collaborative Art in a Time of War*. New York: Oxford University Press, 2014.

———. "*West Side Story* and *The Music Man*: Whiteness, Immigration, and Race in the US during the late 1950s." *Studies in Musical Theatre* 3.1 (2009): 13–30.

Our Story: Jets and Sharks Then and Now: As Told by Cast Members from the Movie West Side Story. Denver: Outskirts Press, 2011.

Ovalle, Priscilla Peña. *Dance and the Hollywood Latina: Race, Sex, and Stardom*. New Brunswick: Rutgers University Press, 2010.

Padilla, Elena. *Up from Puerto Rico*. New York: Columbia University Press, 1970.

Page, Max. *The Creative Destruction of New York, 1900–1940*. Chicago: University of Chicago Press, 1999.

Paredez, Deborah. "'Queer for Uncle Sam': Anita's Latina Diva Citizenship in *West Side Story*." *Latino Studies* 12.3 (Autumn 2014): 332–52.

Peiss, Kathy. *Zoot Suit: The Enigmatic Career of an Extreme Style*. Philadelphia: University of Pennsylvania Press, 2011.

Perl, Jed. *New Art City: Manhattan at Mid-Century*. New York: Knopf, 2005.

Prevots, Naima. *Dance for Export: Cultural Diplomacy and the Cold War*. Middletown, CT: Wesleyan University Press, 1998.

Prince, Harold. *Contradictions: Notes on Twenty-six Years in the Theatre*. New York: Dodd, Mead, 1974.

Pugh, Megan. *America Dancing: From the Cakewalk to the Moonwalk*. New Haven, CT: Yale University Press, 2015.

Relyea, Robert E., with Craig Relyea. *Not So Quiet on the Set: My Life in Movies during Hollywood's Macho Era*. New York: iUniverse, 2008.

Riccio, Vincent, and Bill Slocum. *All the Way Down: The Violent Underworld of Street Gangs*. New York: Simon & Schuster, 1962.

Rivera, Raquel Z. *New York Ricans from the Hip Hop Zone*. New York: Palgrave Macmillan, 2003.

Rodriguez, Abraham. *The Boy without a Flag*. Minneapolis: Milkweed Editions, 1999.

Rosenthal, Jean, and Lael Wertenbaker. *The Magic of Light*. New York: Little, Brown, 1972.

Salisbury, Harrison E. *The Shook-Up Generation*. New York: Harper & Brothers, 1958.

Sanders, James. *Celluloid Skyline: New York and the Movies*. New York: Knopf, 2003.

Sandoval-Sánchez, Alberto. *Jose, Can You See? Latinos On and Off-Broadway*. Madison: University of Wisconsin Press, 1999.

———. "*West Side Story*: A Puerto Rican Reading of America." *Jump Cut* 39 (June 1994): 59–66.

Santiago, Esmeralda. *When I Was Puerto Rican*. Boston: Addison-Wesley, 1993.

Schlesinger, Arthur M., Jr. *The Politics of Hope and the Bitter Heritage: American Liberalism in the 1960s*. Boston: Riverside Press, 1962.

Schneider, Eric C. *Vampires, Dragons, and Egyptian Kings: Youth Gangs in Postwar New York*. New Jersey: Princeton University Press, 1999.

Schwartz, Joel. *The New York Approach: Robert Moses, Urban Liberals, and Redevelopment of the Inner City*. Columbus: Ohio State University Press, 1993.

Schwarzer, Mitchell. *ZoomScape: Architecture in Motion and Media*. Princeton, NJ: Princeton Architectural Press, 2006.

Scott, William B., and Peter Rutkoff. *New York Modern: The Arts and the City*. Baltimore: Johns Hopkins University Press, 1999.

Secrest, Meryle. *Leonard Bernstein: A Life*. New York: Knopf, 1994.

Seldes, Barry. *Leonard Bernstein: The Political Life of an American Musician*. Berkeley: University of California Press, 2009.

Shawn, Allen. *Leonard Bernstein: An American Musician*. New Haven, CT: Yale University Press, 2014.

Shull, Leo. *Angels: The People Who Finance Shows and Films* [1954–58]. New York: Leo Shull Publications, 1959.

Silva, Liana M. "Acts of Home-making: Home and Urban Space in Twentieth Century African American Puerto Rican Cultural Productions." PhD diss., Binghamton University, 2012.

Simeone, Nigel. *Leonard Bernstein: West Side Story*. Farnham, UK: Ashgate, 2009.

———, ed. *The Leonard Bernstein Letters*. New Haven, CT: Yale University Press, 2013.

Smith, Helen. *There's a Place for Us: The Musical Theatre Works of Leonard Bernstein*. Farnham, UK: Ashgate, 2011.

Snyder, Robert W. *Crossing Broadway: Washington Heights and the Promise of New York City*. Ithaca, NY: Cornell University Press, 2015.

———. "A Useless and Terrible Death: The Michael Farmer Case, 'Hidden Violence,' and New York City in the Fifties." *Journal of Urban History* 36.2 (2010): 226–50.

Solomon, Alisa. *Wonder of Wonders: A Cultural History of Fiddler on the Roof*. New York: Metropolitan Books, 2013.

Sondheim, Stephen. *Finishing the Hat: Collected Lyrics (1954–1981), with Attendant Comments, Principles, Heresies, Grudges, Whines and Anecdotes*. New York: Knopf, 2010.

———. *Look, I Made a Hat: Collected Lyrics (1981–2011) with Attendant Comments, Amplifications, Dogmas, Harangues, Digressions, Anecdotes and Miscellany*. New York: Knopf, 2011.

Stearns, Peter. *American Cool: Constructing a 20th Century Emotional Style*. New York: New York University Press, 1994.

Suter, Keith. "Puerto Rico: Beyond 'West Side Story.'" *Contemporary Review* (Winter 2007): 442–48.

Szilard, Paul (as told to Howard Kaplan). *Under My Wings: My Life as an Impresario*. New York: Limelight Editions, 2002.

Taubman, William. *Khrushchev: The Man and the Era*. New York: W. W. Norton, 2003.

Taylor, William R. *Inventing Times Square: Commerce and Culture at the Crossroads of the World*. Baltimore: Johns Hopkins University Press, 1996.

Thomas, Lorrin. *Puerto Rican Citizen: History and Political Identity in 20th Century New York*. Chicago: University of Chicago Press, 2010.

Thomas, Piri. *Down These Mean Streets*. New York: Vintage, 1967.

Vaill, Amanda. *Somewhere: The Life of Jerome Robbins*. New York: Broadway Books, 2006.

Von Eschen, Penny. *Satchmo Blows Up the World: Jazz Ambassadors Play the Cold War*. Cambridge, MA: Harvard University Press, 2004.

Wagnleitner, Reinhold. *Coca-Colonization and the Cold War: The Cultural Mission of the United States in Austria after the Second World War*. Chapel Hill: University of North Carolina Press, 1994.

Wakefield, Dan. *Island in the City: The World of Spanish Harlem*. New York: Houghton Mifflin, 1959.

Wells, Elizabeth A. *West Side Story: Cultural Perspectives on an American Musical*. Lanham, MD: Scarecrow Press, 2011.

West Side Memories. Documentary, directed by Michael Arrick. MGM, 2003.

West Side Stories: The Making of West Side Story. Documentary, produced by Peter Fitzgerald and Melissa Smith (never viewed publicly). Paley Center for Media, 1996.

Whalen, Carmen Teresa, and Victor Vazquez-Hernandez. *The Puerto Rican Diaspora: Historical Perspectives*. Philadelphia: Temple University Press, 2005.

White, Timothy R. *Blue-Collar Broadway: The Craft and Industry of American Theater*. Philadelphia: University of Pennsylvania Press, 2014.

Wiseman, Frederick, producer. *The Cool World* (film, 1963).

Wolcott, James. *Lucking Out: My Life Getting Down and Semi-dirty in Seventies New York*. New York: Doubleday, 2011.

Wolf, Stacy. *Changed for Good: A Feminist History of the Broadway Musical*. New York: Oxford University Press, 2011.

Zadan, Craig. *Sondheim & Co*. New York: Macmillan, 1974.

Zipp, Samuel. *Manhattan Projects: The Rise and Fall of Urban Renewal in Cold War New York*. New York: Oxford University Press, 2012.

Zukin, Sharon. *The Cultures of Cities*. Cambridge, MA: Blackwell Press, 1995.

INDEX

Page numbers in italics refer to illustrations.